CW00672963

# KINGS, MORMAER

# KINGS, MORMAERS, REBELS

*Early Scotland's Other Royal Family*

## JOHN MARSDEN

JOHN DONALD

First published in Great Britain in 2010 by
John Donald, an imprint of Birlinn Ltd

West Newington House
10 Newington Road
Edinburgh
EH9 1QS

www.birlinn.co.uk

ISBN: 978 1 906566 19 7

The author and publishers gratefully acknowledge the support of the Strathmartine
Trust Marjory Anderson Fund towards the publication of this book.

*British Library Cataloguing-in-Publication Data*
A catalogue record for this book is available on request from the British Library

Typeset by Hewer Text UK Ltd, Edinburgh

Printed and bound in Britain by Bell & Bain Ltd, Glasgow

# CONTENTS

# PREFACE

Although not offered as an 'alternative history' of early Scotland, this book does set out to throw some unfamiliar light on the emergence of the medieval kingdom of the Scots from the viewpoint of (what would nowadays be called) the 'opposition benches'. It has not been written, however, as a scholarly monograph for an exclusively academic audience, but is intended instead – as its title and sub-title may have already suggested – for a wider readership.

It does not, for example, assume a fluent command of the languages of early Scotland, and so the use of terms in such tongues as Middle Irish and Old Norse is always accompanied by translation. Names are given in their more recognisable (rather than their archaic) form wherever possible and acute accents are applied to some of those older name-forms simply to indicate the pronunciation of elongated vowels. To which should be added a note that the name *Loarn* is pronounced as two syllables.

It should also be explained that date-numbering in the Irish annals is sometimes misleading and so the year numbers assigned here to annal entries represent what are believed to be the true historical dates of the events recorded. References to those annals and to other early sources are usually contained within the text itself, thus enabling the minimal use of footnotes, almost all of which serve simply to identify and acknowledge quotations from, and references to, the published work of other (invariably much more learned) authors.

A word of grateful acknowledgement is due to staff at the Stornoway headquarters of Western Isles Libraries and the Orkney Library and Archive in Kirkwall – as it is also to my friend Michael Robson of Ness – for their assistance in pursuing queries on my behalf and supplementing the modest resources of my own bookshelves.

A concluding note of acknowledgement is owed to my principal contacts within the Birlinn organisation: specifically to Neville Moir for his good offices in enabling this project, as also to Mairi Sutherland, my commissioning editor at John Donald, and Jacqueline Young, the copy editor on this book, for their unfailing courtesy and co-operation.

JM
Achmore, 2009

# ABBREVIATIONS

| | |
|---|---|
| Anderson, *ESSH* | A. O. Anderson, *Early Sources of Scottish History* |
| Anderson, *SAEC* | A. O. Anderson, *Scottish Annals from English Chroniclers* |
| Bannerman, *Dalriada* | J. Bannerman, *Studies in the History of Dalriada* |
| *CGH* | M. A. O'Brien, *Corpus Genealogiarum Hiberniae* |
| M. O. Anderson, *Kings & Kingship* | M. O. Anderson, *Kings & Kingship in Early Scotland* |
| *SGS* | *Scottish Gaelic Studies* |
| Watson, *Celtic Place-names* | W. J. Watson, *The History of the Celtic Place-names of Scotland* |

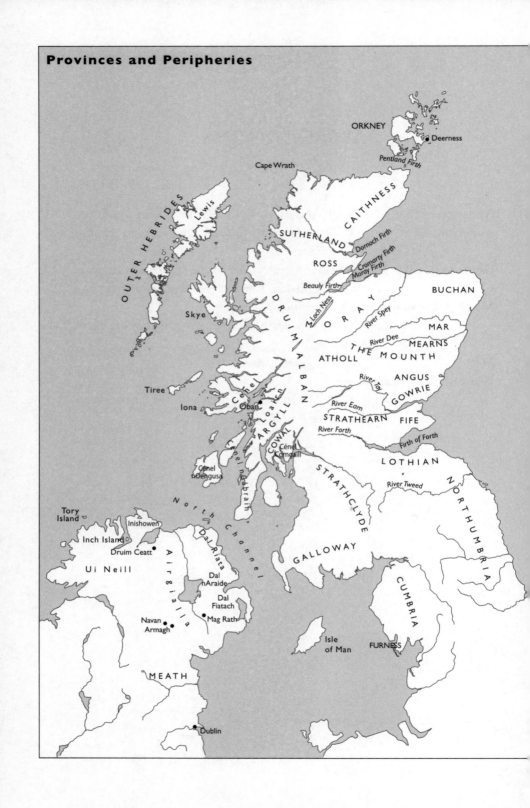

# Provinces and Peripheries

ORKNEY

Deerness

Pentland Firth

Cape Wrath

CAITHNESS

SUTHERLAND

Dornoch Firth

OUTER HEBRIDES

Lewis

ROSS

Cromarty Firth

Moray Firth

Beauly Firth

BUCHAN

Skye

Loch Ness

MORAY

River Spey

MAR

River Dee

THE MOUNTH

MEARNS

Tiree

ATHOLL

ANGUS

Iona

Oban

Loch Awe

River Tay

GOWRIE

Cénel

ARGYLL

STRATHEARN

River Earn

FIFE

Cénel nOengusa

Cowal

Cénel
Comgaill

River Forth

Firth of Forth

LOTHIAN

Cénel nGabráin

STRATHCLYDE

River Tweed

NORTHUMBRIA

Tory
Island

Inishowen

GALLOWAY

Inch Island

Dal Riata

Druim Ceatt

Airgíalla

Dal
nAraide

Dal
Fiatach

CUMBRIA

Ui Neill

Mag Rath

Navan
Armagh

Isle
of Man

FURNESS

North Channel

MEATH

Dublin

Druim Alban

# Alba

Duncansby Head

Thurso
Skitten
Wick

River Oykel

Cyderhall
Tain
Tarbat Ness
Dunskeath
Moray Firth
Burghead
Pitgaveny
Elgin
Garve
Redcastle
Forres
Deer
Stockford
Auldearn
Applecross
Inverness
Raasay
Skye
Mortlach
Essie
River Beauly
River Spey

GREAT GLEN

Abertarff
Lumphanan
Kincardine
Crathie
Fetteresso
River Dee
Mondynes
Dunottar
Stracathro

ARDNAMURCHAN
MORVERN
Loch Linnhe
River Tay
River Isla
Forfar
Mull
Dunollie
Dunkeld
Coupar Angus
Loch Feochan
Dunsinnan Hill
Iona
Seil Island
Monzievaird
Scone
Dundee
Firth of Lorn
Tyndrum
Dundurn
Finglen
Ederline
STRATHALLAN
Loch Leven
Craignish
Dunadd
STRATHCARRON
Loch Fyne
Firth of Forth
Jura
Dumbarton
Edinburgh
Sound of Jura
KNAPDALE
Tarbert
Renfrew
River Clyde
Islay
Bute
Gigha
Ardminish
Lindisfarne
Oa
Arran
River Tweed
Firth of Clyde
KINTYRE
Carham
Roxburgh
Alnwick

Dunaverty

ANTRIM
River Bush
RHINNS
River Bann
Larne
River Tyne
Jarrow
Lough
Neagh
Bangor
Carlisle
Durham
Whithorn
River Wear

# INTRODUCTION

## *Of Kindreds and Kingship*

The accidental death of Alexander III, apparently the result of a fall from horseback along the coast of Fife on a stormy night in the March of 1286, was an event of watershed significance in medieval Scottish history, because none of his offspring survived to claim the succession and the realm was thrust into constitutional crisis. All the subsequent kings of Scotland were to be of ultimately Norman ancestry, with claims to the kingship resting on their descent from marriages to great-granddaughters of David I, and so none would have been able to boast the ancient Scots pedigree which is said to have hailed Alexander on his inauguration in July 1249.

The account of that ceremony preserved in the *Gesta Annalia* (annals appended to John of Fordun's fourteenth-century *Chronicle* but derived from much more closely contemporary sources dated to *c.*1285) tells of the young Alexander, not yet eight years old, brought to Scone by the foremost earls of the kingdom five days after the death of his father and there consecrated into kingship by the bishop of St Andrews before a great assembly of the Scots nobility. As formal proceedings drew to a close, with earls and nobles kneeling in homage before their new king seated on the stone of Scone, 'a highland Scot [evidently a *seanchaidh* or Gaelic bardic genealogist] fell on his knees before the throne and, bowing his head, hailed the king in his mother tongue, reciting . . . even unto the end, the pedigree of the kings of Scots'.

That pedigree, as it is translated from the Gaelic in the *Gesta Annalia*, follows Alexander's royal lineage back through twenty generations from his father Alexander II, the great-great-grandson of Malcolm Canmore, to Gabrán, a grandson of the Fergus Mór, son of Erc, who has long been recognised as the founding dynast of Dalriada, the embryonic kingdom of the Scots in Argyll, on the eve of the sixth century. Indeed, the Gaelic oration extended still further back in time and even beyond the threshold of history to trace the descent of Fergus Mór from names known only from the outer reaches of Irish bardic tradition.

Consequently, Alexander III can be said to represent the last king of Scots in a lineage which linked his forebears of the house of Canmore to the MacAlpin dynasty and thus claimed his ultimate descent from the *Cenél nGabráin* ('kindred of Gabrán') which had borne most of the names entered in the king-lists of Dalriada through the sixth and seventh centuries. It should perhaps be mentioned at this point that the feudal kingship of Scots to which Alexander succeeded in the mid-thirteenth century was of an entirely different character to that of six or seven hundred years earlier, which followed a hierarchical model unmistakably similar to that practised in the Scots' original northern Irish homeland. A tract of eighth-century origin sets out the tiers of kingship in Ireland in a form corresponding to evidence for the Scots of Dalriada found in a later genealogical collection and recognising the Cenél nGabráin as one of four *prímchenéla* ('ruling kindreds'), each with its own king who would have acknowledged another as over-king governing at least two other peoples as well as his own.

All the names entered in the king-lists of Dalriada can be identified as members of three of these *prímchenéla*, so the lists clearly represent a record of over-kings and can thus be read as an index of shifting ascendancies between rival ruling kindreds. While the most obscure of those *cenéla*, the *Cenél nOengusa*, appears never to have held the over-kingship – and, indeed, passes almost entirely without notice in the historical record – the names of members of the *Cenél Comgaill*, a kindred presumably descended from Gabrán's brother and predecessor Comgall, are entered in the lists, initially alternating and on later occasion apparently sharing kingship with the Cenél nGabráin, until the mid-point of the seventh century.

Soon afterwards, however, the king-lists enter a sequence of names from another kindred, the *Cenél Loairn*, which had emerged as a formidable rival to the Cenél nGabráin by the end of the seventh century and was to produce at least four over-kings of Dalriada through the next four decades, thereby establishing a claim on the kingship of Scots which was to be pursued by its descendent houses through the next six hundred years.

By a curious coincidence, the most detailed (even if suspiciously anecdotal) account of the death of Alexander III was set down within thirty years of the event by a prior of the monastery of Lanercost near Carlisle and is preserved in the same *Chronicle of Lanercost* which also contains the only surviving record of another death, that of an infant girl who suffered brutal public execution when her skull was smashed against the mercat cross at Forfar less than twenty years before the coronation of Alexander III at Scone. The fate of that unfortunate child – inflicted as final retribution for a recently suppressed rebellion by her father and elder brothers – was to extinguish the last spark of the MacWilliam claim to kingship which had been sustained in its own right to harass two Canmore kings through half a century, and might be said to have had its deepest roots in an ancient dynastic rivalry inherited from eighth-century Dalriada.

By the end of the first decade of that century when the Cenél Comgaill make their last appearance in the historical record, the Cenél nOengusa having long since passed into oblivion and the Cenél nGabráin, troubled by factional rivalries, having been in steady decline for almost sixty years, the Cenél Loairn had come into the ascendant as over-kings of Dalriada. Yet it was to be an ascendancy constantly beleaguered by their own bitter internecine contention as well as sporadic conflict with the elements of the Cenél nGabráin, all of which would have rendered the Scots especially vulnerable to the Pictish invasions launched in the 730s. All the surviving evidence points to the Cenél Loairn having suffered most grievously from that ferocious onslaught – even to the extent that the kindred would seem to disappear from the historical record after 736.

In their absence, the way lay open for a new ascendancy by a branch of the Cenél nGabráin which had not only been spared the greater impact of the Pictish invasions but was eventually strong enough to carry the war back into Pictland, and by the mid-ninth century they had accomplished so impressive an eastward expansion as to be firmly established in the kingship of the principal Pictish power centre of Fortriu in Strathearn. Meanwhile, and almost entirely unnoticed by the historical record, the Cenél Loairn had made their own migration out of their former territory in northern Argyll and up the Great Glen into Moray. By the end of the tenth century, individuals claimed in later genealogies to have been of kingly Cenél Loairn descent appear as members of the hereditary ruling kindred of that province, styled *mormaers* (or 'great stewards') in Scottish records, but recognised more impressively by the Irish annals – and assuredly also in their own estimation – as kings in the north.

From which it would follow that descendants of the Cenél Loairn of Dalriada had somehow achieved a supremacy over the Picts north of the Grampians, and so should justly be allowed their own share in whatever credit might be due for the 'conquest of the Picts' traditionally attributed to Kenneth mac Alpin – for whom, of course, the genealogies claim descent from the rival Cenél nGabráin. Nowhere in the historical record, however, are these kings in the north noticed in any conflict with the Picts, but instead they are remembered in saga sources for a number of battles fought against Norsemen in defence of the northern frontier of Moray against the advance of the Orkney Norse seeking to extend their mainland territories southward from Caithness.

There is a weight of evidence, then, for what can be recognised as two kingly dynasties of the Scots ruling their own kingdoms to the north and the south of the Grampian mountains, at least until the early decades of the eleventh century, by which time the MacAlpin dynasty in the south had followed a similar pattern to that found also in Ireland at much the same time and eventually established itself in 'high-kingship' of the Scots. Within that scenario, of course, lies the inevitability that the old Cenél Loairn/Cenél nGabráin rivalry would follow the descendants of the two kindreds on their progress out of Dalriada into what had formerly been the lands of the Picts.

As, indeed, it was to do, and so too was their proclivity for internecine contention also brought with them out of the west. The conflict between kinsmen which had bedevilled the Cenél Loairn ascendancy in Dalriada was to persist in Moray and, indeed, with even greater savagery. Similarly hostile rivalries were seen to develop between different branches of the Cenél nGabráin-descended MacAlpin dynasty as it advanced in the direction of high-kingship, a threat of especial concern in the earlier eleventh century to Malcolm II, who had no son to succeed him in the direct male line from Kenneth mac Alpin and so sought to eliminate any potential rival to his daughter's son Duncan as his successor.

When Duncan's less than impressive performance in the kingship provoked the inevitable challenge, it was to come out of Moray and from Macbeth, son of Findláech, whose descent from the first Cenél Loairn over-king of Dalriada is recorded in a genealogy compiled within a century of his own lifetime. There is every reason then to recognise Macbeth's seizure of Duncan's kingship and his subsequent seventeen-year reign in that high-kingship of Scots as the very greatest ascendancy of the Cenél Loairn.

It was, of course, also to be that kindred's last ascendancy, because the violent deaths of both Macbeth and his short-lived successor Lulach (for whom the genealogists claimed a similarly impressive Cenél Loairn pedigree) at the hands of Duncan's son Malcolm, called 'Canmore',[1] not only marked the resurgence of the Cenél nGabráin in the guise of the Canmore dynasty but also signalled the descent of the house of Moray into its terminal decline. Nonetheless, two generations of Lulach's line were to cling on to some measure of power north of the Grampians until the death in battle of his grandson Angus (who is styled 'earl' by a contemporary Scottish chronicler) in rebellion against David I, the last of the sons of Malcolm Canmore who succeeded to their father's kingship.

Even after the fall of Angus and the seizure of his earldom by the crown, a long sequence of members of descendent or otherwise associated kindreds took up the Moray claim and pursued it into the second quarter of the thirteenth century. Therein lies the greater historical significance of the last of the MacWilliam line, because it is possible to trace her ancestry back to the house of Moray, which had borne two high-kings of Scots and claimed direct descent from kings of Dalriada whose own forebears may even have crossed over from Ireland to settle in Argyll before the arrival of Fergus Mór.

---

1    Anglicised from the Middle Irish *cenn mór* ('of the great head').

For various reasons which will become apparent throughout these pages, the documentary record of the Cenél Loairn and its descendent kindreds, preserved as it is across a spectrum of Scottish, Irish, Scandinavian and English sources, is at best uneven and often reliant upon only fragmentary evidence. So this attempt to construct a history of the kings, mormaers and rebels for whom might be claimed descent from the house of Loarn has been trawled, of necessity, from the shadowlands of Scotland's early history – where it must begin at the very beginning . . .

I

# ORIGINS AND EMERGENCE OF THE *CENÉL LOAIRN*

The chronological sequence of Alan Orr Anderson's monumental two-volume *Early Sources of Scottish History* begins with an entry in the *Annals of Tigernach* which is approximately dated to the year AD 501: 'Fergus Mór, son of Erc, with the people of the Dál Riata, held part of Britain; and there he died.'

Despite a shadow of doubt as to the absolute provenance of that annal entry, it would be impossibly difficult to find any other item from the early sources which could stand so well in its place at the starting-point of Scotland's historical record. Evidence as old as the seventh century which remembers Fergus Mór, son of Erc, as founder of the Dalriadic dynasty in Argyll has established his enduring recognition as the very first historical king of Scots.

The most reliable of the Dalriadic king-lists, all of them comparatively late in date but believed to be 'descended from one which must have been extant in Ireland in the eleventh century',[1] accords him a reign of three years, so the annalist's dating of his obituary would place his arrival in Scotland around the year 498. An older list, composed in Middle Irish verse in the second half of the eleventh century and known as the *Duan Albanach* (or 'Scottish Poem'), is not considered to be trustworthy when it accords Fergus a reign of twenty-seven years, yet it is perhaps possible to read that figure as a sum total of his three years in Scotland taken together with his earlier reign as successor to his father as king of the Dál Riata in Antrim. In fact, the only annal record of his father Erc, son of Eochaid Munremar, is an obituary entered in the seventeenth-century *Annals of the Four Masters* at the year 474, a

---

1    M. O. Anderson, *Kings & Kingship*, p.45.

date corresponding so precisely with the *Duan*'s total reign length that it might have been calculated upon just such a premise.

There are references in Armagh sources dating from as early as the beginning of the ninth century which record Fergus himself, together with his father Erc and his son Domangart, as contemporaries of Saint Patrick, whose mission in Ireland is now convincingly assigned to the second half of the fifth century and the year of his death to sometime after 485 in preference to the traditional obituary date of 461. All of which would certainly correspond to the aforementioned dating of the arrival, reign and death in Scotland of Fergus Mór, son of Erc. Yet it is important to notice here that the entry in the *Annals of Tigernach* makes no explicit claim for the advent of Fergus Mór having been the earliest presence of the Dál Riata in Scotland, because – as Anderson stated in his footnote to that annal entry – 'Scots from Antrim had been settling in Kintyre long before 500'.[2]

The name 'Scots', of course, originally meant 'Irish' when it derived from the Latin *Scoti* applied by a fourth-century Roman historian, seemingly in place of the earlier usage of *Hiberni*, to raiders of Irish origin joining the Picts in a concerted attack on the northern frontier of Roman Britain. Whether these Scots were raiding from the island of Ireland itself is unclear, because it is not entirely beyond possibility that there could have been Irish settlement on mainland Britain by that date. Nonetheless Adomnán, abbot of Iona in the last quarter of the seventh century, was apparently following the same Latin usage in his life of Columba (*Vita Columbae*) where he calls Ireland *Scotia* and writes of northern Irish colonists long settled in Argyll as *Scoti Britanniae*, 'the Scots [i.e. Irish] in Britain'.

In that Latin usage, however, *Scoti* represents a generic, or possibly regional, rather than a tribal identity and yet, when all the kings named in Adomnán's *Vita* can be recognised as direct descendants of Fergus Mór, it would follow that his 'Scots in Britain' are to be similarly recognised as descendants of the 'people of the *Dál Riata*'. A note of explanation of the Irish term *dál* (meaning 'division' or 'share') might be timely here, because it indicates a social grouping large enough to include more than

---

2    Anderson, *ESSH*, vol. i, pp.2–3.

one *cenél* (dynastic kindred) as well as any number of lesser kin-groups, all of whom would have taken their common identity from a remote and usually fictitious 'ancestor'. Such then were the Dál Riata, supposedly descended from Cairpre Riata, one of three sons of the mythical 'king of Tara', Conaire Mór. The septs claiming descent from those sons were collectively known as the *Erainn*, who can be justly considered one of the most ancient peoples of Ireland when their name bears a telling similarity to that of *Eriu*, a goddess symbolic of the island itself, and may also be reflected in the Greek *Iernoi* and Latin *Hibernia*, the oldest names for Ireland in the classical sources.

While the traditional region of origin of the Erainn lay in Munster (and genuinely so if they were the same people as the Munster tribe known to the second-century Greek geographer Ptolemy as the *Iverni*), the earliest recorded location of the Dál Riata was found far to the north in what is now County Antrim. There is good reason, nonetheless, for recognition of the Dál Riata as an Irish people of great antiquity and the apparent discrepancy of location is probably best explained by an extension of the application of 'Erainn'. Munster holds the principal concentration of ogam inscriptions – the oldest of them dated to the fourth century – which represent the earliest evidence of Primitive Irish, the 'Q-Celtic' tongue which was to develop into the later forms of the Irish language. Through the seventh and eighth centuries, however, the usage of *Erainn* was superseded by *Goidel* (now 'Gael', but originally a loanword derived from the Welsh *gwydd*, meaning 'wild' or 'savage'), which would suggest 'Erainn' having been broadened from a supposedly ethnic into a specifically linguistic Irish cultural identity. In which case, the inclusion of the Dál Riata among the Erainn can be taken, at the very least, to confirm their language as an elder form of the Middle Irish in which many of the early sources of Scottish history were set down and from which the Celtic bedrock of Scottish Gaelic is ultimately descended.

Be that as it may, the homeland of the Dál Riata at the time of their entry into the historical record lay in the north-eastern corner of Ireland, where their territory of some 450 square miles was centred on the Glens of Antrim. Bounded in the west by the river Bush and to the south by the territory of the Latharna with its southern boundary lying a few miles above the modern port of Larne, the domain of the Dál Riata was contained in the east by the coastline of the Irish Sea and in the north by that of the North Channel, where the heads of Antrim stand just some twelve or fourteen miles off the south-western tip of the Scottish mainland.

As would be expected of island-dwellers, there is substantial historical evidence for the accomplishment of early Irish seafaring, of which the voyager monks of the sixth century and later who ventured far out into the North Atlantic aboard hide-hulled oceangoing curraghs are a prime example. To such a people, the short sea-crossing of the North Channel would have represented a beckoning thoroughfare rather than any impediment and so there can be scarcely any doubt of regular sea traffic, hostile and otherwise, between Ireland and the island-fringed coastline of western Scotland since prehistoric times. Such a likelihood is solidly supported by the numerous references to Irish warriors and wanderers, migrants and exiles making their way into what is now Scotland which are found in so many of the tales, legends and epics surviving only in medieval manuscripts and yet believed to preserve traditions of still greater antiquity.

There is one such tradition with a claim to pre-eminent significance here by reason of its impressive evidence for a migration of the Dál Riata into Scotland long before the appearance of Fergus Mór in the annals at the year 501. The most expansive version of this story, as it can be reconstructed from anecdotes, saga titles and fragmentary references found in Irish sources of various medieval dates, tells how the septs of the Erainn won lands for themselves in Munster.[3] Cairpre Riata's territory was supposed to have been in Kerry and Cork until famine forced him and his people on a northward migration into Ulster – and it was from there that a section of the Dál Riata are said to have crossed over into the land of the Picts.

In fact, the earliest surviving securely dated reference to the same story comes from eighth-century Northumbria where it was included by Bede – the monk of Jarrow internationally respected by contemporaries as an outstanding scholar of his time – in the great history of the English church and people which he completed in the year 731. The

3    Bannerman, *Dalriada*, pp.122–3.

opening chapter of this *Historia Ecclesiastica* includes an account of the peoples of whom Bede knew as the inhabitants of mainland Britain. He first identifies the Britons 'from whom the island took its name', and then tells of the Picts who 'began to settle in the northern part of the island, because the Britons had occupied the south . . .'

> As time passed, Britain received a third people, the *Scoti* . . . and they settled in the territory occupied by the Picts. They left Ireland under the leadership of *Reuda* and either by treaty or by the sword claimed lands among the Picts which are their home to the present day. It is after that leader that they are still known as the *Dalreudini*, because in their language *daal* means 'a part'.

Other than a visit to York and possibly another to Lindisfarne, Bede spent his entire life in the region of Tyne and Wear, so his account of the arrival of the Scots in Britain, which is evidently derived from Irish tradition as also was his account of the Picts, must have reached his monastery on the Tyne through its extensive contacts with the wider ecclesiastical world.

It is quite possible that the story had been brought to Jarrow by Adomnán who is known to have visited Northumbria on two occasions in the 680s, even staying at the monastery for a year on his second visit in 688. Although only in his early teens at that time, Bede might have learned the story at first hand from Adomnán, or otherwise from his abbot Ceolfrith who had conducted extensive conversations with the visiting abbot of Iona. Another likely source of information may have been correspondence with his much-admired English contemporary Ecgberht who spent much of his monastic life in Ireland before passing his latter years on Iona where he died in 729.

The precise identity of Bede's source of information is less important here than the reliable dating and impressive authority of his version of the story, because his *Reuda* is clearly the same person known in the Irish sources as Cairpre Riata, and the more assuredly so when *reuda* has been identified as an elder spelling of the same word dated to *c.*700, thus indicating 'Dalreudini' as an early Latinised form of the Irish *Dál Riata*. It is nonetheless curious, and possibly significant, that Bede's account makes no reference to the earlier migration of the Dál Riata from Munster. He may, of course, have omitted that element of the story simply because it had no immediate bearing on the settlement of the Scots in mainland Britain, but it is also possible that the Munster element, which is almost certainly a fiction devised to underwrite the inclusion of the Dál Riata among the Erainn, was a later accretion which had yet to become a part of the Cairpre Riata legend at the time it found its way to Northumbria.

Bede makes one further reference to the Scots in the first chapter of his history, and it occurs in the closing passage which is clearly describing the Firth of Clyde:

> There is a very long inlet from the sea, which was the ancient boundary between the Britons and the Picts, running inland from the west a great distance, and on it there is a city of the Britons called *Alcluith* [Dumbarton Rock], most strongly fortified to this day. It was to the north of this inlet that the *Scoti* we have mentioned came and made their homeland.

Bede's indication of land 'to the north of this inlet' is usually taken to mean Cowal, which did form part of Cenél nGabráin territory in the later seventh century when it was known as *Crích Chomgaill* or 'Comgall's bounds' and presumably named for Comgall, grandson of Fergus and king of Dalriada *c.*507–38. Yet Bede's geographical reference is so vague as to possibly also encompass upper Kintyre, which lies immediately to the west of Cowal across the slender extent of Loch Fyne and is likewise recorded as Cenél nGabráin territory in the seventh century.

The inhabitants of that region prior to the arrival of the Dál Riata were presumably descendants of the tribe located there by Ptolemy and known to him as the *Epidii*, probably speaking a P-Celtic tongue related to what is known of the Pictish language, yet they cannot be considered 'Picts' in the strict modern application of that name to peoples located much further east and north-east than Kintyre and the Clyde. Even so, Bede did have some knowledge of the Picts of his own time, if only by reason of his abbot's well-recorded contact with their king and churchmen of Fortriu regarding the controversy over the dating

of Easter, so there may well have been some genuine basis for his identification of the original inhabitants of Kintyre and Cowal as 'Picts',
even if only to distinguish them from the north Britons of neighbouring
Strathclyde.

Bede's source of information seems to have left him uncertain as to
whether the 'Dalreudini' had come to occupy their lands in Scotland
'by treaty or by the sword', and yet there is at least one other possible
scenario to offer in place of those two bald alternatives and it lies in the
likelihood of the settlement of the Scots in north Britain growing out
of long-standing earlier contact between peoples on both sides of the
North Channel. There is no reason, of course, to assume that the 'Picts'
of Kintyre were necessarily displaced by the settlement of the Scots
from Antrim, any more than there is to believe that the Picts in the east
simply disappeared after their chieftains had been allegedly entrapped
and butchered by Kenneth mac Alpin in the mid-ninth century. The
more likely course of events is surely that the settlement of some of
the Dál Riata of Antrim in Argyll developed out of that earlier contact
having inevitably involved cultural interchange, and probably also intermarriage which might have prompted early instances of relocation.

Such beginnings would have quite naturally led on to more extensive
kin-based settlement of Scots – probably introducing elements of dynastic
kindreds who established themselves as a local ruling aristocracy – and
eventually to a cultural fusion which culminated in the Gaelicisation of
the indigenous population. It is difficult, nonetheless, to imagine such a
process having been accomplished entirely without contention, and in
that respect also it might be seen to foreshadow the later eastward expansion of the Scots of Dalriada into Fortriu in the later eighth century – and,
at much the same time, northward into Moray.

It is apparent, if only from the context in which Bede placed his
account of the arrival of the Scots in Britain, that he assigned that
settlement to a time remotely distant from his own. So too, his decisive
evidence for the Cairpre Riata story as an 'origin-legend' still current
within some two hundred years of the annalist's date for Fergus Mór's
obituary bears its own testimony to earlier settlement of the Dál Riata in
Scotland, thus laying the groundwork for a realistically historical interpretation of that entry in the *Annals of Tigernach* at 501.

The location of their original homeland in the extreme north-east of Ireland placed the Dál Riata within the province of Ulster which is believed to have extended across a great swathe of the north of Ireland in earlier times and yet, by the end of the fifth century, had been reduced to an area approximately corresponding to the modern counties of Antrim and Down. There the Dál Riata represented one of the three peoples comprising the dynastic group of the *Ulaid* (from which, of course, the name Ulster derives). Foremost among those peoples (and so much so that they were later known as 'the Ulaid') was the Dál Fiatach, another branch of the Erainn whose comparatively small territory was located on the coast of Down and yet lay within fifty miles of *Emain Macha* (now Navan), long renowned in tradition as the capital fortress of ancient Ulster. The ruling kindred of the Dál Fiatach claimed to represent the old kings of Emain who traditionally held sway over all the north of Ireland, and indeed members of the Dál Fiatach do make up two thirds of the names entered in the list of Ulster kings from the sixth to eighth centuries. It should perhaps be explained that this king-list records rulers of the whole province who thus stood at the highest level of early Irish kingship, that of the *rí ruirech* (literally 'king of over-kings') to whom the secondary level of the *ruiri* (or 'over-king') owed submission and paid tribute.

All the names other than those from the Dál Fiatach which are found in that king-list were drawn from an unrelated people, the Dál nAraide who were of *Cruithin* (or, in later Irish, *Cruithne*) stock, a people sometimes, but quite erroneously, referred to as 'Irish Picts', because the name does resemble a Q-Celtic form of the P-Celtic *Priteni* (or 'Briton'). It is fully possible, of course, that the original Cruithin may have been prehistoric settlers from mainland Britain, despite there being no record of any P-Celtic tongue such as those of the Britons and Picts having been spoken in Ireland. The core territory of these Dál nAraide lay in the interior, to the north-east of Lough Neagh with an extension northwards along the Eilne, a narrow corridor between the rivers Bann and Bush, where it ran alongside the western boundary of the lands of the Dál Riata.

The Dál Riata are on record as having paid tribute to the king of the province of Ulster, so their own king would presumably have been accorded the status of a *ruiri*, when his extensive Irish domain must have included a number of peoples (or *tuatha*) owing him submission as its over-king, as also would those cenéla of the Dál Riata who were settled across the water in Scotland. It is against that background that the historical interpretation of Fergus Mór's obituary in the *Annals of Tigernach* comes into focus because – as John Bannerman states with a confidence reflecting the consensus of modern scholarly opinion – 'there is little doubt that it was in the person of Fergus Mór that the Dalriadic dynasty removed from Ireland to Scotland'.[4] By the beginning of the sixth century, then, the ruling kindred of the Dál Riata had relocated from Antrim to Argyll and established itself – although perhaps not entirely without contention – in over-kingship of those northern Irish peoples, presumably its subjects, long since settled there and yet retaining the same sovereignty over its tributary land and people in Ireland.

There is general scholarly agreement also on the political context within which the ruling family of the Dál Riata chose to transfer itself across the North Channel and it is immediately associated with the advance of the Uí Néill and their vassal allies of the Airgialla into Ulster through the fifth century. While the heroic age vividly recalled in the stories of the Ulster Cycle, which is centred around the epic *Táin Bó Cuailnge* ('The Cattle-Raid of Cooley'), has been placed as early as the first century AD, the central subject of the *Táin* is distinctly reflected in the dramatic events of more than four hundred years later, because the story centres around a massive invasion of Ulster, mounted by the forces of the *Connachta* and their allies coming out of the west to seize the great Brown Bull of Cuailnge from the mythical king *Conchobar mac Neasa*. As the Connachta host approached, the fighting-men of Ulster were all magically struck down with a sleeping sickness, leaving the first line of defence of their province in the marvellously capable hands of the hero Cúchulainn.

Much as the Dál Fiatach believed themselves the heirs of the ancient kings of Emain, so modern scholarship recognises the Uí Néill, traditionally descended from Niall of the Nine Hostages, as a later name for

---

4   Bannerman, *Dalriada*, p.73.

a descendent people of the ancient Connachta. Yet when the Uí Néill
swept out of the west in the fifth century there was no Cúchulainn
to bar its advance, the mighty fortress of Emain was destroyed by the
Airgialla and the vast domains ruled by Ulster kings of old reduced to a
remnant mostly contained within present-day Antrim and Down. All of
which depends more heavily on the evidence of tradition than upon the
most reliable sources of historical record, but the political map of the
north-east of Ireland around the date of Fergus Mór's obituary would
show the Dál Fiatach, Dál nAraide and Dál Riata still surviving as an
independent province but almost entirely surrounded by the Airgialla
kingdoms which are in turn encircled by branches of the Uí Néill. 'Such
pressure' – suggests the historian of early Ireland, Gearóid Mac Niocaill
– 'would have given an impulse to the spread of the Dál Riata overseas
to Scotland about the end of the fifth century'.[5]

Perhaps more immediately threatened in the north of Antrim by the
encroaching Uí Néill than were the territories of the Dál nAraide and
Dál Fiatach, the ruling house of the Dál Riata had every reason to fear
a new and formidable overlord and would have sensibly looked to the
lands settled by its subject peoples in Argyll as the location of a more
secure power base. Such a relocation to the mainland would have also
offered potential scope for political expansion beyond anything they
could hope for in Ulster where the superior kingship of the province
was dominated by the Dál nAraide and the Dál Fiatach. In fact, the first
indication of such expansionist ambition on the part of the Dál Riata
was noticed in the annal record within two generations of Fergus' arrival
on the mainland.

Within those two generations also, the emergence of what can now
be recognised as the Scottish kingdom of 'Dalriada' is seen ever more
clearly in the light of the historical record, and certainly insofar as that
new clarity is reflected by the Irish annals. The two such collections
considered to be of especial value for the history of Dalriada are the
*Annals of Tigernach* and the *Annals of Ulster*, both of them believed to
have drawn on a common earlier source, no longer extant but notion-
ally known as the 'Ulster chronicle' because it is thought to have been

---

5    Mac Niocaill, *Ireland before the Vikings*, p.14.

compiled in the monastery of Bangor on Belfast Lough from around the year 740. The significance of this 'Ulster chronicle' for Scottish history lies in its inclusion of material from another lost chronicle compiled in the monastery on Iona through the last quarter of the seventh century until some date between 736 and 741 when this 'Iona chronicle' appears to have been brought to Ireland.

The manuscripts of all the surviving Irish annal collections are of very much later date. The *Annals of Tigernach* – associated with Clonmacnoise yet thought now to have little or no connection with the abbot of that monastery, Tigernach Ua-Broein (d.1088), for whom they are named – survives, but only in fragmentary form, in manuscripts of the fourteenth century. The *Annals of Ulster*, whilst of a later fifteenth-century date, is essentially the work of a single scribe whose work displays the most impressive accuracy, and is thus considered the more reliable of the two annal sets. The oft-aforementioned entry concerning Fergus Mór, for example, is found in the *Annals of Tigernach* (from which it was copied into two later Clonmacnoise collections) and yet appears nowhere in the *Annals of Ulster*, thus casting that shadow of doubt as to its absolute provenance. While the ultimate source of the annal record of the advent of Fergus in Scotland must have lain in Dalriadic tradition, John Bannerman makes a strong case for its inclusion in a recension of the 'Ulster chronicle' made at Clonmacnoise in the early tenth century. Noticing that 'a number of entries in the *Annals of Tigernach* which could have originated in the *Iona Chronicle* are not in the *Annals of Ulster*', he suggests that 'this entry would be an obvious starting point for annals apparently compiled on Iona before 740'.[6]

The obituary of Fergus' son and successor Domangart is entered in both of these sets of annals and in others besides, yet its entry in the *Annals of Ulster* at 506 carries the cautionary qualifier 'as others say', which is taken to indicate the annalist's own suspicion as to the provenance of his source. While both the *Duan* and the king-list accord Domangart a five-year reign (a figure corresponding precisely to the reign-length and obituary date recorded for his father), the annalists have nothing else to tell of him other than hints in their form of words thought to indicate his having

---

6   Bannerman, *Dalriada*, p.74.

died in religious retirement. Only the *Duan Albanach* might have something further to add in its reference to his reign as 'five ever-turbulent years', suggesting some otherwise unrecorded contention which might yet have a bearing here.

It is in their record of the reigns of Domangart's sons and successors, Comgall and Gabrán, that the annals begin to offer greater detail of events in Dalriada, and the reason for this development will reward some investigation. In accordance with the custom of alternating succession between branches of a ruling family, Conall, son of Comgall, became king after the death of his uncle Gabrán in *c.*559. Although the sources preserve few notices of his sixteen-year reign, one event of outstanding importance was the arrival from Donegal of a holy man of princely stock known in Irish as *Columcille*, but more widely remembered by his Latin name-form as Saint Columba of Iona.

Adomnán's life of Columba, set down within a hundred years of his death and recognised as the most authoritative account of the saint, tells of his having stayed at Conall's court very soon after his arrival from Ireland, but of greater significance is the entry in the *Annals of Ulster* at the year 574 (and similarly throughout the Irish annal record) of the obituary of 'Conall, son of Comgall, who granted the island of Iona to Columcille'. Bede, on the other hand and presumably informed by Pictish tradition, believed the island to have been given to Columba by the Picts. Much scholarly effort has striven to reconcile those two apparently conflicting claims, and yet there is quite probably an element of truth in both of them. Iona lies just off the coast of Mull which was inhabited by Dalriadic Scots in Columba's time and so would have presumably been within Conall's gift, but Columba is also known to have visited the court of the powerful Pictish king Bruide, son of Maelchon, in company with other Irish abbots to negotiate safe conducts for their activities in and around Pictland, so it is very likely that he negotiated just such a guarantee for his foundation on Iona.

Of greater significance here is the assurance from the annalists – in agreement with Bede, who dates the foundation to the year 565 – of Columba's greatest monastery having been established within the reign of Conall mac Comgaill. The earliest source of the records preserved in the annals is thought to have been marginal notes of important events entered into 'Easter tables', the calendars with which early monasteries calculated the dating of the Paschal festival for each church year, and such was assuredly the case with the 'Iona chronicle'. Its compilation has been meticulously dated to the period *c.*670–*c.*740 by Marjorie Anderson,[7] which would allow annal entries dated between those years to be considered as a contemporary record, whilst assigning the source of earlier dated entries to notes made in Easter tables from the later 560s or to the collective memory of monastic tradition current at the time of compilation.

Events of a secular character would have been of similar origin, so the increase in number and in detail of annal entries bearing on the history of Dalriada from the reigns of Comgall and Gabrán onwards would correspond to the foundation of the monastery on Iona within living memory of those kings, and particularly so within the orbit of the court of Conall, as their kinsman and successor. When selection of secular entries for inclusion in monastic records must have been influenced, in at least some measure, by kingly patronage, the preservation of those records in later annal collections can be read as a reflection of the political preferences and prejudices of their original monastic source, thus revealing the pattern of relations between the church on Iona and the ruling kindreds of Dalriada.

Close links between the Columban church and kings of the Cenél nGabráin become most evident after the year 574 when Aedán, son of Gabrán, succeeded as over-king of Dalriada following the death of his cousin Conall. Aedán has been recognised as 'one of the greatest warlords in the British Isles during the early Middle Ages, dominating political and military events in northern Britain',[8] campaigning as far afield as Orkney and following up his father's failed attempt at expansion into Pictland with his own more successful intrusion into southern Pictish territory. His long reign extending over more than thirty years can be recognised as the high peak of the Cenél nGabráin ascendancy, and it was an achievement which he owed in great part to the counsel and support – even, in truth, also to the connivance – of Columba himself.

7   M. O. Anderson, *Kings & Kingship*, pp.6–22.
8   Williams, Smyth & Kirby (eds.), *Biographical Dictionary of Dark Age Britain*, p.4.

The most significant such occasion came about in the year after Aedán's succession when the new king, accompanied by the abbot of Iona, met with the powerful king of the northern Uí Néill, Aed, son of Ainmìre (and first cousin to Columba), at Druim Ceatt (the hill now called the Mullagh, near Limavady in County Derry) to resolve the politically anomalous situation of the Dál Riata in Ireland. The true purpose of this meeting, which is remembered as the 'Convention of Druim Ceatt', must have been to extricate Aedán's sea-divided kingdom from any expansionist ambitions on the part of the Dál Fiatach over-king of Ulster, who was excluded from the negotiations despite having only recently taken Aedán's formal submission on behalf of the Dál Riata of Antrim at Island Magee just south of Larne. Yet the actual terms of agreement reached at Druim Ceatt confirmed that the taxes and tribute of the Dál Riata in Ireland should belong to their king in Scotland, but that military obligation went with the land and so belonged to 'the men of Erin' (but without specifying whether to the kings of Ulster or the Uí Néill), and yet the *muir-coblach* (or 'ship-service', meaning that of the formidable Dalriadic war-fleet) should pertain exclusively to the king of Dalriada in Scotland. The long-term mutual benefit of all three provisions both to the Uí Néill in Ireland and the Cenél nGabráin in Scotland attests the far-sighted political acumen of the abbot of Iona on behalf of his own people and in the interest of his new royal patron in Argyll.

Yet Adomnán's account of Columba's part in Aedán's accession to the kingship tells of an unpromising opening of relations between the two men. The choice of successor to Conall lay between Aedán and his brother Eoganán, who would have been Columba's preferred candidate until his nocturnal contemplation of the dilemma of succession was interrupted by an angel insisting that he ordain Aedán as king. When Columba protested on behalf of Eoganán's claim, 'the angel stretched out his hand and struck the saint with a scourge, and its livid mark on his side remained for all the days of his life'. After further appearances of the angel, with the same divine instruction and the threat of further scourging on three consecutive nights, Columba finally complied and consecrated Aedán into the kingship on Iona.

The significance of that ceremony as the first recorded Christian inauguration of a king of Scots is of rather less bearing here than the related insertion into the earliest surviving manuscript of Adomnán's *Vita Columbae* of a quotation from an even earlier (and long since lost) account of the saint set down by Cumméne, abbot of Iona from 657 until his death in 669.

> Cumméne the White, in a book that he wrote about Saint Columba's miraculous powers, said that Saint Columba began to prophesy concerning Aedán and his posterity and their kingdom saying, 'Believe without doubt, Aedán, that none of your enemies will be able to resist you, until you first act deceitfully against me and my posterity. On that account, therefore, give this charge to your sons, that they charge their sons and grandsons and their posterity not to lose from their hands the sceptre of this kingdom through their wicked counsels. For at whatever time they do wrong to me or to my kinsmen in Ireland, the scourge that I have suffered because of you at the hand of an angel will be turned by the hand of God upon them, to their great disgrace; and their men will lose heart, and their enemies will be mightily strengthened against them.'
>
> Now this passage has been fulfilled in our times in the battle of Roth, when Domnall Brecc, Aedán's grandson, laid waste without cause to the province of Domnall, Ainmìre's grandson. And from that day to this they [the people of Dalriada] have continued in subjection to foreigners, which moves the heart to sighs of sorrow.

The battle to which Cumméne referred was fought in 637 at *Magh Rath* (now Moira in County Down) where Domnall, son of the Aed mac Ainmìrech who had met with Aedán at Druim Ceatt, led an alliance of the Uí Néill in an apparently pre-emptive strike against the Ulster king Congal Cáech of the Dál nAraide. Congal, who had long been in contention with the Uí Néill and was anticipating a decisive contest with their forces, had sought support from Domnall Brecc on the basis of an established alliance, which is thought to date back at least as far as the reign of his grandfather Aedán and to have been intended to protect Dalriadic interests in Ireland. The various accounts of Magh

Rath preserved in traditional tales as well as the annals leave it uncertain whether Domnall Brecc himself actually fought in the battle, but there is no doubt that he committed a Dalriadic contingent to the Cruithin forces who suffered crushing defeat in a blood-fray so ferocious as to be remembered in tradition as 'Magh Rath of the Red Pools'. When the fighting was over Congal Cáech, his son, and his sub-king of the Dál nAraide were all numbered among the slain, so it is perhaps unlikely that Domnall Brecc had been with them on the field because it was to be another five years before he met his death in battle against the north Britons of Strathclyde at Strathcarron north of Falkirk.

The annal record of his reign is scarred throughout by defeats and reversals, but none so disastrous for the kingdom of the Scots as was Magh Rath, which probably resulted in their loss of any control over the Irish homeland in Antrim and may also have forced upon Domnall Brecc the indignity of sharing his kingship with the Cenél Comgaill. In fact there is nowhere any doubt that his reign marked the point of downturn from which the Cenél nGabráin ascendancy crumbled into decline. From the viewpoint of the abbot Cumméne, writing about a quarter-century after Magh Rath, all this had been foretold by Columba should any descendant of Aedán mac Gabráin break faith with the saint by making war on his 'kinsmen in Ireland' (specifically the Cenél Conaill branch of the Uí Néill to which both Columba and 'Domnall, Ainmìre's grandson' belonged). Just such a betrayal was what had befallen at Magh Rath and so Cumméne had no hesitation in placing the blame on Domnall Brecc for his kingdom's continuing 'subjection to foreigners' (or *extranei* in the original Latin), meaning overlordship of Dalriada by a neighbouring northern power which, in the 660s, would almost certainly have been Northumbria.

It had been the Angles of Northumbria, under their ferocious pagan warrior king Aethelfrith, who inflicted defeat on Domnall's grandfather at Degsastan (now thought to be Addinston, Berwickshire) in 603, when they threw back an invasion by the Scots apparently intended to stem any further expansion of Aethelfrith's recently unified Northumbrian kingdom into the territory of the north Britons around the Forth. In the event, Degsastan was to be Aedán's last battle, because he is thought to have entered religious retirement through the five remaining years before his death which is entered in the annals at 608. Relations between the house of Aethelfrith and the Scots of Dalriada had evidently improved by 616 when Aethelfrith fell in battle, his kingship passed to a Northumbrian rival, Edwin, and his sons Oswald and Oswy fled the new regime to find sanctuary on Iona.

It was there that they were apparently introduced to the Christian faith and when Oswald returned to Northumbria in 633 one of his first acts after winning back the kingship was to invite churchmen from Iona to found the church on Lindisfarne which became the cradle of Christianity in the north of England. Adomnán expressed great esteem for Oswald, whom he called 'supreme ruler of all Britain', a claim supported by Bede with a specific reference to his sovereignty over Scots and Picts. Yet Oswald had been dead for at least a quarter of a century by the time Cumméne was writing of the Scots in 'subjection to foreigners', so the Northumbrian overlord to whom he would seem to have been referring would have been Oswald's brother and successor Oswy who reigned until 671 and is said by Bede to have 'rendered tributary the Picts and Scots in the northern parts of Britain'. The same overlordship was evidently passed to Oswy's son and successor Egfrith and firmly maintained by him until he was challenged by the Pictish king Bruide, son of Bile, and slain in a decisive defeat of his Northumbrian forces at Dunnichen just to the south-east of Forfar in 685. As a result of that battle, says Bede, 'the Picts recovered their own lands . . . while the Scots living in Britain, and some of the Britons themselves, regained their freedom'.

Had Cumméne lived to hear of the momentous battle at Dunnichen, he would probably have recognised its outcome as the lifting of Columba's curse, but he had been dead for more than fifteen years by 685. Adomnán, on the other hand, would have been especially well-informed on the subject. Since 679 he had been abbot of Iona, where he is said to have had the body of Bruide brought for burial after his death in 693. Not only was he well-acquainted with the Picts, but had earlier been tutor on Iona to Egfrith's half-brother and successor Aldfrith, a son born to Oswy by a princess of the Uí Néill. Aldfrith had only recently returned to assume the kingship after Egfrith's death at Dunnichen, and so it was to his court that Adomnán made his first visit to Northumbria with the purpose of reclaiming Irish hostages held by Egfrith after a punitive raid on Leinster in 684.

By the time he completed his book about Columba – certainly by 697 and possibly five years earlier – Northumbria no longer had any dominion north of the Forth and so it would have been meaningless as well as undiplomatic (bearing in mind his Northumbrian friends) for Adomnán to have included any such reference to 'subjection to foreigners'. Yet when the eminent scribe Dorbbéne, a senior member of the Iona community who had briefly served as its abbot, set down the earliest surviving copy of Adomnán's *Vita Columbae* (possibly shortly before the death of its author in 704 and certainly before 713, the year at which his own obituary is entered in the annals) he chose to insert the passage from Cumméne into Adomnán's text, and his reason for so doing is of signal importance here.

The close links between the church on Iona and the Cenél nGabráin kings of Dalriada would imply a measure of hostility to any rival dynastic kindred, and there is more than one hint of such disfavour specifi- cally directed towards 'people of the tribe of Loarn' in Adamnan's *Vita Columbae*, a work which reflects the Dalriada of its author's own day at least as clearly as that of Columba's era. By the time Dorbbéne was engaged upon his fine manuscript copy of Adomnán's book, however, the Cenél Loairn had supplanted the Cenél nGabráin as over-kings of Dalriada and so, when Cumméne's use of the Latin *extranei* translates equally well as 'strangers' instead of 'foreigners', there is good reason to read Dorbbéne's interpolated quotation as referring to that new political ascendancy established in Dalriada by the first years of the eighth century.

Although surely no more than an accident of coincidence, it is still perhaps worthy of notice that the very first reference to 'the tribe of Loarn' in the *Annals of Ulster* (as also in those attributed to 'Tigernach' and so presumably derived from a contemporary entry in the 'Iona chronicle') is entered at 678, and thus in the year preceding Adomnán's succession to the abbacy of Iona.

Yet the most detailed account of these same people – and, indeed, the earliest recognition of them as a dynastic kindred, if only by reason of its styling them as the 'Cenél Loairn' – has been assigned a date of origin as many as twenty years earlier than that of the annal entry. This evidence – of crucial bearing upon the origin, as well as the emergence, of the Cenél Loairn – is contained in a document known as the *Senchus fer nAlban* ('the history of the men of Scotland', a phrase from its opening sentence) and comprising a civil, military and naval survey interwoven with genealogical matter. Whilst this document is preserved in a number of medieval manuscript collections, none of them older than the fourteenth century, John Bannerman's meticulous examination of its text has shown that 'the extant versions of the *Senchus fer nAlban* derive from a compilation made sometime in the tenth century [which] seems to represent a new edition rather than a mere transcript . . . of a seventh-century original'.

His proposal of a seventh-century date is initially based upon the identity of the latest datable personality named in the *Senchus*: Conall Crandomna, a brother and eventual successor of Domnall Brecc, who is accorded a ten-year reign by the *Duan* and whose obituary is entered in the annals at 660. It would be reasonable then to place the composition of the original *Senchus* in the first decades of the second half of the seventh century. Such a date is further supported by Bannerman's observation that the three factors under negotiation at Druim Ceatt in 575 – essentially taxation, army and navy – are exactly the same as those covered by the survey in the *Senchus*, which leads him to suggest that a similar political crisis might have prompted the composition of the original *Senchus*.[9]

Those same factors of importance to Aedán, Columba and Aed mac Ainmìrech at Druim Ceatt would have been of similar significance to a Northumbrian overlord, and especially so at a time of precarious division of kingship in Dalriada. Such would indeed have been the situation when Oswy of Northumbria 'rendered tributary the Scots in the northern parts of Britain', and particularly during the 650s when Conall Crandomna is said by the *Duan* to have shared his kingship with a 'Dúnchad, son of Dubán'. This Dúnchad (or 'Dondchad') seems to be unnoticed in the annals, but is likely to have been the head of a leading Dalriadic family, probably a branch of the Cenél nGabráin, and quite

---

9   Bannerman, *Dalriada*, pp.39, 155.

possibly the descendant of a son of the Eoganán whom Columba had preferred to Aedán as a candidate for the succession three quarters of a century earlier.[10]

There is one further fragment of evidence to link composition of the original *Senchus* with Northumbrian overlordship of Dalriada and it is found in Bede's *Historia* where he describes the Isle of Iona as 'about five hides in area, according to English reckoning'. So specific an estimate of land area would suggest that his information was drawn from a tribute list akin to the original *Senchus* (and similar to the English 'Tribal Hidage') prepared for a Northumbrian king, probably for Oswy, whom Bede clearly understood to have 'rendered tributary the Scots', or for Egfrith, who evidently inherited that same overlordship from his father and pursued it with no lack of vigour.

It should be said though that there are other estimated dates of origin for the *Senchus* which place it some decades later than Bannerman's proposal, and yet, if the connection with Northumbrian overlordship is accepted, the survey could not have been commissioned and compiled any later than 685. Differing views on dating are to be expected of course, and especially when the state of the surviving text is so suspiciously uneven and riddled with inconsistencies, a condition attributed in no small part to the attentions of its tenth-century 'editor'. Fortunately, John Bannerman's forensic analysis has attempted to extricate as much as possible of the seventh-century content from the apparent disturbances and accretions inflicted upon it some three centuries later.

The core of the original document is presumably to be found in the survey, which is structured upon the base unit of the *tech* (or 'house'). This would have represented the unit of assessment for any rental, taxation or tribute, as well as obligation for military and naval service – as, indeed, is confirmed by the repeated statement of 'two seven-benchers' (i.e. craft for naval service) from 'every twenty houses for a sea expedition'. The military strength of each of the *cenéla* is similarly calculated on the basis of each house being obliged to make a specified contribution to the total manpower mustered for a *slógad* (or 'hosting').

---

10　　M. O. Anderson, *Kings & Kingship*, pp.155–6.

It is perhaps surprising to find only three *primchenéla* – the Cenél nGabráin, Cenél nOengusa and Cenél Loairn – covered by the survey, when four are listed elsewhere, as indeed they are in the set of later genealogies (*Genelaig Albanensium*) appended to the *Senchus*.[11] Yet there is no reference to the Cenél Comgaill in the *Senchus* itself, an omission probably explained by its having been considered as a branch of the Cenél nGabráin at the time of composition. In fact, that explanation would be supported by the text of the *Senchus* where the total of 560 houses of the Cenél nGabráin are located in Kintyre and '*Crích Chomgaill* with its islands', presumably meaning Cowal and its neighbouring islands in the lower Clyde (probably Bute and possibly also the Cumbraes and Arran), all of which might be included within Cenél Comgaill territory.

Apart from that general indication of its territory and its historically corroborated listing of Fergus Mór's descendants through four generations, the *Senchus* survey of the Cenél nGabráin is remarkable for what would seem to be its inconsistencies and omissions in the surviving text, possibly resulting from damage to an earlier manuscript copy, to careless transcription at some stage in transmission or, perhaps more probably, to disturbance of the original text by its tenth-century editor. The apparent underestimate of its expeditionary strength at only three hundred men suggests one example of inconsistency, while an example of omission appears to be the absence of any indication of the distribution of Cenél nGabráin houses, and especially so in comparison to the *Senchus* account of the Cenél nOengusa. In that survey a similar genealogy of four generations from the eponymous 'Oengus Már' names three of his grandsons 'who divided land in *Ilé*' (the same name for the Isle of Islay used by Adomnán), before allocating the houses of the *cenél* on the basis of districts or townships on Islay. Unfortunately, only one of those Islay district names – *Oidech*, a place-name also used by Adomnán and identified as the Oa on the south-eastern tip of the island – has been firmly located on the modern map.

Yet this survey would also appear incomplete when the sum total of houses listed adds up to 350 while the total entered for the Cenél

---

11   See Genealogy 2, p.175 below.

nOengusa alongside those for the other *prímchenéla* at the foot of the *Senchus* is 430. Comparison of those figures suggests a further statistical inconsistency, when the 'expeditionary strength' of the Cenél nOengusa is assessed at a total of 500 men, which is hardly proportionate to the 300 recruited from 560 houses of the Cenél nGabráin.

The survey of the Cenél Loairn following after those of the Cenél nGabráin and Cenél nOengusa in the *Senchus* comprises a detailed account of distribution of houses, yet it differs from the Cenél nOengusa survey inasmuch as it allocates them not to various districts or townships but to individuals who are identified as descendants of the eponymous 'Loarn'. As an unhelpful consequence of such an arrangement, the *Senchus* supplies no indication of the territory of the Cenél Loairn, and so all that is known of its location and extent has been gleaned from Adomnán or references in the annals, with some supplementary support from the study of place-names.

The evidence of those early sources, none of them earlier in date than the last quarter of the seventh century, has been taken to suggest the line separating the Cenél Loairn from the Cenél nGabráin having lain across mid-Argyll, where the hill-fort at Dunadd is thought to have repre-sented the royal capital of Dalriada. By the second quarter of the eighth century, the annals seem to indicate Dunadd held by Cenél Loairn kings, and yet a site of such ceremonial importance would presumably have formerly been in possession of the Cenél nGabráin. Another hill-fort, at Dunollie close by Oban, is firmly identified by the annal record of the early eighth century as a Cenél Loairn stronghold, which it had probably been since earlier times because it lay on the shore of the Firth of Lorn, and the wider application of the name of Lorn to the surrounding coast-land makes its own claim for that region as the heartland of the Cenél Loairn. The same claim finds further support in W. J. Watson's identi-fication of 'Kinelvadon' as the old name for Morvern and a derivation from the Gaelic *Cineal Bhaodain* (or 'kindred of Baodon') whose eponym was almost certainly the same Báetán, son of Eochaid, identified as the ancestor of all the Cenél Loairn kings of Dalriada in four genealogies of dates ranging from the eighth to twelfth centuries.[12]

---

12    Watson, *Celtic Place-names*, p.122; M. O. Anderson, *Kings & Kingship*, p.161.

Adomnán records Scots of Dalriada (who must have been of the Cenél Loairn) further to the north, around upper Loch Linnhe and out on Ardnamurchan, which would have represented their northern boundary fronting on to the north-western domains of the Picts who are said by Adomnán to have been resident on Skye in Columba's time. In view of that extent of Cenél Loairn territory, it would assuredly follow that the outlying islands of the coastland south of Ardnamurchan – specifically Mull, with Iona, and Tiree – would have also been occupied by their people.

Turning back to the *Senchus*, it is interesting to find the survey of the houses of the Cenél Loairn more detailed than that of the Cenél nOengusa, and still more so than that of the Cenél Gabráin, where only the sum total is given at the very foot of its surviving text. The reason for this would appear to have been the listing of Cenél Loairn houses under the names of lesser *cenéla* and of individuals whose descent was of very much greater interest to a tenth-century editor than a civil survey already three hundred years out of date. While the true motive underlying his concern with the genealogy of the Dalriadic *prímchenéla* will bear some further investigation, his attentions in that direction can be blamed at this point for disturbance of the original survey of the Cenél Loairn, and most obviously so when the houses listed under the names of individuals and lesser *cenéla* add up to a sum total no greater than 225, which falls alarmingly short of the figure of 420 entered for the Cenél Loairn at the foot of the *Senchus*.

The original *Senchus* would seem to have identified the Cenél Fergusa Shalaig, the Cenél Cathbath, the Cenél nEchdach and the Cenél Muredaig as the four *cenéla* comprising the dynastic grouping known as the Cenél Loairn and there is good reason to accept their historicity, if only by reason of the Cenél Cathbath's appearance in the annal record of the early eighth century. Yet the extant *Senchus*, having identified their eponyms as four of the 'seven sons of Loarn Mór', lists the house totals for only the first two, the Cenél Fergusa Shalaig and the Cenél Cathbath, assessing them at sixty houses each before proceeding to list smaller totals under the names of individuals who are identified as grandsons and great-grandsons of 'Loarn'.

One of the grandsons is a 'Báitán' identified as a son of Fergus Salach whose eponymous Cenél Fergusa Shalaig takes precedence in the list of septs and would thus represent the line from which kings of the Cenél Loairn were most likely to have been chosen. Yet the similarly named and more reliably historical Báetán (or 'Baodon') who is entered as a son of Echdach, son of Muiredach, in the genealogies appended to the *Senchus* and in the twelfth-century pedigrees of the two kings of Scots descended from the hereditary mormaers of Moray, would have been in the next generation and thus a great-grandson in a different line of descent from 'Loarn'. So it is not difficult to see why John Bannerman came to consider the Cenél Loairn section 'probably the most disturbed of the three' and how his analysis of its genealogical content led him to venture the proposal 'that this section originally consisted of a list of peoples or septs collectively called the Cenél Loairn followed by the names of their respective seventh-century leaders and the number of houses belonging to each. Whether these leaders were in every case the sons and grandsons of the people who appear in the sept names as the present *Senchus* maintains, or whether the hand of the editor should again be detected is not easy to decide, though such a rearrangement of the material would be fully in accord with his apparent methods.'[13]

Yet there is one curious item bearing upon the Cenél Loairn in the *Senchus* which, although probably disturbed from its original placing when it appears as a sudden interruption to the sequence of house allocations, is unlikely to have been of tenth-century invention, especially when it is corroborated by an entry in the *Annals of Ulster* at the year 727. This reference occurs as the final clause of the assessment of the expeditionary strength of the Cenél Loairn at seven hundred men, where it adds that 'the seventh hundred is from the Airgialla'.

The Airgialla, a name already mentioned here as that given to the vassal allies of the Uí Néill on their advance into Ulster, is thought to derive from the Irish term *giall* ('hostage') and therefore to mean 'givers of hostages', which would well describe the relationship of the Airgialla to the Uí Néill. The interpretation of same term in a Dalriadic context was taken at one time to indicate the Cenél Loairn having recruited an indigenous people of Argyll into a similar vassal alliance, but David Sellar's

---

13   Bannerman, *Dalriada*, p.129.

study of the twelfth-century Somerled of Argyll traced his ancestry back to the Uí Macc Uais, a section of the Irish Airgialla located in County Derry.[14] The claim asserted by Clan Donald tradition for Morvern having been the territory of Somerled and his forebears would correspond to an earlier settlement of Airgialla from Ireland in the heartland of the Cenél Loairn, where they presumably accepted a vassal–ally status similar to that of their erstwhile submission to the Uí Néill.

All of which tells a great deal about the Cenél Loairn in the seventh century whilst already hinting at how it was recognised three hundred years later, but leaves open a question of central bearing on the subject of this chapter: who – if such a person ever existed – was the eponymous Loarn?

According to the extant version of the *Senchus*, both he and the Oengus for whom the Cenél nOengusa was named were sons of Erc and brothers to Fergus Mór. Yet, while the historicity of Fergus' own line of descent is corroborated elsewhere in the sources, the *Senchus* account of the 'sons of Erc' is so confused as to deny it any real credibility and so must be suspected of having been a contrivance of the aforementioned tenth-century editorial interference with the original text.

The account of Saint Patrick's visit to Erc, king of the Dál Riata – preserved in two ninth-century Armagh sources, but of possibly earlier origin – tells of twelve sons of Erc, and yet Fergus is the only one mentioned by name. In fact, no other son of Erc is recorded by name until the editor of the *Senchus*, presumably acquainted with the claim for 'twelve sons' preserved in Armagh tradition, took the opportunity to identify the six of them who 'took possession of Alba' as 'Loarn Bec and Loarn Mór, two Mac Nisses i.e. Mac Nisse Bec and Mac Nisse Mór, two Ferguses i.e. Fergus Bec and Fergus Mór'. Yet the form of words in that statement immediately betrays the period in which it was written, because *Alba* had been the Irish name for the whole of Britain until it became applied strictly to Scotland in the tenth century as it is still in modern Gaelic. Thus the entry in the *Annals of Tigernach* – evidently deriving from a source of earlier date when the use of *Alba* in its former sense of 'the whole of Britain' would have been absurd – describes Fergus as having 'held part of Britain'.

---

14    Sellar, 'The Origins and Ancestry of Somerled', p.141.

The six names of 'sons of Erc' are clearly of tenth-century devising, as the text itself effectively admits just a few lines later where it identifies Fergus Mór as having been 'another name for Mac Nisse Mór'. That same dual identity is confirmed by the Armagh source where 'Mac Nisse' is also applied as another name for Fergus, son of Erc. *Nisse* represents the genitive form of the female name *Ness*, and so might be taken for the name of Fergus' mother, even though such a use of 'Mac Nisse' would be unlikely when appearing alongside the use of his patronymic *mac Eirc* ('son of Erc'). In fact, such a possibility is dismissed by the entry of the obituary of Domangart, son and successor to Fergus, in the *Annals of Ulster* and the *Annals of Tigernach* where he is similarly surnamed *mac Nisse*. That would suggest *mac* ('son of') entered in place of an earlier *moccu* ('lineage of') and indicate 'Ness' as the name of an ancestral divinity, possibly even the same *Neas* (earlier *Nes*) who was supposedly the 'mother' of Conchobar mac Neasa, the mythical king of Emain in the *Táin*, and thought to have been the name of a goddess personifying sovereignty.

So it would appear that the editor of the *Senchus* attempted to identify six of the twelve sons of Erc by using the *Mór* and *Bec* formula to double up three names, two of which inconveniently pertained to the original Fergus. At some point, he would seem to have realised that having contrived the eponym of the Cenél Loairn as a son of Erc, he had failed to do the same for the Cenél nOengusa, because the *Senchus* text later states quite plainly: 'Oengus Mar and Loarn and Mac Nisse Már, these are the three sons of Erc.' The necessary adjustment seems to have taken the form of naming one of the other six sons of Erc remaining in Ireland as an 'Oengus, whose seed, however, is in Alba'. Yet even this attempt to claim the eponym of the Cenél nOengusa as a 'son of Erc' is exposed by evidence from the Armagh sources which identifies a Cenél nOengusa already established within the Dál Riata while Fergus was still living with his father Erc in Ireland. Consequently, whoever might have been the Oengus for whom that *cenél* had been named, he could hardly have been a son of Erc and, indeed, it is fully possible for his descendent Cenél nOengusa to have been a branch of the Dál Riata which was already settled on Islay before Fergus re-located its ruling house from Antrim to Argyll.

Much the same must almost certainly also apply to the Cenél Loairn, because if the eponym of the Cenél nOengusa could not have been a son of Erc, then the claim by the *Senchus* for 'Loarn' having been the name of one (or two) of the others was almost certainly another invention attributable to that tenth-century editor. Yet, while the personal name Oengus was not at all uncommon in early Ireland, the earliest datable record of anyone by the name of Loarn is that found in the extant *Senchus*. Nonetheless, the poet of the *Duan*, writing in the late eleventh century and presumably informed by the *Senchus*, not only acknowledged Loarn as a son of Erc but went still further to accord him a ten-year reign as the predecessor of Fergus Mór. John Bannerman dismisses the *Duan* entry of Loarn's kingship as 'fiction',[15] and quite reasonably so, especially when the earliest surviving king-list, that known as the *Synchronisms* and attributed to Fland of Monasterboice who died in 1056, somehow manages to put Oengus in place of Domangart as Fergus Mór's successor. Even so, there is still something about the form of words used by the *Duan* to describe Loarn's reigning 'with distinguished renown in the kingdom of *Oirir Alban*' (literally 'the coastland of Alba', but plausibly rendered as 'Argyll' by A. O. Anderson[16]) which might be taken to hint at some recollection, not necessarily of 'Loarn' himself, but of a Cenél Loairn ascendancy in Argyll before the arrival of Fergus Mór to claim over-kingship of earlier Dalriadic settlements.

Yet there remains an apparent absence of any genuinely historical evidence for the eponym of the Cenél Loairn, a situation which invites such serious doubt as to his even having been a living person that the origin of the name must be sought elsewhere. One possibility is of Loarn having been an ancestral divinity similar to the Ness associated with Fergus Mór, his son Domangart, and the legendary Ulster king Conchobar. W. J. Watson identified the name Loarn (or *Loern*) as a derivation from the older Celtic *Lovernos*, meaning 'fox' and preserved in the name of a Gaulish chieftain as well as ancient Welsh place-names,[17] which could indicate the eponym of the Cenél Loairn as having been a prehistoric, even shamanic, animal totem.

---

15    Bannerman, *Dalriada*, p.74.
16    Anderson, *ESSH*, vol. i, p.2.
17    Watson, *Celtic Place-names*, p.121.

An alternative possibility has been more recently suggested by Alan Bruford who points to the modern Gaelic form of the place-name Lorn being *Latharna* and thus identical with the name of the early Irish *tuath* whose territory around Larne lay immediately to the south of the Dál Riata. 'It is tempting to wonder whether they [the Cenél Loairn] were Dál Riata at all or settlers from a neighbouring tribe, and the form Loarn is itself an invention to muddy the record.'[18] It is tempting indeed – and especially so when a Lorn man is still today known in Gaelic as a *Latharnach* – because pursuit of that line of inquiry would lead to the proposal of an origin for the Cenél Loairn at extreme variance from that found in the *Senchus*.

If 'Loarn' does represent a later form of Latharna, then its origin lies in a distinct regional identity rather than an otherwise unrecorded eponymous ancestor. In which case it is fully possible that 'Cenél Loairn' represents a formal style, maybe even one first applied in the compilation of the civil/military survey at the core of the original seventh-century *Senchus*, for a number of *cenéla* collectively known to Adomnán – and similarly to the compiler of the immediately contemporary 'Iona chronicle' which assuredly provided the source for the annal entry at 678 – as 'the people of the tribe of Loarn'.

It is considered to be of signal importance that there is nowhere in the *Senchus* any reference to a 'Cenél Fergusa', and the dominant ruling kindred is named, not for its supposed founding dynast but for his grandson, as the Cenél nGabráin. That alone would suggest the Cenél Loairn, like the Cenél nOengusa, having been an earlier northern Irish settlement who came under the over-kingship of Fergus Mór following his arrival in Scotland at the end of the fifth century.

The proposal of their original homeland around what is now Larne – and thus just outside the southern border of the Irish territory of the Dál Riata – might appear inconsistent with their submission to a Dalriadic over-king and yet it need not necessarily have been so, because the political circumstances of Latharna in Ireland at that time are uncertain. The eleventh-century *Lebor na Cert* (or 'Book of Rights') records its king having paid tribute directly to the provincial king of Ulster, while the

---

18    Bruford, 'What happened to the Caledonians?', p.66, n.82.

'Tripartite Life' of St Patrick, compiled in the late ninth century, places the Latharna within the territory of the Dál nAraide. Yet the political situation of northern Ireland when those records were set down was greatly changed from that of the fifth century and earlier, and it is not impossible that a *tuath* such as the Latharna might have been in some wise and at some time tributary to the over-king of the neighbouring Dál Riata. Had that been the case before Fergus Mór transferred the ruling house of the Dál Riata to Argyll – and probably done so with the prospect of expansion in mind – he might well have taken the opportunity to resume sovereignty over a branch of the Latharna already settled in Scotland. Neither is it unimaginable that he may have needed to overcome initial resistance – and thus possibly sown the seed of later contentious rivalry between the Cenél Loairn and Cenél nGabráin.

The homeland of the Latharna may also have a further significance here, because its location on the coastline of the Irish Sea would have offered an approach to the lower Clyde encouraging settlement on its northern shore, plausibly on the Cowal peninsula whence they could soon have crossed over Loch Fyne into mid-Argyll. Subsequent expansion to the north would soon have extended their territory to the coastland of the Firth of Lorn and beyond, where Adomnán certainly knew them to be resident in his own day, if not already so in Columba's time a hundred years earlier. There is, of course, another correspondence between such a scenario for Cenél Loairn settlement and Bede's version of the Cairpre Riata legend, which he believed to represent the earliest Scots settlement on mainland Britain.

That same legend, already established in Irish tradition by the time it was brought to Bede's notice, was evidently still current in the tenth century when the editor of the *Senchus* chose to make reference to it as one of his accretions to the original text. An obvious interpolation when it occurs out of sequence between the end of the Cenél Loairn survey and the concluding summary of house totals for the three *prímchenéla*, the line tells how 'a hundred and fifty men, the ship expedition, went forth with the sons of Erc, the third fifty was Corpri and his people'. Cairpre Riata was still remembered even in the eleventh century, if only on the evidence of one of the genealogies appended to the *Senchus* when it traces the pedigree of Constantine III (d.997) through the Cenél nGabráin to the ancient Dál Riata in Ireland and manages to enter a *Corpri rigfhotaì* some ten generations before Fergus Mór.

All of which can only be read as an attempt by a tenth-century scribe confronted with a seventh-century survey of Dalriada and finding within it genealogical matter which he sought to revise, rearrange and rewrite in order to create a new 'origin-legend' for the embryonic kingdom of the Scots, presumably intended to replace the earlier one centred upon Cairpre Riata. His original text was concerned with three ruling kindreds and so his plan, quite logically based upon the age-old concern with kinship characteristic of the Gael, was to contrive a family relationship between his preferred founding dynast Fergus Mór, son of Erc, and the supposed eponyms of the three *prímchenéla*. He would seem to have used the same device elsewhere in the *Senchus* where he claims his fictitious 'Fergus Bec', son of Erc, to have 'had one son, Setna, from whom are the Cenél Conchride in Islay'. Recognising this as an obvious invention by the tenth-century editor, John Bannerman suggests that 'there may have been such a kindred on Islay in his day whom he wished to connect with the ruling family of Dál Riata'.[19]

When it came to the three *prímchenéla* entered in the original text, he would have had no problem with the Cenél nGabráin which he would have certainly known to have been named for and directly descended from the Gabrán, son of Domangart and grandson of Fergus Mór. It only remained for him to contrive a similar relationship for the supposed eponyms of the Cenél nOengusa and Cenél Loairn, and so he simply invented brothers named Oengus and Loarn to be included with Fergus among the 'twelve sons of Erc' of whom he had assuredly learned from the Armagh sources.

The question remains as to why a tenth-century scribe should have gone to such extraordinary lengths of contrivance and invention with fragments of genealogy interwoven into a civil, military and naval survey, itself of such remote antiquity as to be virtually meaningless some three hundred years after it was compiled.

The answer to that question is of key significance in the wider context of this book because it must lie within the political context of the later

---

19   Bannerman, *Dalriada*, p.130.

tenth century when the MacAlpin kings who claimed direct descent from the Cenél nGabráin rulers of Dalriada were already advancing towards a high-kingship of Scots. The major impediment to their achievement of such an ambition lay north of the Grampians where the ruling kindred of Moray claimed descent from the kings of the Cenél Loairn in Dalriada and clung tenaciously to their independence. While these kings in the north do appear on occasion to have submitted, if only with reluctance, to a measure of overlordship from the south, they may yet have been prepared to challenge the house of MacAlpin for high-kingship of Alba.

A document of impressive antiquity which could be adapted to show a close blood-kinship binding the ancestors of those two rival ruling families might have been thought a useful device in forestalling such a challenge should it ever be raised against any present or future genera-tion of Cenél nGabráin-descended kings of Scots. If such had indeed been the true purpose behind the rewriting of the *Senchus fer nAlban*, it was to prove of little avail in the following century when the high-kingship of Scots was seized by a man who could claim to be a direct descendant of the kings who had achieved the first ascendancy of the Cenél Loairn more than three hundred years before.

## II

## KINGSHIP IN DALRIADA

Even though the kindreds who made up the dynastic group recognised by the original *Senchus* as the Cenél Loairn had very probably been settled in Argyll before the arrival of Fergus Mór in the last years of the fifth century, there is no reference to the 'people of the tribe of Loarn', nor to any individual named in their genealogies, to be found in the annal record until the year 678. While it is impossible to know how much of that apparent invisibility can be justly blamed on the disregard of an Iona chronicler for the activities of a dynastic kindred suspected as a rival to his community's favoured Cenél nGabráin, it might still be possible to discern from the early sources at least some hint of the presence of the Cenél Loairn in Dalriada before the last quarter of the seventh century.

Indeed, some historians have read a hint of contention into the entry in the *Annals of Tigernach* at 501, where Fergus Mór is said to have 'held [*tenuit*] part of Britain', if the use of the word *tenuit* is taken to imply an element of force having been involved. As suggested earlier, it is fully possible that some degree of coercion might have been exerted by Fergus and his following to secure his acceptance as over-king had there been elements of resistance from earlier Dalriadic-related settlements in Argyll – and not least amongst them the forebears of the Cenél Loairn. If such really is the implication of that annal entry, then it could well find an echo of support in the *Duan Albanach* where the reign of Fergus' son and successor Domangart is described as 'five ever-turbulent years'. The emergence of an untested successor to a recently deceased over-lord would seem to have served as the opportunity for a whole series of challenges to MacAlpin and Canmore kings of Scots staged by rival claimants of Cenél Loairn descent in later centuries. If so, then even the tenuous possibility of a Cenél Loairn challenge to the succession of the pious Domangart having represented the first example of a family tradition later taken up by a long line of Moray rebels throughout the eleventh and twelfth centuries is just too tempting to be allowed to pass unnoticed here.

A more substantial connection with the Cenél Loairn has been sought in an annal entry at the end of the reign of Domangart's son Gabrán when it records 'the flight of the Scots (*Albanach*) before Bruide, Maelchon's son, king of the Picts' sometime between 558 and 560. This Bruide, who was described as 'most powerful' by Bede, has a genuine claim to recognition as the first properly historical king of Picts, and not only on the strength of the annal evidence because he is also mentioned by Adomnán on a number of occasions, most importantly here that of Columba's visit to his fortress in the year following the saint's arrival in Scotland.

That 'flight of the *Albanach*' – assuredly meaning Dalriadic Scots – is found in the *Annals of Tigernach* at *c*.559 and also in the *Annals of Ulster* where it is entered twice, first at the year 558 and again at 560. Even though that entry is placed beside the obituary of Gabrán in all three instances, there is no reason to suppose an immediate connection between the two events, especially if the flight from Bruide implies an element of conflict, because there is no indication of violent death in the form of words used by any entry of Gabrán's obituary. So too, the sequence of the two events differs across the annal record where the *Annals of Tigernach* place Gabrán's obituary before the flight from Bruide and the second entry in the *Annals of Ulster* follows that same sequence even though their earlier notice reversed that order. Neither is the sequence of those events the only difference between the annalists' description of them, because the first Ulster entry follows the meaning of the Tigernach annalist's Irish *teiched* with its use of the Latin *fuga* – both words translating as 'flight' – and yet the second entry chooses the term *immerge* which means a 'shifting of ground' or, perhaps, 'withdrawal'. The difference between the two is of real significance because whereas 'flight' might imply a rout or, at least, a defeat in battle, *immerge* would indicate ejection, and not necessarily by direct force, of a Dalriadic attempt at expansion into Pictish territory.

Adomnán provides the earliest evidence for the geographical feature separating the domains of the Picts from those of the Scots (at least on the mainland) having been 'the mountains of the spine of Britain' (*montes dorsi Britannici*), by which he meant the line of peaks ranging up from Ben Lomond to Ben Nevis, if not still further north into Sutherland, and more usually known by its Gaelic name-form of *Druim Alban*, 'the ridge of Alba'. Adomnán's account of Columba's visit to Bruide tells of the saint's travelling beyond the 'spine of Britain' – presumably by boat along the lochs and rivers which effectively form a waterway along the greater extent of the Great Glen – to reach Bruide's fortress above the river Ness (convincingly identified as the timber-laced hill-fort of Craig Phadrig overlooking the city of Inverness). If Craig Phadrig really did represent Bruide's capital fortress, Adomnán's evidence would well correspond to Bede's description of Columba's activity having been in 'the kingdoms of the northern Picts . . . separated from the southern territories of the Picts by a range of steep and rugged mountains', by which was meant the Grampian range anciently known as the Mounth (from the Gaelic *Monadh*, or 'The Mountains').

All of which could be taken to indicate Bruide in kingship over 'the northern Picts' and to locate his kingdom north of the Mounth where any move towards territorial expansion on the part of the Dalriadic Scots would have been more realistically attempted from the north of Argyll than Kintyre. On the basis of that premise it would be reasonable to suggest the Scots driven out of Pictland in the mid-sixth century as having been ancestors of the Cenél Loairn who were indeed to accomplish just such a migration and settlement north of the Grampians a few hundred years later. However reasonable such a proposal might appear, it was almost certainly not the case because – as Marjorie Anderson observed – 'Gabrán seems to have been remembered for expeditions far to the east of Argyll' and so it is more likely that 'the flight of the Scots before Bruide, Maelchon's son, king of the Picts' entered in the annals alongside Gabrán's obituary 'may have been the end of an attempt by Gabrán and his people to settle in Pictish territory'.[1]

W. J. Watson found impressive support for the same proposal in the Welsh sources which preserve ancient material relating to the North

---

1    M. O. Anderson, *Kings & Kingship*, p.138.

Britons, and especially in their genealogies where a *Luan* or *Leian*, one of the twenty-five daughters of a north British prince called Brachan (*Brychan*), is said to have been a wife of Gabrán, king of Dalriada in Scotland, and the mother of Aedán. Further support is found in verses of the sixth-century bard Taliesin where he tells of Gwallawg, another prince of the North Britons and an ally of the celebrated Urien of Rheged, warfaring in *Prydyn* ('Pictland'), specifically in *Gafran* and in 'the quarter of *Brychan*'. Despite *Gafran* being the name-form by which Gabrán of Dalriada was called in the Welsh genealogies, 'the Gafran mentioned in the poem was evidently a district, and the only district anywhere which can be meant is Gowrie'. Watson goes on to deduce that Gabrán would have been a man in his fifties by the time he succeeded his brother Comgall as king of Dalriada and, while nothing is recorded of his earlier life, his son Aedán is known to have been closely associated with the Britons north of the Forth and may even have been born and raised amongst them. 'If Gabrán's wife was the daughter of a Brachan of Forfarshire, he himself may have ruled the district adjacent to Forfarshire on the west, namely *Gafran* or Gowrie' before he succeeded to the kingship of Dalriada.'[2]

Whether or not Bruide's power-base was centred on the Moray Firth, Adomnán indicates his over-kingship extending northwards to Orkney and there is no reason to doubt the territorial ambition of such a powerful king of Picts having been directed at least as far to the south as Forfarshire, especially when he himself is thought to have been of part-British descent. In which case, the death of the ageing Gabrán would have offered an immediate opportunity for pursuit of such ambitions, and the Scots who fled 'before Bruide, Maelchon's son' would more probably have been elements of the Dalriadic nobility associated with, if not related to, Gabrán and settled in Gowrie to govern on his behalf until driven back across the Druim Alban by the advent of a new Pictish overlord. Thus they would certainly not have been of the Cenél Loairn.

There is just one further fragment of evidence from the annal record prior to the year 678 with a distinctly probable bearing on the Cenél Loairn and it occurs in the reign of Gabrán's nephew and successor,

---

2   Watson, *Celtic Place-names*, pp.111–13.

Conall, son of Comgall. An entry in the *Annals of Ulster* at *c.*568 records 'a campaign in *Iardoman* [an early name for the Inner Hebrides] led by Colmán Bec, son of Diarmait, and Conall, son of Comgall'. What had brought Colmán Bec, of the Southern Uí Néill and king of Meath, to join Conall on a seaborne campaign in the Hebrides is unspecified, although some form of alliance secured by a marriage contract is perhaps the most likely explanation. Of greater importance here, however, is the supplementary detail offered by the annals in the twelfth-century *Book of Leinster* where the destinations of Conall's fleet are specifically identified as the islands of Seil and Islay.

The entry of the same expedition in the *Annals of the Four Masters* also identifies Seil and Islay as its targets and adds that Colmán and Conall 'took from them many spoils', which would suggest the operation having been an intimidatory tribute-gathering venture directed against recalcitrant lesser kings. While the evidence of the *Senchus* points to the Cenél nOengusa having been the target group on Islay, the close proximity of Seil island to Oban would place it within the territory of the Cenél Loairn, which would propose both of those two *cenéla* having found – or placed – themselves in contention with Conall, son of Comgall, by the later 560s.

More than a hundred years were to pass before the annalists had occasion to notice the Cenél Loairn, and this time by name although with an irksome shortage of supporting detail. An entry in the *Annals of Ulster* at the year 678 records 'a slaughter of the tribe of Loarn in *Tirinn*', and the same entry is made at the same year in the *Annals of Tigernach* but with some further detail added as a gloss to the effect that this slaughter was inflicted in a battle 'between Ferchar Fota and the Britons, who were the conquerors'. As far as I am aware, no location of 'Tirinn' has been identified or even suggested and it is difficult to imagine any late seventh-century scenario which could put the Cenél Loairn of northern Argyll into conflict with Britons (presumably those of Strathclyde). Neither have I come upon any detailed scholarly examination of the problem, excepting only a few comments by Marjorie Anderson where she recognises the Tigernach gloss as 'a manifest dislocation, suggesting that the extra details were carelessly incorporated from additions written in a margin or between lines', probably deriving from 'a tale of Ferchar

Fota' and yet implying that he 'was remembered in his own right, and not simply as the father and grandfather of succeeding kings'.[3] Nonetheless, it is as the ancestor of succeeding kings that Ferchar *fóta* ('the tall') is of greater importance here, because the appearance of his name in the annals, when taken together with the evidence of the Cenél Loairn genealogies appended to the *Senchus*, can be said to represent the first notice of early Scotland's 'other royal family' in the historical record.

Other than that suspect interpolation in the *Annals of Tigernach*, the only notice of Ferchar in the annal record is his obituary which is entered at 697, thus placing his death in the same year as that of Eochaid, grandson of Domnall Brecc and the last of the Cenél nGabráin to hold the kingship of Dalriada, albeit only for a year or two, before it passed to the Cenél Loairn. Yet the Dalriadic king-list and the *Duan Albanach* not only enter Ferchar Fota immediately before Eochaid but accord him a twenty-one year reign which scarcely corresponds to the evidence of annal record. It is perhaps possible that the editor of the list – who was, of course, working some centuries after the event – had confused the Ferchar of the Cenél Loairn with an earlier Ferchar, variously linked with the Cenél nGabráin and the Cenél Comgaill, who may have briefly held the kingship of Dalriada in 629, but whose obituary is entered in the *Annals of Ulster* at the implausibly late date of 693. While the possibility of such scribal confusion cannot be discounted, A. O. Anderson's alternative proposal that the twenty-one year kingship credited to Ferchar Fota in the *Duan* as well as the later king-lists 'must include his previous reign in Lorn' would seem to be the more convincing explanation of the conflict of evidence from the sources.[4]

Whatever might have been the true origin of that apparent confusion, its mere existence bears testimony to the parlous state into which the kingship of Dalriada had descended through just two generations of succession to the ill-starred Domnall Brecc. The weakening of the Cenél nGabráin would seem to have allowed a new independence to the Cenél Comgaill when they are included as one of the four *prímchenéla* in the eighth-century genealogies appended to the *Senchus*, while their

---

3   M. O. Anderson, *Kings & Kingship*, pp.38, 179.
4   Anderson, *ESSH*, vol. i, p.202.

omission from the survey at the core of the original *Senchus* indicates their having been subsumed into the Cenél nGabráin by the second half of the seventh century. Yet there can be no doubt of the Cenél Loairn having been the foremost beneficiary of the decline of the Cenél nGabráin, because by the year 710 when the Cenél Comgaill make their last appearance in the annal record the sons of Ferchar Fota had been in the ascendant for over a decade.

If Ferchar was indeed the first of his dynasty to achieve over-kingship of Dalriada, his reign could not have been of more than a few months in duration because Eochaid is included among the signatories to the *Cáin Adomnáin* ('Adomnán's Law of the Innocents') which was adopted in Ireland in 697, and so he was evidently king of Dalriada at the time. Before that year was out, however, Eochaid had been slain (almost certainly by the Cenél Loairn, despite there being no notice of warfare in the annal record), Ferchar Fota had also died (presumably of natural causes at an advanced age), and the appearance of Ferchar's son Ainbcellach in the king-lists confirms him as over-king of Dalriada. Despite the precise sequence of those events in that year 697 being left unclear by the annalists, there is nowhere any doubt among modern historians that the succession of Ainbcellach signifies the full achievement of Cenél Loairn ascendancy in Dalriada.

That ascendancy was to survive into the fourth decade of the eighth century and yet appears to have been only rarely untroubled by contention from one quarter or another. Whilst it had to withstand more than one challenge in arms from the Cenél nGabráin and was ultimately doomed by a ferocious Pictish onslaught, the earliest troubles besetting the house of Ferchar Fota appear to have sprung from a vicious internal rivalry which was to drive Ainbcellach out of power and into exile within twelve months of his succession to the kingship. Summary in the extreme and sparing in detail, the annal record of his reign comprises just two events, both of them entered in the *Annals of Ulster* at the year 698. The first of these simply records 'the burning of Dunollie', while the second offers just a little more information when it tells of 'the expulsion of Ainbcellach, son of Ferchar, from the kingship; and he was taken, bound, to Ireland'.

The two events were undoubtedly connected, because Dunollie (or

*Dún Ollaigh*) which is generally recognised as having been the capital fortress of the Cenél Loairn would seem also to have represented the principal stronghold of Ainbcellach's family and their followers at the end of the seventh century. Nick Aitchison's military history of early Scotland points to abundant evidence for the strategic importance of such hill-forts found in the annal record of the subsequent decades when it notices only three land battles and another fought at sea, while forts are mentioned in at least nine entries, most of them recording burnings, destructions and sieges related to contention between and within the principal cenéla. Aitchison suggests that it was the character and proximity of this conflict – as well as the importance of its outcome to relations between the kings of Dalriada and the community of Iona – which rendered it of such particular interest to the Iona annalists.[5]

In that same orbit of Iona, it may be of some significance that the emergence of the Cenél Loairn ascendancy was closely concurrent with the abbacy of Adomnán, whose writings seem to display so little warmth towards the people of Lorn. Adomnán's differences with his own community over the vexed question of the dating of Easter are usually suspected as the reason for his absences from the monastery on Iona, whether on visits to Ireland and Northumbria or on extensive travels around Pictland. By 697, however, he was effectively 'retired' to Ireland – and reasonably so when he would have been already in his seventies by that time – yet it is tempting to wonder whether the imminent rise of the Cenél Loairn might have played its own part in prompting that retirement to his home country in Donegal. He was eventually to return to Iona, however, but only shortly before his death there in 704, and it can have been scarcely accidental that his successor Conamail, son of Failbe, was the very first abbot of Iona whose ancestry was unrelated to Columba's people of the northern Uí Néill. Instead, as John Bannerman has astutely observed, Conamail was of the Uí Macc Uais, which was very probably the same branch of the Airgialla which is linked to the Cenél Loairn by the *Senchus*.[6]

Such then was the political context within which the Iona chronicle

---

5   Aitchison, *The Picts and the Scots at War*, pp.108–9.
6   Bannerman, *Dalriada*, p.117.

was being compiled in the last years of the seventh century and yet, in view of the monastic community's concern about secular events so close at hand, it is unfortunate that the source for those entries in the *Annals of Ulster* at the year 698 seems to have omitted identification of the party responsible for the burning of Dunollie and the expulsion of Ainbcellach. It may, of course, have been considered so obvious as to be unnecessary at the time, because the subsequent annal record leaves the least doubt that the events of 698 represented the opening conflict in an apparent civil war between rival families within the Cenél Loairn. Even though he is not mentioned by name in the annals until 701 – when the *Annals of Ulster* enter 'the destruction of Dunollie by Selbach' – it was assuredly that same Selbach, another son of Ferchar Fota, who was responsible for driving his brother out of the kingship and into exile in Ireland, a fate presumably considered less reprehensible on the part of a kinsman than any act of more extreme violence. The burning of Dunollie can be recognised, then, as a blatant act of war directed at his brother's family by Selbach, his kinsmen and their followers. Likewise, the subsequent expulsion of Ainbcellach can be attributed to Selbach and an element of his following, quite probably a warband of the Airgialla who are on later record as a component of Selbach's forces and would have been ideally placed to 'take [Ainbcellach] bound, to Ireland' where he could have been conveniently held in exile among their own people in Derry.

Even with Ainbcellach out of the picture – at least for the time being – there is a distinct indication of his family having sustained their resistance to Selbach for the next three years and, presumably, until his 'destruction' of their power base of Dunollie. Later in that same year the Ulster annals record 'the slaughter of the tribe of Cathba', assuredly the same Cenél Cathbath included among the Cenél Loairn in the *Senchus* and presumably allied to Ainbcellach's faction, which would suggest their 'slaughter' as a 'mopping-up operation' conducted by Selbach's warband in suppression of such dissident elements as remained among the Cenél Loairn kindreds.

Whether or not Selbach can be recognised as Ainbcellach's immediate successor in the kingship of Dalriada has been the subject of some scholarly disagreement because a 'Fiannamail, grandson of Dúnchad' is styled 'king of the Dál Riata' in his obituary entered in the *Annals of Ulster* at 700. In his obituary as it is entered in the *Annals of Tigernach*, however, the same Fiannamail is styled 'king of the Dál nAraide'. If that entry can be blamed on scribal error and he was actually a king of the Dál Riata, then the inclusion of his name with that of Eochaid among the signatories to the *Cáin Adomnáin* would indicate him as king of the Dál Riata in Antrim, thus leading to the proposal that he also assumed kingship of the Dál Riata in Scotland after the exile of Ainbcellach. Yet that suggestion is placed in doubt by the absence of his name from any of the Scottish king-lists, and especially so when Selbach is entered immediately after his brother in the *Synchronisms*, which represent the earliest surviving form of the supposed original Dalriadic king-list. On the other hand, Selbach is omitted from the *Duan*, while the later and apparently dislocated Latin lists enter in his place an 'Eogan' who is entirely unknown to the contemporary annal record.

Notwithstanding those apparent contradictions in the early sources, the American historian Benjamin T. Hudson, who takes an especial interest in the Cenél Loairn and its descendent kindreds, has no doubt that 'Selbach's family was supreme' after 698.[7] Even though Selbach does not appear again, at least by name, in the annal record for more than a decade after his first notice at 701, he had evidently used those years to establish himself in sufficiently confident control over rival elements of the Cenél Loairn to take a warband deep into Cenél nGabráin territory. An entry in the *Annals of Ulster* at the year 712 records his besieging *Aberte* (now Dunaverty), a coastal fort at the southern tip of the Mull of Kintyre where it would have stood guard over the nearest point of landfall for a crossing from Antrim. In the course of his advance down the Kintyre peninsula, Selbach or some contingent of his forces struck at another key stronghold of the Cenél nGabráin on the evidence of the same Ulster annalist's entry of 'the burning of *Tairpirt Boitter*' (a fort which probably stood on the same site as the later medieval castle at Tarbert on Loch Fyne) earlier in the same year.

This campaign of intimidation was assuredly aimed at the extension of Selbach's kingship to the Cenél nGabráin, which would further suggest

---

7   Hudson, *Kings of Celtic Scotland*, p.20.

the entry in the annals at the year 714 of his having 'built Dunollie' (or, more probably, 're-built' the stronghold after its destruction of thirteen years before) with the purpose of establishing his own capital fortress in the heartland of the Cenél Loairn. For all that achievement, however, he would seem not to have entirely extinguished some smouldering embers of family rivalry which were to flare up five years later when his brother Ainbcellach had returned to Scotland from his Irish exile and apparently raised a force capable of bringing Selbach to battle at Finglen on the Braes of Lorn near Lochavich. In their entry at the year 719, the annals tell of 'the battle of Findglen [between] two sons of Ferchar Fota; and there Ainbcellach was slain on the fifth [more correctly, 'the fourth'] day of the week, the Ides of September' (i.e. Wednesday, 13th September in 719).

Just a few weeks later Selbach was confronted by another challenge, this time from the Cenél nGabráin, which is entered in the annals as 'the battle of *Ardda nesbi*, on the sea [located by W. F. Skene off the Point of Ardminish on the Isle of Gigha[8]] between Dúnchad Bec with the tribe of Gabrán and Selbach with the tribe of Loarn; and Selbach was defeated, on the second before the Nones of October, the seventh [more correctly, 'the sixth'] day of the week [i.e. Friday, 6th October in 719].[9] And certain nobles fell in it.'

Although Selbach suffered defeat in that sea-fight (incidentally, the first real naval battle on record in the British Isles), it was evidently not to deprive him of the over-kingship of Dalriada because the obituary of Duncan Bec, entered in the annals just two years later, recognises him only as 'king of Kintyre' which would indicate his sovereignty having extended no further than the core territory of the Cenél nGabráin. So, if Dúnchad had indeed been challenging Selbach for the kingship of Dalriada, his victory at sea was not so decisive as to achieve that ambition.

There is a further point which will have its own bearing on the context of that engagement if it can be taken to suggest such naval warfare – or,

---

8    Skene, *Celtic Scotland*, vol. i, p.285.
9    Both of these dates from the annals at 719 are as corrected by Anderson, *ESSH*, vol. i., pp.218–19.

at least, its likelihood – having been of somewhat wider occurrence than is indicated by the annal record. Such might very well be implied by the annal entry of Selbach's rebuilding of Dunollie just five years earlier, because that hill-fort occupying a headland on the north side of Oban had the benefit of a natural harbour and secure anchorage in the shelter of the island of Kerrera. So too – as Nick Aitchison has observed – Oban Bay's strategic command of the confluence of the Firth of Lorn with the Sounds of Kerrera and Mull would have well qualified Dunollie as 'an ideal base for naval operations around the coasts and isles of Dalriada'.[10]

The reign of Selbach, son of Ferchar Fota, was certainly the longest, and arguably the most successful, of any Cenél Loairn king of Dalriada, yet it was he himself who brought it to an end in 723 when he retired into religion after passing the kingship to his son Dúngal. Although Selbach was certainly no longer a young man by that date, subsequent events do not indicate his decision to have been made on grounds of sickness or advancing senility. So Benjamin Hudson's suggestion that 'the guilt of kinslaying may have been the reason for Selbach's retirement into religious life' is more than plausible, and especially so in view of the annalist's use of the particularly vicious term *iugulatus* (literally 'throat-cutting') in the entry of Ainbcellach's death in battle just four years earlier.[11]

Other than the building of *Ailen mic Craich* (presumably an island fortification) in 724, there is no annal entry of any event of specific bearing on the reign of Selbach's son and successor until 726, at which year the *Annals of Tigernach* record 'Dúngal cast from his kingdom' and, some lines later, add 'Eochaid, son of Eochaid, began to reign'. If those two entries are in some wise connected, then the kingship of Dalriada might be thought to have been passed back to the Cenél nGabráin. If such was indeed the case (and it is by no means certain that it was so), Eochaid's kingship was to face a challenge within months, on the evidence of an entry in the *Annals of Ulster* at 727 indicating Selbach having emerged from his monastic retreat to bring a formidable alliance to 'the battle at *Rosfoichne* between Selbach and the *familia* of Eochaid,

---

10    Aitchison, *The Picts & the Scots at War*, p.115.
11    Hudson, *Kings of Celtic Scotland*, p.21.

*nepos* [grandson?] of Domnall Brecc', to which the annalist adds 'and there some men of the Airgialla [presumably with Selbach's forces] fell'. While the location of the battle has been plausibly identified by Skene as 'the promontory of Feochan, at the mouth of Loch Feochan [to the south of Oban and just above Seil island]',[12] other matters remain in doubt. The 'Eochaid, son of Eochaid' who 'began to reign' in 726, was the son of a grandson of Domnall Brecc, so *nepos* would be more accurately translated as 'descendant' (depending, of course, on which of the two Eochaids was intended by the annalist). Nonetheless, *familia* is a curious term and may even be read to indicate a Cenél nGabráin warband of his late father's following, because it is fairly apparent that the younger Eochaid was not himself present at the battle. Neither is there any distinct indication of its outcome, which would suggest it as effectively inconclusive and thus indecisive as regards the rival claims to kingship of Dalriada.

Whether or not he had returned to his monastery after the battle, Selbach had only a few years to live on the evidence of his obituary entered at 730 in the *Annals of Ulster*. His son Dúngal, however and although unnoticed by the annals since being 'cast from the kingship' in 726, was still very much alive on the evidence of 'the burning of *Tairpirt Boittir* by Dúngal' entered in the *Annals of Ulster* at 731. It is unclear whether this aggression was an impulsive gesture of vengeance on behalf of his recently deceased father or whether it was intended as a challenge for the over-kingship of Dalriada. If the latter, it would appear to have been an unsuccessful one on the evidence of Eochaid's recognition as 'king of Dalriada' in his obituary entered in the *Annals of Tigernach* at the year 733. On the other hand, the same obituary is entirely absent from the *Annals of Ulster*, and its form of entry in the much later *Annals of the Four Masters* recognises Eochaid only as *toísech* ('chieftain' or even, possibly, 'nobleman'), a style which led Benjamin Hudson to his suggestion that the regal title accorded Eochaid 'could be a later amendment' to the Tigernach entry.[13] If so, then the over-kingship may have collapsed by 733 and the kingdom effectively fragmented

---

12    Skene, *Celtic Scotland*, vol. i, p.286.
13    Hudson, *Kings of Celtic Scotland*, p.22.

into the dominions of its *primchenéla* who were themselves beset by rivalry between their descendent branches.

There is, however, the alternative possibility of kingship of Dalriada having passed back to the Cenél Loairn and to the line of Ainbcellach in the person of his son Muiredach, who is noticed by the annal record at the year 733 but only as having 'assumed the kingship of the tribe of Loarn'. In fact, those entries are the only occasion on which the annalists specifically style any member of the Cenél Loairn as a king, and then only of his own *cenél*, although a later entry in the *Annals of Ulster* can be read to indicate his having been king of Dalriada (although in quite exceptional circumstances) by 736. Nonetheless, Muiredach is certainly recognised as such by the *Synchronisms*, as also by the *Duan Albanach* and later king-lists where he is accorded a three-year reign which would correspond acceptably well to the subsequent course of events.

Whether Muiredach was indeed king of Dalriada or whether he had merely reclaimed kingship of the Cenél Loairn, there is dramatic evidence for the rival line of Selbach having been still active, and very much at large, in 733. The entry in the *Annals of Ulster* at that year tells how 'Dúngal, Selbach's son, profaned Tory island when he dragged Bruide from it; and on the same occasion he invaded the island of *Cuiren rigi* [probably Inch, off Inishowen]' – all of which might be better explained with some background detail.

Both of those islands mentioned by the annalist lie off the Donegal coast where they housed small monasteries of typically Irish character, and the Bruide who was dragged out of what would thus have been a monastic sanctuary can be recognised as the son of Oengus, the powerful king of Picts who will yet have his own dramatic part in the story of the Cenél Loairn. Entries at the same year in the *Annals of Tigernach* and, with still more helpful detail, in the *Annals of the Four Masters* tell of a fleet brought from Scotland to Ireland as a mercenary force to support Flaithbertach of the Cenél Conaill in defending his high-kingship of the Uí Néill against the rival Cenél nEogain and their Ulster allies.

This expedition of 733 represents the first record of Dalriadic Scots engaged in warfare on the island of Ireland for very nearly a hundred years, and yet their fate on this occasion bears an ironic resemblance to that suffered in 637 by the contingent sent by Domnall Brecc to join

Congal Cáech's Ulster forces at 'Magh Rath of the Red Pools', because the Tigernach annalist records 'a great slaughter made of them in the island of Oine'. Of most immediate bearing at this point, however, is the plausible identification (by the editor of the *Annals of the Four Masters* as also in the later *Annals of Clonmacnoise*) of the 'island of Oine' as Inishowen, because it can be taken to suggest Dúngal having accompanied the mercenary fleet on its crossing to Ireland and at some point having made a diversion, presumably in company with his own warband, to the island monasteries in pursuit of Bruide.

While Dúngal's absence in Ireland would assuredly have offered his cousin Muiredach the opportunity to reclaim kingship of the Cenél Loairn for the family of Ainbcellach, there is nothing in the annal record of the year 733 which even hints at the origin of Dúngal's apparent feud with the Pictish prince, so any attempt to suggest such an explanation must look into the earlier history of Picto-Scottish relations. In fact, there is no record of conflict involving the Scots of Dalriada with their Pictish neighbours to be found anywhere in the early sources between the second half of the sixth century and the fourth decade of the eighth century, by which time Bruide's father Oengus, son of Fergus, had emerged as an apparent 'high-king' of Picts – or, at least, as over-king of those south of the Mounth.

It should perhaps be said at this point that what Benjamin Hudson refers to, and with justified scepticism, as the 'so-called king lists' very probably give a false impression of Pictish kingship by grouping together into a neat sequence the names of provincial kings, some of whom must have been reigning simultaneously within the same generation and competing with each other for wider overlordship. Indeed, the annal record would indicate dynastic rivalries similar to those besetting the Scots in the early eighth century having also been found, and at much the same time, among the Picts, whose dynasties seem to have ties to specific provinces.[14] On occasion throughout the historical period, individual Pictish kings appear to have established a supremacy over their rivals which bears comparison to that attributed in Columba's time to Bruide, son of Maelchon, and by the second quarter

---

14    Hudson, *Kings of Celtic Scotland*, p.23.

of the eighth century it was Oengus, son of Fergus, who had achieved such a pre-eminence.

On his ascent to that pinnacle of power, Oengus had fought and won a whole series of battles with three rivals, the first of them an Elpin who was defeated, and whose son was slain, at *Mónid chroibh* (Moncrieff Hill, the site of a hill-fort at the confluence of the Tay and Earn, south-east of Perth) in 728. Shortly afterwards, Elpin was to suffer a second rout 'in a pitiful battle', according to the Tigernach annalist, at *Caislen credhi* (most recently and convincingly recognised as Crathie in Braemar), and there lost his territories to Nechtan, son of Derile, who was to be defeated in his turn by Oengus in the following year when his tax-gathering expedition appears to have been ambushed just west of Tyndrum.

Some five years earlier this Nechtan seems have been forced into monastic retirement by the Drust who followed him into the kingship of Fortriu (the province which appears to have represented the power centre of Pictish kingship since the last quarter of the seventh century). Nechtan had come out of his monastery in 726 but only to be made captive by his successor and presumably held until Drust himself was driven from the kingship by Elpin later in the same year. In 728, Nechtan appears to have won back his kingship by his defeat of Elpin at 'Caislen credhi', but only until the following year when he suffered his own final defeat at the hands of Oengus. Later that same year Oengus was to face a third rival in the person of the seemingly indefatigable Drust, whom he is said by the very late, and perhaps less than reliable, *Fragmentary Annals of Duald MacFirbis* to have already beaten in no fewer than three battles. Whatever the truth of that claim, this was to be Drust's last defeat because he was slain at *Druim Derg Blathuug* (Drumderg, in the Forest of Alyth, to the north of Blairgowrie and west of the river Isla), leaving Oengus without rival in the kingship of Fortriu and overlord-ship of the Picts by the end of the year 729.

It was against that background of turbulent political change in early eighth-century Pictland that Marjorie Anderson put together her scenario of the source of acrimony which had arisen between Dúngal and Oengus' son Bruide by 733. As far as I am aware, her proposal represents the only substantial attempt to make sense of a feud which was to have the most dramatic consequences for the Cenél Loairn and is thus deserving of a summary outline here before venturing to suggest an alternative reading of the same sequence of events.

Mrs Anderson's proposal is based upon the apparent practice of exogamy among the Picts having been the underlying premise of the supposed matrilineal succession of Pictish kings; or, in plainer English, Pictish princesses either married, or otherwise bearing offspring, to fathers from the ruling kindreds of neighbouring peoples, so that the right to kingship hinged upon the descent of the successor through the female line. While this matrilineal model of Pictish succession enjoys neither universal nor unqualified endorsement among modern historians, it was believed by Bede to have been the case in his own time and his acquaintance with the Picts in the eighth century must allow his evidence all the authority due to its contemporaneity. Even so, such a system of matrilineal succession can present problems of interpretation of the Pictish king-lists, particularly where a king is identified as the son of someone whose name might be that of a mother, when that of a father would usually be expected. Nonetheless, the lists do contain examples of seventh-century Pictish kings who can be reliably identified as sons of non-Pictish fathers. One such is the Talorcan, son of Eanfrith of Northumbria, and another the Bruide, son of Bile, king of Strathclyde – while the later Talorcan, who was a son of the aforementioned Oengus and reigned in the 780s, would seem to represent the first recorded instance of a Pictish king whose father had also been king of Picts.

So too, as Benjamin Hudson suggests, the ancestry of Oengus himself 'may reflect the intermarriage found among the English, Irish and Picts'. There is a fragment of evidence found in an old Irish genealogy which can be taken to propose Oengus, son of Fergus (as he is called in the Irish sources, but whose Pictish name-form of *Onuist*, son of *Urguist*, is found in Pictish king-lists) as ultimately descended from the Eoganachta of Munster, a claim assuredly linked to tales and legends telling of Irishmen active among the Picts in the east of Britain. One of those legends makes specific reference to a semi-historical early Irish king having battled in *Circenn*, a Pictish province comprising the region later known as Angus and the Mearns, and that implied association with

Oengus might be taken to explain why an eighth-century Irish list of the 'ales of kingship' should have included 'red ales like wine . . . around the fields of Circenn'.[15]

All of which lends support to Mrs Anderson's identification of Pictish kings whose fathers' names are to be found in the Dalriadic king-lists and genealogies, including amongst them the aforementioned Drust and Elpin, both of whom she identifies as sons born to the elder Eochaid, grandson of Domnall Brecc, by a sister of the Nechtan who, like them, had been deprived of his kingship by Oengus. While Nechtan, whose obituary is entered in the annals at 732, is thought to have ended his days in monastic retirement, Mrs Anderson suggests that the Elpin driven from kingship in Pictland in 728 had fled into Dalriada and to the court of his half-brother, the younger Eochaid who died in 733, leading on to her convincing identification of the *Alpin* who is entered as Eochaid's successor in the Dalriadic king-lists as the *Elpin* who had lost his Pictish kingship to Nechtan five years earlier.

If so, then this Alpin (whom she believes to have held kingship of the Cenél nGabráin at the same time as Muiredach, son of Ainbcellach, was king of the Cenél Loairn) would have been a full brother to the Drust killed in battle with Oengus at Drumderg in 729. Yet Drust's earlier loss of his kingship in Pictland is entered in the *Annals of Tigernach* at 726 and thus in the same year as 'Dúngal was cast from his kingdom', which led Mrs Anderson to surmise 'that Drust took refuge with Dúngal in Lorn . . . and that Drust's attempt to regain the kingship in 729 was made with Dúngal's support'. On the basis of that possibility – which would follow the suggested pattern of flight taken by Drust's supposed brother Elpin, but otherwise hinges upon what may be nothing more than pure coincidence – she goes on to propose that it might have been by his alliance with Drust that 'Dúngal had incurred the enmity of Oengus' some four years before the annals had occasion to notice his apparent feud with Oengus' son Bruide.[16]

It must be said, though, that there are problems with that proposal. Such an alliance would have been more usually based either on kinship

15   *CGH*, p.196; Hudson, *Kings of Celtic Scotland*, p.26.
16   M. O. Anderson, *Kings & Kingship*, p.184.

or marriage obligation, neither of which are either known or likely to have applied in this instance. Neither would the other plausible basis of political advantage or ambition seem to apply in the case of Dúngal, who had much more to lose than to gain by contention with so powerful and aggressive a warlord as Oengus, and if he had been tempted to such a hazardous venture so far east of Druim Alban, it is scarcely likely that he would have escaped the same fate suffered by Drust at Drumderg.

Neither would that proposal strictly correspond with the account of events found in the annal record, where there is nowhere any indication of Dúngal having incurred the enmity of Oengus prior to his seizure of Bruide from Tory island. So it would follow that whatever the origin of the hostility which prompted Dúngal to that dangerously provocative abduction in 733, it would seem to have been immediately directed at the son, and not – at least not yet – to have involved the fearsome father, so an alternative explanation might be found in the activities of Bruide, son of Oengus, before his discovery in and removal from that monastic sanctuary. In fact, he is first noticed in the annal record just two years earlier in 731, and most reliably by the entry at that year in the *Annals of Ulster* of 'a battle between the son of Oengus and the son of Congus, but Bruide conquered Talorc, who fled'.

While this Talorc is noticed on only two occasions by the annalists, his father Congus is known from one of the eighth-century genealogies which are appended to the *Senchus* and throw their own informative light on the relative status of the four Dalriadic *prímchenéla* a couple of generations before the appearance of Talorc in the annal record. For example, the prominence of Ainbcellach at the head of the eighth-century genealogy of the Cenél Loairn can assuredly be taken to reflect its ascendancy in the 700s. Of more immediate significance at this point is the genealogy supplied for the Cenél nGabráin, because where it might be expected to list the kingly descent from Gabrán through Aedán to Domnall Brecc and his successor kings it traces instead another branch of the same family from a Gartnait who is named in the original *Senchus* as one of the sons of Aedán. While evidence of fragmentation of the Cenél nGabráin in the early eighth century is only to be expected, perhaps it is not quite so surprising to find the descendants of Gartnait overshadowing those of Domnall Brecc in the first decades of the eighth century in the light of the annalist's curious styling of the '*familia* of Eochaid' in 727.

Perhaps more surprising, though, is the unmistakably Pictish character of the name Gartnait, which can be taken to identify him as a son born to Aedán by a Pictish mother. The name Talorc (of which Talorcan is recognised as the diminutive form), applied by the annalists to the son of Congus who appears to have been the principal representative of the line of Gartnait by the early 730s, is also of a distinctly Pictish character which would suggest him too as the son of a woman of the Picts, a line of descent which might yet have bearing on the eventual fate of Talorc, son of Congus.

It is unfortunate that the annal record of the family of Gartnait is so sparse by comparison with that of the more prominent kingly branch of the Cenél nGabráin, an imbalance which might once again be explained in terms of the political preference of the monastic community which produced the 'Iona chronicle'. That same bias in what is believed to have been a principal source for much Scottish material in the Irish annals – which has already been discussed here with regard to their record of the Cenél Loairn – led Marjorie Anderson to identify 'a group of about a dozen entries, some of them found only in the *Annals of Ulster*, concerning Skye and the family of Gartnait, which on geographical grounds, might plausibly be attributed to Applecross annalists'.[17]

The monastery of Applecross (from *Apor Crossan*, 'the confluence of the river Crossan') in Wester Ross was founded by Maelrubha, an Irish monk from Bangor, in 673. Whilst nothing is known of any political orientation of Malrubha's community in its early years, its connection with Bangor would suggest the probability of annalistic records compiled there having found their way to Ireland and to inclusion in the original 'Ulster chronicle' by a route quite independent of the Columban monastic network. So, when all the evidence for the location of the family of Gartnait links them to the Skye island group, the source of the record of their activities preserved in the *Annals of Ulster* would most probably have originated in Applecross, thus rendering entries dated to 673 and later the status of contemporary record. Even so, it is from a source of

---

17   M. O. Anderson, *Kings & Kingship*, p.11.

tradition rather than the formal historical record that the descendants of
Gartnait are better known, and specifically from the 'Tale of Cano, son
of Gartnait' (*Scéla Cano meic Gartnáin*) which is thought to have been
compiled in the eleventh century from materials of ninth-century origin.

Although too anachronistic to be considered of real historical value, the
story tells of a Cano, son of Gartnán (the diminutive form of Gartnait),
who was a 'son of Aed, son of Gabrán' and lived on the islands of Skye and
Raasay. Aedán is said to have slain Cano's father 'Gartnán' and would have
killed Cano too had he not fled Skye and escaped to Ireland, so it is possible
that the tale might still preserve a genuine tradition recalling contention
between branches of the Cenél nGabráin. Interestingly, the entry in the
annals at 668 of 'the voyage of the sons of Gartnait to Ireland with the
people of Skye' would seem to support the story (even whilst underlining
its anachronism when Aedán's obituary is entered at a date sixty years
earlier), and a second entry at 670 recording 'the people of Gartnait came
[back?] from Ireland' would appear to take it a stage further on.

The Gartnán of the 'Tale of Cano' would seem to have been intended
as the same son of Aedán, son of Gabrán, who is recorded in the *Senchus*,
and also in its appended eighth-century genealogy which traces a line of
descent from that Gartnait through his son Cano (called *Cano garb*, or
'Cano the rough') and Cano's son *Consamla* (probably a corruption of
*Consamail*) to Congus, father of the Talorc who is first noticed in the annal
record at 731. Yet John Bannerman points to a Cano whose violent death
is entered in the annals at 688 and who appears to have been the son of a
Gartnait, king of Picts, whose obituary was entered in the annals twenty-
five years earlier when he is identified, and also in the Pictish king-lists, as
the 'son of Domelch'. Bannerman goes on to suggest that 'Domelch was
perhaps his mother and therefore Aedán's Pictish wife', adding that a king
of Picts whose father was a king of Dalriada would have been 'in complete
accord with the Pictish system of matrilineal succession' and pointing
to examples of other Pictish kings with non-Pictish fathers. Nonetheless,
when it comes to the fourth generation of descent from Gartnait, he can
confidently confirm that the annal entries 'relating to Talorc leave . . . no
doubt that he belonged to Dalriada rather than to Pictland'.[18]

---

18   Bannerman, *Dalriada*, pp.92–4, 109; see also Genealogy 2, p.175 below.

Nonetheless, there is surely some connection between the Pictish element in the pedigree of the family of Gartnait and its association with Skye, which was believed by Adomnán to have been Pictish territory when Columba visited the island in the second half of the sixth century and would have still been considered as such for another two hundred and fifty years, especially by an ambitious king of Picts in the second quarter of the eighth century. Yet at the same time the descendants of Gartnait appear to have been the ascendant branch of the Cenél nGabráin and enhancement of that status among the dynastic kindreds of Dalriada might well have prompted them to reassert or to extend their lordship within the Skye island group. Such an ambition would have encouraged them to form some sort of alliance with the Cenél Loairn whose northern frontier on Ardnamurchan looked towards those islands. There would also have been common ground upon which to base such an alliance at a time when Dúngal's Cenél Loairn had long been in conflict with Eochaid, whom Talorc would have recognised as the representative of a rival branch of the Cenél nGabráin with which his own family appears to have had its own history of contention. Indeed, Dúngal's burning of the hill-fort at Tarbert in 731 represents an act of aggression against Eochaid which might well have been made in support of, or in alliance with, Talorc.

If any such arrangement had been in place in that year, Talorc would have had urgent need of a Cenél Loairn ally on another occasion – whether before or more probably after the Kintyre adventure – when he was brought to battle by Bruide, son of the Oengus who had only recently despatched the last of his rivals to achieve his full ascendancy in the kingship of Picts. It may have been that Oengus saw in Talorc yet another potential rival with a matrilineal claim on that kingship, but a no less likely point of contention between Bruide and Talorc might well have centred around the overlordship of Skye. In which case, the probability would have been of Oengus, who is on record as having deployed close kinsmen as his military commanders, having sent his son to assert control over islands which he assuredly considered to be westerly offshore outposts of Pictish territory.

Just such a mission would have been accomplished when – in the words of the annalist – 'Bruide conquered Talorc, who fled'. Yet it is particularly unfortunate that the annal record supplies no reliable indication of the whereabouts of the conflict – and particularly so when the Tigernach annalist appears to locate it in 'Muirbolg', but only because he had conflated two different battles, the other being a defeat of the *Cruithne* (presumably the Dál nAraide) by the Dál Riata which was, of course, fought out in Ireland. Neither is the destination of Talorc's flight indicated by any annalist (although it may yet be deduced from their further notice of him three years later), nor is there even a hint at Dúngal having been in any wise involved, yet when he appears in the annals two years later he is scouring the island monasteries of the Donegal seaboard in hostile pursuit of Bruide.

Whether that hostility was rooted in Bruide's 'conquest' of Talorc or in some other cause which had passed unnoticed by the annalists, Dúngal's grievance must have been serious indeed to warrant the consequences of his chosen course of satisfaction. He must have realised, for instance, that to profane the sanctuary of the monasteries of Inch and Tory would risk his incurring the wrath of the powerful Uí Néill under whose protection those holy places were kept secure. Which raises the question as to why a Pictish warrior prince should have taken himself off to an Irish monastic sanctuary within a year or two of his triumph in battle in Scotland. Benjamin Hudson believed it having been to escape from Dúngal,[19] but that does seem less than likely in view of the available evidence and so there must have been another, even quite different, reason which has been lost to history. Whatever was the reason for Bruide's resort to sanctuary, his choice of a monastery in Ireland instead of one of the many presumably available to him in Pictland might be taken to support the claims preserved in Irish tradition for his father's Munster ancestry.

In the event it was to be Dúngal's offence against the son of the king of Picts, rather than his profaning of holy places, which incurred the devastating vengeance which was to prove ultimately fatal for himself and disastrous for the Cenél Loairn. It began in the following year of 734, when the *Annals of Ulster* record 'Dun Leithfind [an unidentified fort, presumably in Dalriada] was destroyed after the wounding

---

19    Hudson, *Kings of Celtic Scotland*, p.21.

of Dúngal; and Dúngal fled into Ireland to be out of the power of Oengus'.

While Dúngal was escaping 'the power of Oengus', another target of Pictish hostility was less fortunate on the evidence of another entry in the annal record of the same year: 'Talorc, son of Congus, was taken by his own brother who gave him into the hands of the Picts and he was drowned by them.' In an imaginative effort to make up for the annalists' short measure of supporting detail, Marjorie Anderson raises the possibility of Talorc, son of Congus, having been a son of the same Pictish mother (whom she identifies as a sister of Nechtan) as Drust and Elpin, the two rivals earlier disposed of by Oengus. She goes on to suggest that Talorc's flight from his defeat by Bruide might thus have taken him to Kintyre where he found refuge with his uterine half-brother Elpin, who was to shortly reappear as the 'Alpin' entered in the king-lists as Eochaid's successor in the kingship of the Cenél nGabráin. That undeniably plausible scenario inevitably leads her to ask: 'Was his brother, who betrayed him to the Picts, the Alpin who had formerly held the Pictish kingship and was now, I have suggested, part-king of the Dál Riata?'

While her parallel proposal that Talorc – assuming he had the same matrilineal claim on the kingship of Fortriu (effectively over-kingship of Picts south of the Mounth) as Alpin and Drust – 'would have been equally a rival of Oengus' is perhaps less convincing in the context of the year 733, she is surely correct in her suggestion that 'the handing-over of Talorc may have been done under a direct threat of force'.[20] As to the motive for that seizure under threat, the inference that Oengus' campaign was primarily driven by his vengeful fury at the abduction of his son, taken together with the evidence for Dúngal having been its principal target, must indicate the greater likelihood of it having been Talorc's guilt by association – and probably, as suggested earlier, in the form of an alliance – with Dúngal.

There is only one other notice in the annals which bears on the events of the year 734 and it is entered in the *Annals of Ulster* before the reference of Dúngal's flight to Ireland, where it records a 'Talorcan, son of

---

20    M. O. Anderson, *Kings & Kingship*, pp.183–4.

Drostan, taken and bound near Dunollie'. This Talorcan – who is styled
'king of Atholl' elsewhere in the annals and so might be recognised as a
provincial king under military obligation to Oengus – might probably
have been leading his own contingent of the Pictish forces when he was
'taken and bound [presumably, but not necessarily, by a Cenél Loairn
warband] near Dunollie'.

Before moving on from the events of 734 to their dramatic sequel two
years later, there remains the question of the whereabouts of Bruide, son
of Oengus, after he had been dragged out of his monastic sanctuary. The
one absolute certainty, in view of the irrefutable evidence of his obituary
entered in the annals at 736, is that he was still alive in 734. It might be
assumed that he was held captive by Dúngal, presumably somewhere in
Argyll and probably in Dunollie, in which case his rescue would have
represented an urgent – if not, indeed, the very first – objective of the
Pictish invasion of Dalriada. Yet there is no reference to his release in the
annal record of the campaign, which mentions only the destruction of
the unidentified Dun Leithfind and the wounding of Dúngal before his
flight to Ireland.

The capture of Talorcan of Atholl near Dunollie, however, might just
possibly indicate an unsuccessful Pictish assault on that stronghold, which
could be taken to suggest Oengus' forces having come up against a more
determined resistance from the Cenél Loairn than they had anticipated.
Indeed, had Dunollie been the place where Bruide was thought to have
been held and had it been so well-defended as to repulse an attempt to
release him, there would have been every reason for Oengus to launch the
further onslaught with the stronger forces and seemingly greater malice
which he was to throw against Dalriada two years later.

The entry in the annals at 736 supplies a concise but still usefully
detailed account of the dramatic events of that year: 'Oengus, son of
Fergus, king of the Picts, devastated the territories of Dalriada, and
won Dunadd, and burned Creic; and he bound with chains two sons of
Selbach, namely Dúngal and Feradach.'

If vengeance was still the motive driving Oengus to war against
Dalriada, it may have been news of the return of Dúngal from Ireland
which had prompted this second onslaught because he clearly was a

prominent target of the campaign, and this time there was to be no escape from the chains with which Oengus had him bound. The son and successor of Selbach makes no further appearance in the annal record and it would seem quite certain that he was put to death very soon after falling into Pictish hands. There is, however, genuine reason to doubt the same fate having befallen his brother Feradach, who seems to have had no part in the seizure of Oengus' son and who might yet be found in the later annal record under a different name-form and in an unexpected context.

As to the fate of Bruide, who has been unnoticed by the annalists since his abduction three years earlier, nothing more is known other than the entry in the annals of a plain obituary with no explanatory detail but as a distinctly separate entry at the year 736. It may have been that he had been released from captivity somewhere in Argyll by this second Pictish onslaught, if not in the earlier raid which would appear to have been aimed more directly at Cenél Loairn territory. If so, then the likelihood must have been of his having died very shortly afterwards, perhaps as a result of privations suffered in captivity. Yet Nick Aitchison offers a more dramatic interpretation of the brief obituary found in the annals when he discerns an implication of Bruide having been 'deliberately killed by Dúngal', either in revenge for the Pictish attack or to prevent his liberation by his father's invading army, unless he had been put to death earlier in the year and it had been this which provoked Oengus to his onslaught on Dalriada.[21]

There are other references in the annal record of 736 which can be read in the light of the wider historical context to propose a motive beyond mere vengeance or retribution having lain behind Oengus' strategy in 736, and not least what appears to have been the initial direction of his attack into the traditional heartland of the Cenél nGabráin in upper Kintyre as distinct from the territory of the Cenél Loairn lying further to the north. There is, on the other hand, the likelihood of the Cenél Loairn having extended their southern boundary rather further into mid-Argyll during the period of their ascendancy, as would certainly have been the case if the *Creic* burned by the Picts in 736, and identified

21    Aitchison, *The Picts and the Scots at War*, p.152.

by W. F. Skene as the fort on the promontory of Craignish overlooking the Sound of Jura,[22] was the same *Ailen mic Craich* built in 724, and thus in the first year of Dúngal's reign.

Although the annals do not actually specify the place where Dúngal and his brother were captured by the Picts having been either Creic or Dunadd, one of those would seem to be implied and the more likely of the two may well have been Dunadd. Be all that as it may, there is ample reason to recognise Oengus' seizure of the strategically sited hill-fort generally thought to have been a focal ceremonial site of the over-kings of the Dál Riata as a gesture intended to signify his conquest of the kingdom of the Scots. So too, the unmistakably Pictish outline of a boar carved into the famous rock slab on the crest of Dunadd, which also bears a deeply etched footprint supposedly used in the ritual inauguration of kings, has been convincingly assigned to this same period of Pictish domination of Dalriada and can thus be taken to represent the same gesture cut in stone.

All of which suggests the possibility that his presumed initial motive of seeking vengeance for Dúngal's treatment of Bruide might have served Oengus as a pretext for a greater ambition to impose Pictish overlordship on the Scots of Dalriada, an objective never attempted by any king of Picts before him and yet suggesting itself as tempt-ingly achievable by the second quarter of the eighth century. Just some two decades earlier, the inclusion of the Pictish church within the Columban monastic federation centred on Iona would have presented a formidable diplomatic obstacle to any such aggression against the kingdom which held Columba as its patron saint. That constraint had been effectively removed since 717, the year at which the annals enter the 'expulsion of the community of Iona across the spine of Britain by Nechtan' (during his earlier reign in Fortriu and as a result of his adoption of the Roman practice recommended by Bede's abbot in Jarrow).

There was, of course, a more immediate signal of Dalriada as a kingdom ripe for conquest by an ambitious neighbouring warlord and it lay in the long-running contention between, and within, its

---

22    Skene, *Celtic Scotland*, vol. i, p.290.

dynastic kindreds which had resulted in the fragmentation of any effective over-kingship of the Scots by the 730s. Yet it was very probably a 'backs-to-the-wall' reaction to the Pictish onslaught of 736 which was to produce the first evidence of a real over-king in Dalriada since Dúngal had been driven from power ten years earlier – and it came in the person of his cousin Muiredach, son of Ainbcellach, who was said by the annals to have been elected king, although only 'of the Cenél Loairn', in 733.

In a separate entry which follows their notices of the burning of Creic, winning of Dunadd, capture of Dúngal, and death of Bruide, the *Annals of Ulster* enter 'the battle of Cnocc Coirpri in Calathros, at Etarlindu, between the Dál Riata and Fortriu; and Talorcan, son of Fergus, pursued the son of Ainbcellach who fled with his host; and in this encounter many nobles fell'. The site of this 'battle of Cnocc Coirpri' is not immediately apparent, because there is an earlier record of Domnall Brecc having suffered one of his defeats at a place also called Calathros but thought to have been on Islay which would have been an unlikely point of contact between Muiredach's force and the invading Picts. W. J. Watson found a more helpful clue to the location of the battlefield in the place-name *Etarlindu* which he identified as Ederline just south of Loch Awe and thus credibly situated for a stand against an enemy advancing north out of Knapdale towards Oban and the surrounding coastland of Lorn.[23]

It would seem then that Muiredach (who presumably was the 'son of Ainbcellach' intended, although not actually named, by the annalists) had somehow mustered an army from his own and, presumably also, from other Dalriadic *cenéla* – a feat bearing its own testimony to his effective status as over-king of Dalriada – to confront the Pictish advance towards the heartland of the Cenél Loairn. In fact, it is not entirely beyond possibility that the emergence of a Cenél Loairn king unexpectedly capable of recruiting forces from other *cenéla* of 'the Dál Riata' might have prompted the invading Picts to extend their campaign northward into the lands of Lorn.

Also significant is the annalist's evidence for the Pictish force having been led by Oengus' brother Talorcan, because it could be taken to indicate Oengus having delegated command to his kinsman in order to allow his own return to Fortriu, a decision which Benjamin Hudson

---

23  Watson, *Celtic Place-names*, p.105.

suggests 'might have been due to the necessity to remain on guard against rivals in Pictish lands'. Indeed, 'even possible former allies could have been suspect' in the light of the entry in the annals at 739 of 'Talorcan, son of Drostan, king of Atholl . . . drowned by Oengus', presumably on grounds or suspicion of treachery of one sort or another.[24]

He may, however, have been otherwise distracted from the campaign in the west if he had received some form of warning from Northumbria where the kingship was soon to change hands when the saintly Ceolwulf (to whom Bede had recently dedicated his *Historia*) abdicated in favour of his more warlike first cousin Eadbert before entering into monastic retirement on Lindisfarne. Eadbert, who is acknowledged by an eminent modern authority on Anglo-Saxon England as 'the last Northumbrian king to lead effective expeditions beyond the northern border',[25] would have been undoubtedly recognised by Oengus as a real potential threat. So, indeed, he proved to be on the evidence of the twelfth-century English historian Symeon of Durham, who is thought to have been informed by a lost northern chronicle and tells of Eadbert having been at war with the Picts (presumably around the Forth) in 740 when a Mercian attack on Northumbria caused him to abandon a campaign which might otherwise have led him into conflict with Oengus.

Whatever might have been the true nature of its surrounding circumstances, the rout at Cnocc Coirpri clearly represented not only the last, and most decisive, defeat inflicted upon the Scots by the Pictish invasions of the 730s, but also the final act in the ascendancy of the Cenél Loairn in Dalriada. There is a collateral significance, however, in the absence of any reference to the Cenél nGabráin in the annal record of that year 736, because such an absence would indicate their ruling house – possibly still headed by the same Alpin who had earlier suffered at the hands of Oengus in Pictland – having laid low in the south of Kintyre and left the Cenél Loairn to bear the greater heat and burden of the Pictish onslaught. In which case, and

---

24    Hudson, *Kings of Celtic Scotland*, p.28.
25    Stenton, *Anglo-Saxon England*, p.92.

as Benjamin Hudson has suggested, the Cenél nGabráin's 'obscurity came at a propitious time',[26] because the subsequent course of events was to allow them to recover their former ascendancy within the next generation.

Through the following fifteen years, however, it would be realistic to assume the Scots having remained under at least some measure of Pictish domination and yet there is no indisputable entry in the annal record which would associate Oengus with Dalriada after the year 736. The one apparent exception is a bald entry of 'the hammering of Dalriada (*percutio Dalriata*) by Oengus, son of Fergus' which is found only in the *Annals of Ulster* at 741, but where it is suspected by Marjorie Anderson as 'just possibly a misplaced duplication' of events more widely and reliably entered five years earlier.[27] An extension of her very reasonable suspicion might venture to suggest Ulster, rather than Iona, as the source of that entry and its original form having been as a reference to the arrival in Bangor of the 'Iona chronicle' brought to Ireland in, or before, the year 741 with the purpose of finding a safe refuge for valued manuscripts considered to be at risk from that 'hammering . . . by Oengus'.

Whatever might have been the concerns which distracted the mighty king of Picts from personal involvement with the war on Dalriada in 736, he had evidently redirected his ambitions towards Strathclyde by the end of the subsequent decade and assigned command of operations in that theatre to his brother Talorcan. An entry in the *Annals of Tigernach* at 750 records 'a battle between Picts and Britons, in which perished Talorcan, son of Fergus, and his brother; and there was slaughter of the Picts along with him'. The same conflict is also entered in the *Annales Cambriae* (or 'Welsh annals' and thought to preserve contemporary eighth-century source material) which record Talorcan having been slain in 'the battle of *Mocetauc*'. While the site of the battle – known by variant name-forms in the Welsh and Irish sources and possibly somewhere in the region of Dumbarton – remains otherwise unidentified, its outcome was quite certainly a decisive defeat for the

---

26   Hudson, *Kings of Celtic Scotland*, p.22.
27   M. O. Anderson, *Kings & Kingship*, p.186.

Picts and one which is probably reflected by another entry at the same year of 750 in the *Annals of Ulster* which simply and bleakly records 'the ebbing of the sovereignty of Oengus'.

Oengus himself would live on for more than a decade, allowing him time enough to avenge his brothers' deaths as he was to do in 756 when he forged an alliance with Eadbert of Northumbria to attack *Alcluith*, the capital fortress of the Strathclyde Britons on Dumbarton Rock, and – according to Symeon of Durham – seemingly forced the Britons to accept terms. While the obituaries entered in the annals at 761 still confirm Oengus as 'king of Picts' (or even as 'king of Alba' in the *Annals of Tigernach*), there is good reason to believe that it was the 'ebbing of his sovereignty' eleven years earlier which allowed Aed Find of the Cenél nGabráin to free Dalriada from Pictish control.

There is no further mention of Muiredach, son of Ainbcellach, in the annal record after the rout of his army at Ederline in 736, and so it must be assumed that he was slain in the flight from the field of battle. Of somewhat greater significance here is the fact that no clearly identified member of the Cenél Loairn appears to have been noticed in the annal record after 736. Yet the first unmistakable evidence of the resurgence of the Cenél nGabráin is the entry in the *Annals of Ulster* at 768 of 'a battle in Fortriu between Aed and Cinaed', because this battle had evidently been carried into the very heart of Pictland by Aed Find, a son of Eochaid and thus a king of Dalriada in direct line of descent from Gabrán, grandson of Fergus Mór.

The 'Cinaed' against whom he fought that battle is known in the Pictish king-lists as *Ciniod* and identified as the son of *Uuredech*, a name which suggested itself to Marjorie Anderson as a Pictish form of Feradach and led her to suggest the intriguing possibility that the brother of Dúngal of Lorn who had been captured with him in 736 went on to make his peace with Oengus and to seal their reconciliation by marrying his sister, thus becoming the father of a later king of Fortriu.[28]

Whether or not the line of Selbach had indeed found its way into the ruling house of Fortriu by the second half of the eighth century (and the suggestion is far too plausible to be dismissed out of hand), the

---

28    M. O. Anderson, *Kings & Kingship*, pp.185, 189.

other branch of the Cenél Loairn had followed its own course out of Argyll and northwards into Moray, because it is there that the descendants of Ainbcellach reappear in the early eleventh century as hereditary mormaers of Moray recognised as kings in their own right north of the Mounth.

## III

## MORMAERS IN MORAY

It should be said at the outset of this chapter that when the descendants of the Cenél Loairn kings of Dalriada do eventually appear in the Irish annal record of the earlier eleventh century, there is nothing in those first notices which immediately identifies them as such. Nonetheless, all the individuals named by the annalists are of presumably Dalriadic origin and ancestry, if only on the evidence of the unmistakably Gaelic (or, more properly, Middle Irish) character and form of their personal names and patronymics.

Some indication of their status is supplied by the titles accorded them which undoubtedly signify lordship over the land, and so too is their location confirmed when that land is firmly identified as the province of Moray. The title given by one annalist, however, can differ from that applied to the same individual by another, and even when both are telling of the same event. In the first of these entries, for example, a Findláech, son of Ruadrí, is styled 'mormaer of Moray' by the *Annals of Tigernach* and yet recognised as 'king of [or, perhaps, in] Alba' by the *Annals of Ulster* in their entries of his death at the hands of 'the sons of his brother Máelbrigte' in 1020.

While those titles and their application will bear further consideration later, two other factors indicated by these earliest appearances of the house of Moray in the annal record are of immediate bearing at this point, because both are so strikingly reminiscent of the earlier history of the Cenél Loairn in Dalriada. The first is the fact that all the named individuals clearly belong to branches of the same kindred, while the second is the evident contention between those two families, which appears to have flared up again twelve years later when the *Annals of Ulster* notice the death of 'Gillacomgain, son of Máelbrigte, mormaer of Moray . . . burned with fifty of his men' in 1032.

70

Such similarities cannot be taken as decisive evidence of origin, of course, and especially when intra-dynastic contention was so rife as to have been virtually characteristic of ruling kindreds in early medieval Scotland. Yet, when later records assert a credible claim for the direct descent of these apparently hereditary lords of Moray from the kingly family of the Cenél Loairn in Dalriada, it would suggest the vicious rivalry between the sons of Ferchar Fota having been so endemic as to have been carried by their descendants out of Argyll and into Moray where it continued to bedevil their family history three centuries on. There are occasions, however, when the early sources do seem to fore-shadow the future whilst at the same time reflecting a greater antiquity than that of the events they record, and the very first entry of the house of Moray into the annals certainly might be read as one such instance.

The son of the Findláech noticed at the year 1020 was to become high-king of Scots twenty years later and is unrivalled even today as the best-known of all Scotland's kings. He was, of course, Macbeth and it is an early record of his ancestry, preserved alongside a related pedigree tracing the lateral lineage of his successor Lulach, which represents the principal documentary evidence for the direct descent of the house of Moray from the old Cenél Loairn kings of Dalriada. The oldest sources of those genealogies are two Irish manuscript collections compiled in the twelfth century, the earlier of them known (from its Bodleian Library catalogue entry) as 'Rawlinson B 502', the other being the slightly later *Book of Leinster* containing a copy of the same two pedigrees which supplies a generation missing from the Rawlinson version of one of them.[1] The longer of these two genealogies descends Máelsnechtai, son of Lulach (who was himself the son of the Gillacomgain noticed in the annals at 1032), from Ainbcellach, son of Ferchar Fota. Its companion pedigree traces the descent of Macbeth from another branch of the same lineage, but only as far back as Ainbcellach's great-great-grandson Morgán, where it would evidently have conjoined with the lineage of Máelsnechtai and Lulach.

In view of the crucial role of these records in linking the Cenél Loairn of Dalriada to its descendent kindreds in Moray, it should be said that

---

1    *CGH*, pp.329–30; see also Genealogy 4, p.177 below.

their reliability does not enjoy the unanimous acceptance of modern historians. However, the most balanced assessment I have yet found is that offered by David Sellar, a foremost authority on old Scottish genealogies who suggests that 'it has perhaps not always been realised how close the earliest surviving record of his pedigree is to Macbeth's own time. Macbeth died in 1057, his relative and eventual successor as mormaer of Moray, Máelsnechtai, in 1085. Their pedigree appears already in the Irish manuscript Rawlinson B 502, compiled about 1130, the very year in which the last mormaer of their kin, Angus, the nephew of Máelsnechtai, was killed at Stracathro in Angus, fighting the forces of David I. Given these dates, it seems reasonable to assume that the genealogy of Macbeth preserved in Rawlinson B 502, and repeated in various later manuscripts, is the official pedigree which Macbeth himself put about and wished to be believed – a political document which can be safely backdated to his reign . . . Whether or not this claim has a sound genealogical basis – and the possibility should not be ruled out – the fact that the claim was made at all is evidence that the house of Loarn and its kings had not been forgotten in eleventh century Scotland, and that there was political advantage to be gained in claiming descent from them.'[2]

When the proximity of those pedigrees to living memory of the last generation they record is taken together with the age-old (and still prevalent) great concern of the Gael with ancestry and kinship, there would seem to be ample reason to allow them a genuinely 'sound genealogical basis'. Indeed, were they to be granted the same forbearance generally afforded to the descent of the MacAlpin kings from the Cenél nGabráin (despite the doubtful historicity of the eponymous Alpin, father of Kenneth), then the fully credible direct descent of Macbeth and Lulach from Ferchar Fota might enjoy a similarly wide acceptability.

The same really cannot be said for the evidence of the later Latin king-lists when they enter the names of an 'Eogan', a 'Selbach', and a 'Dúngal', identified respectively as the son, grandson, and great-grandson of Muiredach, son of Ainbcellach, and listed as his successors

---

2    Sellar, 'Highland Family Origins', p.104.

in alternation with Cenél nGabráin kings through the second half of the eighth century. Even though these three reigns are not included among those listed in the *Synchronisms* and *Duan Albanach*, it has been suggested that information about them may not have come to light until the twelfth century and thus been unavailable when earlier lists were compiled in the previous century.[3] When the existence of these three supposed kings is uncorroborated by any contemporary record, the greater likelihood must surely be that these names and reigns are simply repetitions of those of earlier Cenél Loairn kings which had been interpolated into the later lists, presumably with the intention of constructing a spurious pattern of neatly alternating kingship.

Indeed, the 'Eogan' might be recognised as the most glaring example of this process, because the name does not occur in any genealogy of the Cenél Loairn and is found in association with that kindred only in the *Senchus* survey where an 'Eogan Garb' is named as a son of Fergus Salach and attributed thirty houses. When the name first appears in the Latin king-lists, however, an 'Eogan' identified as 'Ferchar Fota's son' is entered as the successor to Ainbcellach at the point where the older lists and the annals all confirm Selbach having followed his brother into the kingship. Curiously, both the name and exact reign-length of that genuinely historical Selbach are found in the Latin lists, but not until a much later point in the eighth century when a 'Selbach, Eogan's son' is entered with a twenty-four year reign as successor to a son of Aed Find. This surely must have been a deliberately misplaced entry of the name and reign of the real Selbach, Ferchar Fota's son, whose obituary is entered in the annals at 730, and the same would also apply to the seven-year reign of 'Dúngal, Selbach's son' when it is entered as that of a successor to another son of Aed Find.

While it is not at all unusual for the same given name to occur regularly through any number of generations of Gaelic families – and at least as regularly in modern times as in early medieval antiquity – such a custom of naming is invariably intended as a gesture in commemoration of some honoured family member. Consequently, it would have been scarcely imaginable for two generations of descent from Muiredach,

---

3   Hudson, *Kings of Celtic Scotland*, p.130.

Ainbcellach's son, to have been given the names Selbach and Dúngal in honour of members of a rival branch of the same kindred – and especially when the earlier Selbach was believed to have slain their forebear Ainbcellach in battle.

The absence from the annals of any reference to these supposed descendent successors to Muiredach cannot, in itself, be said to deny their existence. Even had they actually existed, they might well have escaped the notice of the annalists, because no trace of any name entered after Ainbcellach in the Cenél Loairn genealogies is found in the annals until the last quarter of the tenth century and there is no specific notice of a recognisable member of that kindred (excepting only the solitary and highly suspect entry of an obituary of Muiredach in the very late *Annals of the Four Masters* under the year '771') in the annal record of all the years between 736 and 1020.

There are, of course, perfectly plausible explanations for this three-hundred-year 'black hole' in the contemporary record of the Cenél Loairn. The removal of the 'Iona chronicle' to Ireland sometime before 741, and presumably in flight from the 'hammering of Dalriada' by the Picts, would undoubtedly have greatly depleted the flow of Scottish material into the Irish annals. Thus the activities of a kindred whose territory lay in the further north of Argyll would have been more likely to pass unnoticed by the compilers of the 'Ulster chronicle' in Bangor than would those of one – such as the Cenél nGabráin who appear to have been located in the south of Kintyre – remaining in closer proximity to, and presumably contact with, the Irish coast. By the time the Cenél Loairn had relocated to the Highlands their activities would have been still further remote from notice by the Irish chroniclers – and so all due weight must be given to Benjamin Hudson's proposal that 'if one were to suggest a date for the beginning of the move by at least some of the Cenél Loairn up the Great Glen to the lands round the Moray Firth, then the mid-eighth century should be considered'.[4]

Some support for such a date has been discerned from the study of place-names because, while the Gaelic tongue must have found its way into Moray and Ross with Irish monks active thereabouts since the sixth

---

4    Hudson, *Kings of Celtic Scotland*, p.28.

century, the establishment of a ruling aristocracy from Dalriada would have been reflected in the emergence of names including the Gaelic elements *baile* ('township') and *achadh* ('field') which are taken to signify an early phase of settlement. Working from that premise, W. F. H. Nicolaisen's study of the distribution of such name-types in Moray and beyond provided him with 'evidence for ascribing the earliest Gaelic settlement in this northernmost part of Scotland and neighbouring areas to the ninth century'.[5]

The name Moray (or *Moireabh* in modern Gaelic) first appears in the annals in its Middle Irish forms of *Mureb* and *Muireb* which are thought to derive from the early Celtic *mori-treb* meaning 'sea settlement'. There is, however, no recognisable form of Moray in the oldest list of the provinces of the Picts – that found in the *Leabhar Breathnach*, an Irish version of Nennius' *Historia Britonum* dated to the eleventh century – which derives their names of *Cat, Cé, Cirig* (or *Circenn*), *Fíb, Fidach, Fotla* and *Fortrenn* (or *Fortriu*) from those of the assuredly mythical 'seven sons of Cruithne'. The earliest record of the location of those provinces, which together comprise the greater part of the Scottish mainland north of the Forth and east of Druim Alban, is preserved in *De Situ Albanie*, a twelfth-century tract said to have been informed in part by Andrew, bishop of Caithness, who is known to have died in 1184.

Of the seven provinces, those of Circenn (Angus and the Mearns), Fotla (Atholl and Gowrie), and Fortriu (Strathearn and Menteith) have already been mentioned, while Fíb is immediately recognisable as Fife. Of rather greater bearing here are the more northerly provinces of Pictland, and of these 'Cat' has been convincingly identified with Caithness and south-east Sutherland, whilst the location of 'Cé', which was placed by the bishop in Mar and Buchan, is considered less certain by more recent scholarship. 'Fidach' – a name surviving in that of Glen Fiddich beside Dufftown,[6] and perhaps meaning 'the wooded country' – is identified with Moray and Easter Ross and so it would have been the Picts of that province who were first brought under the

5   Nicolaisen, *Scottish Place-names*, pp.176–8.
6   Watson, *Celtic Place-names*, p.115.

lordship of a Dalriadic kindred newly arrived from the lands of Lorn. If the Cenél Loairn had begun their migration into Moray by the later eighth century, then they would have been moving into the provinces of Pictland north of the Grampians at much the same time as – or just possibly even before – the Cenél nGabráin were establishing themselves in the kingship of Fortriu.

More than twenty years after Aed Find's incursion into Fortriu in 768 – and his battle with Ciniod, son of the 'Uuredech' who has been convincingly identified as the former Cenél Loairn prince Feredach – it was Aed's nephew Constantine, a son of his brother Fergus, who became the first of the Cenél nGabráin known to have ruled over both the Picts and the Scots.

The evidence of the annal record and king-lists for Constantine mac Fergusa (or *Castantin*, son of *Urguist*, in his Pictish name-form) has been variously interpreted by historians. The Pictish character of his given name, for example, would indicate his mother having been a Pict and has been taken to suggest his earlier life having been spent east of Druim Alban. Such a proposal would thus correspond to the Ulster annalist's description of Constantine's 'conquest' of a rival to win kingship of Fortriu in 789 (or possibly 790) as 'a battle among the Picts', yet an alternative interpretation has suggested that such a recognition actually obscures a decisive victory for the Scots whose earlier raiding had become an effective 'invasion' of the Pictish kingdom of Fortriu before the last decade of the eighth century.[7] Whether by sheer force of arms which overwhelmed Pictish kingly families left grievously weakened by the ascendancy of the warlike Oengus half a century before or by the assertion of some supposed matrilineal claim, the advent of Constantine quite certainly launched an ascendancy of the Picto-Scottish 'house of Fergus' of which two generations of Cenél nGabráin descent were to be both kings of Fortriu and overlords of Dalriada through the most part of half a century.

None of which need have had very much bearing on the Cenél Loairn, who were advancing, if not already consolidating, their own lordship north of the Mounth and thus far outwith the dominion of

---

7    Hudson, *Kings of Celtic Scotland*, p.29.

the kings of Fortriu. Writing some sixty years before that first notice of Constantine in the annals, and thus with a closely contemporary authority, Bede described 'kingdoms of the northern Picts separated from the southern territories of the Picts by a range of steep and rugged mountains'. So too, the obituary of a *Dubthalorc* ('Black' – or perhaps 'Young' – Talorc, who was quite possibly a son of the mighty Oengus) entered in the *Annals of Ulster* at 782 recognises him as 'king of the Picts this side of the Mounth', which led Marjorie Anderson to suggest the possibility 'that the kings to the north were no longer recognising the kings of Fortriu as their superiors'.[8]

Not since Adomnán wrote of Columba's visit to Bruide, son of Maelchon, at Craig Phadrig in the second half of the sixth century had there been any reference in the early sources which might be taken to associate any king of Picts with Moray or any other province north of the Grampians. The most prominent Pictish king in the seventh century, for example, was another Bruide, the son of Bile, whose victory at Dunnichen in 685 had freed the Picts, Scots and Britons from subjection to the Angles of Northumbria. While this Bruide is thought to have had an ancestral claim on the kingship of Circenn, his power centre apparently lay in Fortriu, as did that of Oengus, son of Fergus, in the following century, by which time the kingship of Fortriu can certainly be taken to represent a greater overlordship of Picts – and yet only of those south of the Mounth.

There is nonetheless abundant archaeological evidence – ranging from many fine symbol stones of the incised 'Class I' type to the formidable coastal fort of Burghead on the shore of the Moray Firth north-east of Forres – for an impressive Pictish culture having flourished in Moray throughout two and a half centuries after the last reference to any king of Picts north of the Grampians. While there are numerous notices to kings of Fortriu – and, in one instance, to a king of Atholl – in the annal record, there is nowhere any mention of a 'king of Fidach', so it may have been that Pictish lords of Moray in the seventh and eighth centuries were known not as kings but as 'mormaers'. This title – from the Old/Middle Irish *mór-maer* which would translate as 'great steward'

---

8    M. O. Anderson, *Kings & Kingship*, pp.191–2.

– first appears in the Irish annals in the earlier tenth century and is invariably applied only to Scots, yet it is thought to have been of Pictish origin because when the title occurs in Scottish records it is usually found in association with former Pictish provinces such as Angus and Buchan. Eventually those who would have been earlier styled 'mormaer' were accorded the title of 'earl' (derived from the Norse *jarl*), and yet when the *Annals of Connacht* enter the inauguration of Robert Bruce as king of Scotland at the year 1306, his title 'earl of Carrick' is rendered as *mormaer Cargi* (the Irish genitive form of Carrick).

It is more than likely, of course, that descendants of the Cenél Loairn kings of Dalriada continued to recognise themselves as kings in Moray, as indeed they are most often styled by the Irish annalists – and, as the historian David Kirby has suggested, their styling as mormaers 'may have been how Kenneth mac Alpin's descendants preferred to think of them'.[9] However those different forms of title might be read, the reappearance of members of the Cenél Loairn in the annal record assuredly confirms their establishment in the lordship of Moray by the earlier eleventh century, and yet there is nowhere any account of how or when they had achieved such power and prominence.

The possibility that an incoming Dalriadic nobility might have raised itself to power north of the Mounth by intermarriage with a native ruling aristocracy is effectively denied by the absence of any given name of recognisably Pictish character either in the annal notices or the genealogies of the Cenél Loairn-descended house of Moray. The alternative scenario then must be of their having achieved ascendancy by force of arms, as the Cenél nGabráin appear to have done in both phases of their effective conquest of the Pictish kingdoms to the south. There is no reference to any conflict between Pict and Scot in Moray in the annals, or elsewhere in the early sources of ninth-century Scottish history, an omission which might, once again, be reasonably explained by warfare in remote places having simply passed unnoticed by the chroniclers.

There may, however, be evidence of such conflict cut into stone and preserved in the battle scene carved on the reverse face of the cross-slab which stands twenty feet tall on the outskirts of Forres where it

---

9    Kirby, 'Moray – prior to *c*.1100', p.20.

is called by the comparatively recent and historically unhelpful name of 'Sueno's Stone'. This carved slab (of the later Class III type, which includes no Pictish symbols) has been reliably dated to the ninth or tenth century and suggested by the archaeologist Anna Ritchie as the work of 'a Pictish sculptor possibly working for a Scottish patron'.[10] Of the many and various interpretations of the conflict and carnage depicted in extraordinary detail on 'Sueno's Stone', one of the most convincing is the proposal that it may have 'marked the final victory north of the Mounth by the Scots over the Picts'.[11] Whether or not this was the decisive contest of arms by which the descendants of the Cenél Loairn kings of Dalriada achieved their new ascendancy in Moray, there is a further – and parallel – likelihood that whatever conflict there might have been between the Picts and Scots of Moray through the ninth century, it would probably have been abandoned when both peoples found themselves confronted by the advance of a common enemy out of the further north.

However unaffected they may have been by political developments in Fortriu on the eve of the eighth century, the one event in the reign of Constantine which must have been of great concern to the Cenél Loairn – at least some of whom would probably have still been in Argyll at that time – was the initial wave of the Scandinavian impact which was to direct so great a part of the subsequent course of Scotland's medieval history.

The first record of viking raids on Scotland is entered in the *Annals of Ulster* at the year 794 where 'the devastation of all the islands of Britain by the gentiles' is usually interpreted as a Norwegian fleet operating out of forward bases in Orkney or Shetland and rounding Cape Wrath to ravage the Outer Hebrides. In the next raiding season the northmen returned to pillage Skye and 'devastate' Iona en route to raiding island monasteries around the Irish coast. The monastery on Iona was attacked again in 802, and in 806 when the slaughter of sixty-eight monks seemingly forced the abbot and the greater part of his surviving community to relocate to Ireland where a new monastery was being built for them at Kells in Meath in 807.

---

10    Ritchie, *Invaders of Scotland*, p.52.
11    Sellar, 'Sueno's Stone and its Interpreters', p.107.

The effective transfer to Ireland of what had so long been the spiritual centre of the kingdom of the Scots is thought to have prompted Constantine to his foundation of a new royal church at Dunkeld. Even while that monastery was being built, and certainly before Constantine's death in 820, the northmen were an increasing presence along the coast and the coastland of Argyll because what had begun as pirate nests were fast developing into permanent Scandinavian settlements along the western seaboard. Indeed, and as Alfred Smyth has pointed out, 'whole households from Scandinavia must have been settling down to fish and farm in the Isles by the end of the first quarter of the ninth century'.[12] While a branch of the Cenél nGabráin had certainly moved east into Pictland before the first viking raids on the coast of Argyll, and the Cenél Loairn may have similarly begun to move into Moray by that time, it is probable that their migration in greater numbers up the Great Glen had been made in the first quarter of the ninth century and thus quite probably, in at least some measure, as a reaction to the advent of the northmen.

Within twenty years of Constantine's death, his successor kings east of Druim Alban were to suffer their own repercussion of the Scandinavian impact, and with disastrous consequences on the evidence of the entry of 'a battle by the gentiles against the men of Fortriu' in the *Annals of Ulster* at the year 839. The reason why the annalist supplied no indication of the whereabouts of that battle (which was presumably fought somewhere on the Scottish mainland) was probably the greater significance of its more prominent fatal casualties. These are identified as Constantine's nephew Eoganán who had succeeded to the kingship just two years earlier, Eoganán's brother Bran, and Aed, son of Boanta, who is entered in the Dalriadic king-list and so would presumably have been Constantine's representative in the west. 'And others fell,' adds the annalist, 'almost without number.'

As a result of what appears to have been its initial hostile contact with the Scandinavian presence in Scotland, the ruling house of Fortriu had been effectively obliterated in a massacre of its forces by what was undoubtedly a warband of Hebridean Norse, and one which may have

---

12   Smyth, *Warlords and Holy Men*, p.148.

been in alliance with the *Cináed mac Alpín* who succeeded to the king-ship of Dalriada in the following year and subsequently eliminated as many as five Pictish rivals to become the sole ruler of the Picts and Scots by 848. He is, of course, better remembered as Kenneth mac Alpin, who may have been a great-grandson of Aed Find but assuredly did belong to a branch of the Cenél nGabráin which had remained in the west, and probably in Kintyre, when the family of Aed's brother Fergus had relocated itself to Fortriu.

Kenneth is justly acknowledged as founder of the dynasty which was to supply Scotland with its long line of medieval kings who claimed descent from Fergus Mór through the Cenél nGabráin kings of Dalriada. There is however one great achievement long attributed to Kenneth and yet to which he can be allowed no exclusive claim, and that is his 'conquest of the Picts'. In his concise account of Moray before the year 1100, David Kirby recognises that it must have the Cenél Loairn, not the Cenél nGabráin, who conquered northern Pictland and goes on to propose that 'the double-pronged attack on the Picts not only helps explain their collapse but reveals why two important separate and opposing kingdoms emerged among the Scots after 848'.[13]

Not until a full hundred years after that date is there any record of a MacAlpin king having intervened against the 'men of Moray', most of whom must have been of Pictish origin and yet by the tenth century had long since absorbed the culture and tongue of their Gaelic ruling kindred. From which there emerges a distinct likelihood that the long contention between mormaers of Moray who regarded themselves as 'kings in the north' and the MacAlpin dynasty's advance towards a high-kingship of Scots may have reflected an earlier acrimony between Picts north and south of the Mounth which was at least as old as the rivalry between the Cenél Loairn and Cenél nGabráin in Dalriada.

Even within the reign of Kenneth mac Alpin (who died in 858) the northern and western isles and coastland of Scotland can be recognised as an integral sector of the orbit of Scandinavian expansion, and one which was soon to be drawn under Norwegian political control centred on the jarldom of Orkney. The ambitions of the Orkney jarls were not

---

13    Kirby, 'Moray – prior to *c*.1100', p.20.

to be long contained within their northern isles and soon extended across the Pentland Firth to the Scottish mainland. By the last quarter of the ninth century, Caithness and Sutherland were effectively a territory of the Orkney Norse who were already looking further to the south, and particularly to the rich woodland of Ross which offered them an abundance of the much-needed ship-timber they had found in such short supply on the virtually treeless northern isles.[14]

It was that direction of their land-seeking which brought the Orkney jarls into inevitable conflict with the Gaelic lords of the northern Highlands, who consequently begin to appear in the sagas and related Icelandic sources which can thus supply evidence for the whereabouts, activities and identities of the descendants of the Cenél Loairn some hundred and fifty years after they had vanished from the Irish annal record. The most part of that evidence is found in *Orkneyinga Saga*, a 'history of the jarls of Orkney' thought to have been completed in 1234–5, but initially set down (under its elder title of *Jarls' Saga*) some-time around 1200 by an Icelander whose name is not known but who was undoubtedly linked to the important cultural centre at Oddi in southern Iceland which had especial connections with Orkney during the last decades of the twelfth century and early years of the century following. The *Saga* identifies the first of the jarls of Orkney as Sigurd, called *inn riki* ('the mighty') and said to have been granted the jarldom by his brother Rognvald, who was jarl of Moer in the west of Norway and apparently the first Norwegian overlord of the northern isles of Scotland.

For all their value and vigour, the Icelandic sagas were written as literature rather than history, and chronology is not their greatest strength. Thus the dating of Sigurd's death must rely upon the expertise of modern historians, whose varying estimates would enter his obituary as early as *c*.870 or some two decades later (and perhaps more accu-rately) around the year 892. Of greater interest here than its precise date, however, are the circumstances of his death which provide a vivid conclusion to the account of his career in *Orkneyinga Saga*. Sigurd is said – by that saga and by others – to have formed an alliance with

---

14    Crawford, *Earl & Mormaer*, pp.11–16.

Thorstein Olafsson, usually called *raudr* ('the red'), which is probably the reason why their achievements came to be so widely recorded by Icelandic saga-makers because, while Thorstein's father was Olaf the White, Norse king of Dublin, his mother was Aud Ketilsdottir, called *djúpaudga* ('the deep-minded') and well-remembered as the founding matriarch of a prominent family based at Laxardal in Iceland.

The claim made by Snorri Sturluson's thirteenth-century *Heimskringla* for Thorstein and Sigurd having 'plundered in Scotland' is thought to be corroborated by the Scottish annotated king-list usually known as the 'Chronicle of the Kings' (from a twelfth-century source, but thought to preserve much older material) which tells how 'the northmen wasted Pictland' in the reign of Donald II, Constantine's son and a grandson of Kenneth mac Alpin, who succeeded to the kingship in 889. This raiding evidently resulted in the conquest of the northern mainland claimed for Thorstein and Sigurd by a number of sagas, but most concisely by *Heimskringla* which specifies their acquisition of 'Caithness [*Katanes*] and all Sutherland [*Suðrland*] as far as *Ekkjalsbakki*', meaning the bank of the river Oykel which has thus been taken to mark the line where land-taking by the Orkney Norse fronted on to the territory of the mormaers of Moray.

*Orkneyinga Saga* claims still more extensive conquest for Sigurd when it adds '*Maerhaefi* [Moray] and *Ros* [to] all of *Katanes*', and even claiming him to have built a stronghold 'in the south of Moray', but more probably interpreted as 'south of the Dornoch Firth', and it would appear to have been this bold foothold which brought him into contention with a *Melbrikta*, '*jarl* of the Scots'. When the two arranged to settle their differences with forty men apiece in a place unspecified by the saga-maker but evidently south of the Oykel, Sigurd sought the advantage by means of mounting two warriors on each of forty horses, and successfully so when 'a fierce fight' left Melbrikta (a name clearly recognisable as the Norse form of the Gaelic *Máelbrigte*) and his men dead on the field.

In a grisly celebration of his victory, Sigurd had all the enemy corpses decapitated and their heads slung from his men's saddles, whilst reserving the head of Melbrikta as his personal trophy. Unfortunately for Sigurd, his victim had a tooth so prominent that he was known as *Melbrikta*

*Tönn* ('Máelbrigte Tusk') and so unclean that when the 'tusk' scratched Sigurd's calf as the head swung from his saddle he would appear to have contracted blood-poisoning. 'Pain and swelling rose around that wound and brought him to his death. And Sigurd the Mighty is buried in *Ekkjalsbakki*.' The same place of burial is confirmed in *Heimskringla* and further supported by a remarkable item of place-name evidence, because on the north side of the Dornoch Firth and downstream from where the Oykel widens out into the estuary stands a farm now called Cyderhall. The name has been traced back through its elder form of 'Sidera' to the original Old Norse *Sigurdar haugr*, meaning 'Sigurd's howe' or burial mound, which is traditionally located and still visible (although as yet unexcavated) just some half a mile north-west of the modern farm.[15] The greater historical significance of Sigurd's place of burial lies in its evidence for *Ekkjalsbakki* as the southern frontier of Norse expansion, because it would have been surely unthinkable to have laid an Orkney jarl in earth outwith the bounds of his own lordship.

All of which also makes its own contribution to the little that is known of the descendants of the Cenél Loairn in the ninth century, because there can be the least doubt as to the 'Melbrikta' of the saga having been a notable member of that kindred. The name Máelbrigte occurs again (recurring in a later generation as was, and is, the custom of Gaelic nomenclature) in the aforementioned Moray genealogies where a Máelbrigte, son of Ruaidri, is entered as the grandfather of Lulach and the brother of Macbeth's father Findláech. The name of the same Máelbrigte is found twice more in the annals: at 1020 where his sons are accused of the murder of their uncle Findláech and at 1029 in the *Annals of Ulster* where the obituary of Máelbrigte's son Malcolm styles him as a 'king of Scotland'. There is further evidence for the name's currency among members of the Cenél Loairn-descended house of Moray preserved in the 'Gaelic notes' inserted, by different hands and at different times between the later eleventh and mid-twelfth centuries, in a ninth-century manuscript of gospel texts called 'The Book of Deer' purely by reason of the notes beginning with a foundation legend

---

15  Crawford, 'Making of a Frontier', pp.38–9; *Scandanavian Scotland*, pp.58–9.

for the monastery of Old Deer in the north-east of Aberdeenshire.[16] The majority of these notes record grants made to the monastery by regional magnates, including gifts of lands and estates by Máelbrigte's son Malcolm and by another Máelbrigte, son of Cathal, who is recorded in no other source. Thus the Máelbrigte slain by Sigurd might be recognised as the earliest on record in a line of that name which was to continue for at least two hundred more years.

After the death of Sigurd the Mighty and the short reigns of two successor jarls who failed to constrain the activities of local viking chieftains, Rognvald of Moer agreed to allow his youngest son Einar to cross to Orkney and assume the jarldom sometime around the year 900. Einar – who is described by *Orkneyinga Saga* as 'tall and ugly, and although one-eyed still the most keen-sighted of men' – slew the two foremost viking reprobates and took control of all the island territories, yet is best remembered in saga tradition as *Torf-Einar* on account of his having been 'the first to cut *torf* (peat) for fuel at *Torfnes* in Scotland'. *Torfnes*, a place mentioned again on two later occasions in the saga, has been convincingly identified as Tarbat Ness on the coast of Easter Ross, and so the significance of Einar's peat-cutting is more likely to have been as a bold demonstration of the Orkney Norse claim to Ross south of the Oykel than as the discovery of a new source of fuel.

Torf-Einar's successor was his son Thorfinn, who is distinguished from his great-grandson, the second jarl of that name, by his cognomen *hausakljúfr* meaning 'skull-cleaver'. Thorfinn's only real importance here, however, lies in the background of his wife Grelaug who is identified in both *Heimskringla* and *Laxdaela Saga* as a grand-daughter of Thorstein the Red. Thorstein is said by *Laxdaela Saga* to have made peace with the Scots after establishing himself in Caithness and eastern Sutherland, but the Scots apparently broke faith with that truce when they slew Thorstein, probably some time in the later 880s. After his death, his mother Aud had a ship built secretly in Caithness and sailed with her family and others to Orkney where she gave Thorstein's daughter Groa in marriage to a Scots noble who is identified in *Heimskringla* as

---

16 Translated, edited and analysed by K. H. Jackson in his *The Gaelic Notes in the Book of Deer*, 1972.

*Dungadr*, who was assuredly a man of some prominence if, as seems likely, he was the 'Duncan' commemorated in the name of Duncansby Head at the far north-eastern point of Caithness.

The implications of all this for the Cenél Loairn are considerable because they would propose Dungadr as a Gaelic Scot in some measure of lordship as far north as Caithness by the last decade of the ninth century, and his daughter Grelaug having been of sufficiently noble standing to become the wife of a jarl of Orkney in the first half of the century following. Of further importance here, though, is the name *Dungadr* itself which is recognisable as the Norse form of the Gaelic *Donnchad* (anglicised as Duncan), a name occurring again in the last quarter of the tenth century and in the direct line of descent from Ainbcellach – which could be reasonably taken to indicate the earlier 'Dungadr of Caithness' having been of that same branch of the Cenél Loairn.

Thorfinn Skull-cleaver became jarl of Orkney during the later years of the reign of Malcolm I, the son of Donald II and – most importantly here – the first of the MacAlpin kings to be reliably recorded on an aggressive campaign north of the Mounth. Malcolm's entry in the *Chronicle of the Kings* records his reign of eleven years (943–54) and goes on to state that 'Malcolm went with his army into Moray, and slew Cellach', who was presumably ruler of the province and thus effectively the Cenél Loairn king in the north at that date. The next line of the *Chronicle* entry makes specific reference to the seventh year of Malcolm's reign, and so the raid on Moray can be assigned to a date prior to 949 and may even have been one of his first acts on becoming king. David Kirby has proposed Malcolm's motive as having been vengeance for the death of his father Donald in 900, which is located at Forres by the later king-lists,[17] but that location is placed in doubt by the earlier evidence of the *Prophecy of Berchán* when it tells of the Gaels having turned against 'the rough one' (as it calls Donald II) secretly 'on the path above Dunottar. He is on the brow of the mighty wave, in the east, in his broad gory bed.'

Dunottar is thought to have been the principal stronghold of Donald's

17    Kirby, 'Moray – prior to *c.*1100', p.21.

family and is said by the *Chronicle of the Kings* to have been 'destroyed by the gentiles' (presumably in the course of Sigurd and Thorstein's raiding) towards the end of Donald's reign. If that might have been taken to imply Donald having been slain by vikings, the specific reference to Gaels in the *Prophecy of Berchán* would clearly suggest otherwise and there is no doubt that the location of Dunottar would have offered it as potentially vulnerable to raiding from Buchan and the Moray coastland, thus retaining a measure of credibility for the suggestion that Malcolm's father had been slain by the Cenél Loairn. This *Prophecy of Berchán* represents a valuable source of independently informed and comparatively contemporary evidence for kings of the Scots, especially those of the tenth and eleventh centuries, which will be referred to again and so might bear a note of introduction here.

It should first be explained that the *Prophecy of Berchán* cannot be read as a 'prophecy' in the literal sense of the term, because the format of history presented as prophecy had been current in the Irish literary tradition since at least as early as the time of Adomnán in the later seventh century. Neither can the entire text be attributed to a 'Berchán' when only its opening section, comprising an account of the first Scandinavian impact on Ireland, is thought to represent the work of the ninth-century churchman Berchán of Clonsast. He is still of particular interest here, however, because the genealogy of 'Berchán, prophet and bishop and poet' in the *Book of Leinster* makes him a great-grandson of Ainbcellach of the Cenél Loairn.[18]

The greater part of the 'prophecy' attributed to Berchán is, in fact, a history in Gaelic verse of Irish and Scottish kings (only one of them properly identified by name) from the ninth to the eleventh centuries, of which the author has been identified by Benjamin Hudson as the *Dubthach Albanach* ('Duthac the Scotsman') who is called 'chief confessor of Ireland and of Scotland' by his obituary entered in the *Annals of Ulster* at 1065.[19] Thought to have been of a noble Scottish family, Duthac studied in Ireland and later returned to his homeland where he was consecrated as 'chief bishop of Scotland'. Associated with

---

18    Anderson, *ESSH*, vol. i, p.xxxvi.
19    Hudson, *The Prophecy of Berchán*, p.121; see also Anderson, *ESSH*, vol. ii, p.10.

the church of Dornoch by the *Breviary of Aberdeen*, he was buried at Tain where he is still revered as the local patron saint, so it would be reasonable to assume that his acquaintance with the Highlands would have made him familiar with the topography and traditions of Dunottar. Thus, if Duthac of Tain was indeed the eleventh-century 'continuator' of the *Prophecy of Berchán*, its evidence for the location of Donald's death would be rendered all the more trustworthy.

As to the victim of Malcolm's supposed vengeance, there is no record of a Cellach in the Moray genealogies, presumably because his branch of the Cenél Loairn had no connection to the lines of descent which bore Macbeth and Lulach. But if – in accordance with Gaelic custom – the name occurred again in succeeding generations of the same family, there may be a link between the Cellach slain by Malcolm and two of the 'three mormaers of Scotland' named as Cellach, son of Findghan, and Cellach, son of Bairedh, in an entry in the *Annals of Tigernach* at 976 bearing upon warfare in Offaly. It would not be at all unusual to find the same name given to cousins and so these two Cellachs might well have been nephews of the Cellach slain in Moray some thirty years earlier. Why they should have been in Ireland is unexplained, but of greater interest here is the identity of the third mormaer – Donnchad, son of Morgand – and not only because the name Donnchad echoes that of Jarl Thorfinn's father-in-law, but because the name of this Donnchad's father links him firmly to the kingly branch of the Cenél Loairn.

The 'Morgand' of the annal entry was assuredly the same *Morgán* whose name is entered in the Rawlinson pedigrees of Macbeth and Lulach, and stands also at the head of the second Cenél Loairn gene-alogy appended to the *Senchus*.[20] All of which can be taken as impressive evidence for Morgán's stature, not only as the ancestor of future kings but in his own right and in his own time of the mid-tenth century. Two more of his sons are found among the donors of land recorded in the *Book of Deer*, the first of them a Muiredach who is styled as mormaer and as toísech, while the other, a Cathal, is given no form of title, yet both can be safely assigned to the later tenth or very early eleventh centuries. Although Morgán himself is nowhere noticed in the

---

20　　See Genealogies 2 and 4, pp.175, 177 below.

annal record, a memorial of his importance has been found in a fragment of place-name evidence because Longmorn, near Elgin in Moray,
is thought to derive from *Laundemorgan* meaning 'Morgán's clearing'.[21]

It is quite possible then that Morgán may have succeeded the Cellach
slain by Malcolm as king of the Cenél Loairn, but if he did so then he
still cannot be justly accused of having avenged his predecessor's death,
despite the claim made by later annotated king-lists, and by Fordun's
*Chronicle*, for Malcolm having been killed by 'the men of Moray'. The
earlier and more reliable *Chronicle of the Kings* quite specifically states
that 'the men of the Mearns slew Malcolm in Fetteresso', which lay
fairly close by his stronghold of Dunottar and would correspond to
the lines bearing on Malcolm's death in the *Prophecy of Berchán* when
they refer to 'an expedition upon the brow of Dunottar; the Gael will
shout about his grave'. The claim made in the later sources for Malcolm
having been slain by the 'men of Moray' might perhaps be better understood as a reflection of the new era of hostility between rival dynasties
north and south of the Mounth which had been ushered in by his strike
into Moray and was to continue through the two succeeding centuries.

This effectively 'bipartite' kingship of Scots which was to continue
into the first half of the eleventh century has led to problems with the
interpretation of references to 'kings of Scots' in the sagas, the first of them
found in the context of conflict between sons of Thorfinn Skull-cleaver
in the early 980s. Much of this contention is blamed by *Orkneyinga Saga*
on Ragnhild, a daughter of the famous Erik Blood-axe and wife to no
fewer than three of Thorfinn's five sons, but her murderous intriguing
was of rather greater interest to the saga-maker than of any real bearing
here. Suffice it to say that Ragnhild had already disposed of her first two
husbands and was married to their brother Ljot whose succession to the
jarldom was resented by a fourth brother named Skuli.

Skuli is said by the saga to have crossed over to Scotland where he
was given the title of 'jarl' by an (unnamed) 'king of Scots'. Having
raised a warband in Caithness, he returned to Orkney where he refused
to negotiate with his brother and instead insisted on a battle in which
he suffered defeat. Subsequently, Skuli fled back across the Pentland

---

21    Barrow, 'Macbeth and other mormaers of Moray', p.112.

Firth, 'first over to Caithness and then south to Scotland'. Ljot followed in pursuit and raised his own forces in Caithness where Skuli came to meet him 'with a large following provided by the king of Scots and Jarl *Magbjóðr*' (apparently an earlier 'Macbeth'). Which immediately – and not least by reason of the name given to the Scots 'jarl' – raises the question of which 'king of Scots' was intended by the saga-maker.

These events can be dated to *c.*984–5, and so they would have fallen within the reign of Kenneth II, the son of Malcolm I who certainly strove to exclude the rival branch of the MacAlpin line from the kingship and has been seen as the instigator of the move towards a 'high-kingship' of Scots. Yet the saga claims only that Skuli was 'given the title of jarl by the king of Scots', which need have been nothing more than a gesture of courtesy on Kenneth's part because the jarldom of Orkney was not to lie within the gift of any Scottish king for another five hundred years. It is not impossible that Kenneth may have had his own ambitions for kingship north of the Mounth, but if he did then they passed quite unnoticed by all the early sources. Kenneth might, nonetheless, have allowed Skuli a warband as an escort, and this might have formed a part of the force supplied to him by 'Jarl Macbeth'.

Beyond that speculation lies the alternative possibility that the 'king of Scots' who gave the title to Skuli was a Cenél Loairn-descended king in Moray who was seeking to support his own sympathetic and grateful contender for the Orkney jarldom. The Moray genealogies would indicate the king (or mormaer) having been either Ruadrí or his father Domnall in the mid-980s, which raises the question of the status of 'Jarl Macbeth', whose title given by the saga might simply be taken to indicate a noble, although assuredly a member of the ruling kindred, were it not for the subsequent narrative which distinctly portrays him in the role of a mormaer of Moray.

The saga goes on to tell of the Orkney brothers in battle once again, this time in the Dales of Caithness where Ljot won the decisive victory which left Skuli dead on the field. The location of these 'Dales' (*Dalir*) is of bearing here because, as Barbara Crawford has pointed out, 'later evidence suggests that the Dales of Caithness and Sutherland were considered to be separate areas from Caithness proper. Indeed the name Caithness [deriving from the *nes*, or 'headland', of the province of *Cat*] may initially have been applied only to Duncansby Head, becoming more extensive as the Scandinavian settlement grew.'[22] That Norse perception of a 'bipartite Caithness' may well be rooted in the older Pictish division of provinces into two parts which is thought to be reflected in the evidence of *De Situ Albanie* for the 'seventh *regione* [or 'province'] of Scotland' being 'Caithness, to this side of the mountain, and beyond the mountain, because the mountain of Mound divides Caithness through the middle'. In this case 'the Mound', although similarly derived from the Gaelic *monadh*, cannot mean the Grampian range and so almost certainly refers to the mountains flanking the river Helmsdale, which would indeed appear to 'divide Caithness through the middle'.

That sketch of the political geography would perhaps explain why the saga tells of Ljot having exploited the defeat of Skuli and his allies to extend his own control over Caithness and this having led to 'trouble with the Scots . . . [when] Jarl Macbeth came north with a great army and met with Jarl Ljot at *Skíðamýrr* in Caithness. Ljot was outnumbered but fought so well that all the Scots left alive took flight.' The Norse had also taken casualties 'and Ljot himself had suffered a wound which led to his death' soon after his return to Orkney. The location of this blood-fray at *Skíthmór* – identified as the moor beside Skitten farm a few miles north-west of Wick – is of significant bearing because it would appear to have been the customary cockpit of contention between the Orkney Norse and Scots of Moray, as it was to be again some fifteen years later.

On that later occasion, the jarl at the head of the Orkney forces was the Sigurd, son of Hlödvir and grandson of Thorfinn Skull-cleaver, who is widely remembered in saga tradition, and not least by reason of the magical raven banner which was promised to always bring him victory in battle whilst bringing death to the man who carried it for him on the field. So it was to do on the day when Sigurd brought to Ireland the great host of northmen he had mustered, from as far afield as Iceland and as near to hand as Man and the Hebrides, in support of the Norse king of Dublin allied to the king of Leinster against Brian Boru, the powerful and ambitious king of Munster, in the battle of Clontarf

---

22  Crawford, *Scandinavian Scotland*, p.65.

fought on Good Friday in the year 1014. The blood-fray at Clontarf was
to be Sigurd's last battle because, when the man he ordered to take up
his standard refused the command after three bearers had already been
slain, Sigurd himself tore the raven banner from its pole and thrust it
into his own clothing. Very shortly afterwards, of course, he was struck
by a spear and fell dead on the field while the shield-wall formed by his
warriors crumbled into flight from the fray.

The precise date of Sigurd's death is reliably recorded by the entry of
the battle of Clontarf in the closely contemporary *Annals of Innisfallen*,
but *Orkneyinga Saga* can offer only the most approximate indication of when he was first given the raven banner by its placing of the
story just before the conversion of Orkney to Christianity in 995. By
which date and although portrayed in the saga as a relatively young
man, Sigurd was nonetheless already jarl of Orkney and 'ruling over
several dominions . . . powerful enough to defend Caithness against the
Scots and to go on viking expeditions each summer, raiding through
the Hebrides, Scotland and Ireland'. On this occasion, however, he had
been challenged by a Scottish *jarl* named *Finnleik* to fight on a given
day at Skitten and, fearing he would be facing odds of at least seven to
one, he sought the counsel of his Irish mother, who is said by the saga
to have been a sorceress. After making mock of a son so timid that she
ought to have raised him in her wool-basket, he was presented with the
raven banner into which she had woven her craft of sorcery.

If the greater importance of the story to a medieval Orcadian audience
lay in its reference to Sigurd having had to give back their land-rights
to the Orkney farmers before they would follow him to the battle, the
connection to the raven banner, which is elsewhere particularly associated with Clontarf, would nonetheless imply a vivid memory of the
battle itself in local tradition. Nora Chadwick's study of the skaldic
verses called *Darraðarljóð* ('The Lay of Dorrud') – which are preserved
only in *Njal's Saga* where they are specifically associated with Clontarf
– suggested to her that 'the poem had been transferred to its present
position in the saga from its original context in connection with the
battle of Skíthmór. Its localisation in Caithness would speak strongly in
favour of this . . . The references to the "young king" contained in the
poem still remain obscure, but the reference to the "standard" would

be highly appropriate to the Raven Banner which is in the process of being woven, especially in view of the words which follow immediately and which clearly refer to the owner: "We shall not suffer him to lose his life" – words which could not be appropriate to the battle of Clontarf in which he was killed.' She goes on to suggest that the prophecy contained in the lines 'lands will be ruled by new people who once inhabited outlying headlands' would be 'very appropriate to the Orkney *jarls*, the successors of Thorfinn, Sigurd's grandfather'.[23]

If she is correct, then the exceptionally sanguinary character of the poem – and not least its image of the entrails of slain warriors being woven on a loom – bears its own gruesome testimony to Sigurd's battle on Skitten moor having been vividly remembered in Caithness tradition on account of its ferocity and slaughter. *Orkneyinga Saga*, however, has no more to say of the battle itself than that it was Sigurd who won the victory while three standard-bearers were slain, and nothing at all to say of the fate of his opponent. The *Finnleik* of the saga is, of course, the Findláech, Ruadri's son, who is recognised as 'king of Scotland' by his obituary entered in the annals which further confirms that, although defeated at Skitten, he not only survived the battle but outlived Sigurd by a full six years. By way of postscript to the annal notices of Findláech's obituary, Benjamin Hudson points out that the *Annals of Tigernach*, which are 'not entirely reliable for the early eleventh century', are quite alone in styling him 'mormaer of Moray' when the annals in the *Book of Leinster* and the *Annals of Loch Cé* both follow the *Annals of Ulster* in recognising him as a king.[24]

While the entry of Findláech's obituary at the year 1020 represents the first appearance of an identifiable member of the kingly line of the Cenél Loairn in the annals for almost three hundred years, the circumstances of his death at the hands of the sons of his brother Máelbrigte supply clear testimony for the kindred having been again entangled in its own civil war out of which one of those sons of Máelbrigte was to emerge in the ascendant. Malcolm (or *Máel coluim*, a name originally meaning 'follower of Columba') apparently claimed kingship in the

---

23    Chadwick, 'The Story of Macbeth', *SGS*, vol. 7, p.22.
24    Hudson, *Kings of Celtic Scotland*, p.134.

north after the murder of his uncle and ruled until he died a seemingly natural death in 1029, the year at which his obituary in the *Annals of Tigernach* recognises him as *rí Alban*. Purely by accident, of course, his nine-year rule in the north coincided quite precisely with the middle decade of the reign of another 'Malcolm, king of Scots', the son of Kenneth II who had won kingship in the south when he slew his cousin and predecessor Kenneth III at Monzievaird on the banks of the Earn to the west of Crieff in 1005.

This Malcolm, the second king of Scots to bear that name, represents a figure of signal importance in Scotland's history and is generously recorded across all the early sources, not least by the *Annals of Tigernach* where he is recognised as 'the glory of all the west of Europe' in his obituary entered at 1034. The Malcolm of Moray, on the other hand, is noticed in his own right by the annalists on just one occasion, that being the entry of his obituary at the year 1029. Both of these Malcolms are clearly identified – and helpfully distinguished from each other by use of patronymics – in the notes to the *Book of Deer* where the grant of *Elerc* (now Elrick in the parish of Old Deer) from *Mal-Coluim mac Mal-Brigte* is entered immediately after the gift of a 'king's dues' in Biffie (just south-west of the monastery) and other estates by *Mal-Coluim mac Cinaed* (who is clearly Malcolm II).

Unlike the careful naming of Gaelic names by the monastic scribe who entered those notes, the references made in *Orkneyinga Saga* to a *Melkolm skota-konung* ('Malcolm, king of Scots') in association with the jarls Sigurd the Stout and his son Thorfinn (who is usually distinguished from his skull-cleaving predecessor as 'Thorfinn the Mighty') have left opinion starkly divided as to which of the two Malcolms was the one intended. The saga states quite plainly that 'Jarl Sigurd married the daughter of Malcolm, king of Scots, and their son was Jarl Thorfinn', then goes on to say that 'Thorfinn was only five years old when his father was killed and living with his grandfather, King Malcolm of Scotland . . . [who] gave Thorfinn Caithness and Sutherland [and] granted him the title of *jarl*'.

The same claim, which is reiterated at a later point in the saga, led Benjamin Hudson to conclude that 'the correct identification of Thorfinn's grandfather is Malcolm mac Máelbrigte of the Cenél Loairn [because] not until the reign of David I would the line of Malcolm II have any claims on the lands of Caithness and Sutherland'. He goes on to propose that an alliance between Sigurd and Malcolm mac Máelbrigte (presumably one sealed by the marriage) was an effort by both sides to remove an area of conflict which was draining their resources.[25] His view is sturdily argued and should perhaps command a sympathetic endorsement here, as indeed it would have done were it not for the chronological problems weighing against unqualified acceptance of what would otherwise have been a most convincing case.

Whilst acknowledging that chronology is not usually thought to be the greatest strength of the sagas as an historical record, the dates indicated by *Orkneyinga Saga* in its account of Thorfinn are scarcely ever contradicted, and indeed often corroborated, by other sources considered more reliable. The death of Sigurd at Clontarf, for example, is securely assigned to Good Friday in 1014 and as there is no reason to doubt the saga's claim for his son Thorfinn having been five years old at that time, he must have been born within a year of the Eastertide of 1009. Thus his father's marriage to the 'daughter of Malcolm, king of Scots' must have been consummated by the midsummer of 1008, when Malcolm II had already held his kingship for three years, and yet another twelve years were to pass before the murder of his uncle Findláech allowed the other Malcolm to claim kingship in Moray.

Of no lesser bearing is the date assigned to the division of the Orkney jarldom agreed between the young Thorfinn and his brother Brusi, because the saga states that 'this happened at the time when Cnut ruled Norway and Olaf [Haraldsson, formerly king and later patron saint of Norway] was a fugitive abroad'. The saga-maker's dating at this point can be considered all the more trustworthy because Rognvald Brusason, Thorfinn's nephew with whom he was later to share the jarldom, had been with Olaf in Norway and accompanied him on his flight (as 'a fugitive abroad') to Russia in 1028/9, before returning with him to Norway in the spring of 1030 to fight at Stiklestad where Olaf was slain on the last day of August in that same year.

Having survived the battle and rescued Olaf's young half-brother Harald (later famed as 'Hardrada') from the field, Rognvald returned first

---

25    Hudson, *Kings of Celtic Scotland*, pp.135–6.

to Russia before coming home in *c*.1037 to Orkney where his adventures would have been assuredly well-remembered in the oral tradition which later informed *Orkneyinga Saga*. All of which renders the evidence of the saga the more valuable here when it states that Thorfinn's grandfather 'the king of Scots died some time after the reconciliation of Thorfinn with his brother Brusi' which its narrative has already effectively dated to 1029–30. Thus Malcolm, son of Máelbrigte, whose obituary is entered at 1029, must have died while 'Olaf was a fugitive abroad', while the king of Scots who died 'some time' after that date is more likely to have been Malcolm II, who lived on for six more years until his death in the year 1034. 'Some time' is, of course, only a very dubious chronological approximation, but if the dates suggested by *Orkneyinga Saga* can be accepted, then its evidence must suggest Malcolm II having been the more probable 'king of Scots' said to have been Jarl Thorfinn Sigurdsson's grandfather. While it is not unlikely that the five-year-old Thorfinn would have been placed in the safety of his grandfather's court while his father went to war in 1014, the jarldom of Orkney certainly did not lie within the gift of a king of Scots, and the 'title of jarl' granted by Malcolm to his grandson would have been some nominal equivalent to that of a Norse *jarl* which was simply intended to assure Thorfinn of the Scottish king's recognition of his future lordship over Caithness and Sutherland.

If, as Alexander Grant has suggested, the political purpose underlying the marriage of Malcolm's daughter to Sigurd of Orkney was the extension of his kingship of Alba beyond the Grampians by the creation of 'an alliance which pressurised Moray from both north and south',[26] it can be similarly interpreted as a stratagem intended to ensure the supremacy of the Cenél nGabráin-descended MacAlpin kings over the Cenél Loairn-descended house of Moray. There is every reason to believe that Malcolm did achieve such a supremacy, even though the evidence supplied by the earlier sources for his having done so depends almost entirely on fragments. For their own part, the later king-lists and chronicles seem to assume that the ascendancy he sought to secure for his own line of MacAlpin descent was a culmination of the natural

---

26   Grant, 'The Province of Ross and the Kingdom of Alba', p.101.

order of things and – certainly by the later twelfth century – any challenge raised by, or on behalf of, a rival dynasty was to be condemned as 'wicked rebellion against a natural lord'.[27]

There may, however, be hints of Malcolm's ambitions on Moray to be found in the ecclesiastical orbit, wherein the Cenél nGabráin had found legitimating support ever since Columba had inaugurated Aedán into the kingship of Dalriada on Iona in 574. One such may be the plain and simple acknowledgment of Malcolm II's generosity preserved in the notes in the *Book of Deer*, while another might be discerned from Fordun's claim that Malcolm 'in the seventh year of his reign [1011–12], established a new episcopal see at Mortlach [now a part of Dufftown]'. Whether or not this had really been the gesture of gratitude for his earlier defeat of 'a great army of Norwegian invaders' somewhere in the same locality that Fordun says it was, there is probably rather greater value in his following reference to Malcolm's 'desire to extend the territory of the diocese from the stream or river called the Dee to the river Spey' because that would imply the bishopric as a statement of his own sovereignty extending into the very heart of Moray.

The most impressive fragment of evidence from the earlier sources might be recognised in the entry of his reign in the *Duan Albanach* as 'thirty years verses proclaim Malcolm as king of the Mounth'. The reference to the Mounth must surely allude to the age-old significance of the Grampian range as the boundary between kings and kingdoms to its north and south, and can thus be taken to claim Malcolm having achieved overlordship of the house of Moray. The means by which he attained that pinnacle of his sovereignty might just possibly be the subject of cryptic lines from the *Prophecy of Berchán* (which calls him *Forránach* or 'the Aggressor') which tell of 'the day he goes to battle with the kin-slayers, to a swift morning leap at the Mounth'. Once again, and as in the *Duan*, the poet's use of the Gaelic *Monadh* could be taken to refer to some venture into Moray, which in turn would infer the 'kin-slayers' having been the sons of Máelbrigte who are said by the annals to have slain their uncle Findláech in 1020.

---

27 As the *Chronicle of Melrose* described Somerled of Argyll's 1164 rebellion against Malcolm IV.

Perhaps then there may be more evidence for Malcolm's achievement of overlordship north of the Mounth than is immediately apparent in the notice of the burning of Gillacomgain 'along with fifty of his men' entered in the *Annals of Ulster* at the year 1032. As the brother of that other Malcolm, the son of Máelbrigte whose supposedly peaceful death is entered in the annal record at a date just three years earlier, Gillacomgain might be thought to have been the presumptive successor to the same title and lordship. Yet while Malcolm is styled 'king' by his obituary in the *Annals of Tigernach* at 1029, his brother is acknowledged only as 'mormaer' by the *Annals of Ulster*, a source considered quite specific in its use of titles and thus worthy of trust when it reflects the diminished status which would have been the inevitable consequence of submission to a high-king of Scots.

While there is nowhere any suggestion by the annalists of Malcolm II having had a part in the burning of Gillacomgain, even though the last of Máelbrigte's sons would certainly qualify as one of the 'kin-slayers' referred to by the *Prophecy of Berchán*, the king it knows as 'the Aggressor' could have had his own personal reason for vengeful satisfaction at that infliction of a fiery death. The same reason would also have significant bearing on his achievement of overlordship of Moray if – as later references have led more than one eminent modern historian to suggest – 'peace in the north was bought for the price of a marriage' between Findláech, son of Ruadrí, and a kinswoman – either a sister or a daughter born out of wedlock – of Malcolm II.[28]

All of which will bear further consideration in the following chapter, because it was the son of that marriage who was to slay Malcolm's chosen successor and seize the high-kingship of Scots – not least by right of his claim to direct descent from Ainbcellach – thereby achieving the last and highest peak of ascendancy for the Cenél Loairn.

---

28    Cowan, 'The Historical MacBeth', p.121; see also Anderson, *ESSH*, vol. i, pp.579–80 and Hudson, *Kings of Celtic Scotland*, p.137.

IV

# HIGH-KINGSHIP IN ALBA

'Malcolm, Kenneth's son, a most victorious king, reigned for thirty years. And he died at Glamis, and was buried on Iona.' Thus the *Chronicle of the Kings* entered the reign and obituary of Malcolm II, the son of Kenneth II and the last king of Scots in direct male line of descent from Kenneth mac Alpin. It was no less than fitting that Malcolm should have been laid in earth on the holy island which is said (at least by the *Chronicle*) to have been the traditional burial place of Scottish kings since the founding dynast of the house of MacAlpin had been laid in its earth in 858.

Whether Malcolm is the more justly acknowledged by the Tigernach annalist as 'the glory of all the west of Europe' or by the Berchán poet as 'the Aggressor', his achievement of high-kingship of Scots can scarcely be denied. The decisive victory over a Northumbrian host at Carham in 1018 had established the river Tweed as his southern frontier and the dominion of the north Britons centred around Strathclyde was effectively reduced to a province of the kingdom of the Scots. By the time the apparent submission of Moray had extended his sovereignty north of the Grampians, the reign of Malcolm II had come to represent the very pinnacle of MacAlpin ascendancy.

The great concern of his later years, however, would appear to have lain in securing that high-kingship for his own branch of MacAlpin descent, and especially because Malcolm II had no son to succeed him. Indeed, the very last recorded act of his reign as it is entered in the *Annals of Ulster* at 1033 tells of his killing 'the son of the son of Boite, son of Kenneth'. This 'Boite' – a Latinised form of the Gaelic *Bodhe* – is usually identified as the son of Kenneth III, son of the Dubh who had been the brother of Malcolm's own father Kenneth II. If so, then Boite's grandson would have been of the *derbfine* (the immediate kin-group

99

of a formerly reigning king) and yet, when he represented the fourth generation of that descent, would have been the very last of that family to retain a claim on the succession. The elimination of that last claimant from the rival branch of the MacAlpin dynasty would thus have secured the succession for Malcolm's grandson Duncan (*Donnchad*), the son of his daughter Bethoc who had been given in marriage to Crinán, hereditary lay abbot of the royal church of the house of MacAlpin at Dunkeld and evidently holder of a powerful political office comparable to that of a royal steward or chamberlain.

A reference to Duncan as 'king of the Cumbrians' in two English chronicles of the twelfth century indicates his having been given lordship over the dominion formerly held by the Britonic kings of Strathclyde, the last of whom had been killed at Carham in 1018 whilst fighting in the battle as Malcolm's allied client king. Duncan's appointment to the kingship of Cumbria/Strathclyde is taken to signify his recognition as the *tanaise* ('expected one'), the chosen successor to his grandfather as high-king of Scots. Such indeed he was to become, because it was Duncan, son of Crinán, who did claim the succession after the death of Malcolm in the last week of November 1034 and went on to reign for almost six years. Little is known of the greater part of his reign, all of which was to pass entirely unnoticed in the Irish annals until their entry of his obituary at the year 1040. There were, however, events occurring in the year or two before that date which were of particularly local interest to the Northumbrian sources, and fortunately so because they are of substantial bearing here.

The most dramatic of these events was Duncan's only recorded military venture, which is most fully described in the *History of the Church of Durham* set down within seventy years of the event by Symeon of Durham. A wider-ranging chronicle – of Durham origin but only 'attributed' to Symeon – mentions an attack on Cumbria by Eadulf, a son of Earl Uhtred, who succeeded his brother as ealdorman of Bamburgh in c.1038, and it may have been this raid, probably made shortly after Eadulf came to power, which provoked Duncan to retaliate by laying siege to Durham in 1039, or possibly early in 1040. Duncan may even have been seeking to improve on his grandfather's unsuccessful siege of the same cathedral city some thirty-three years before, but if so he not only failed in that attempt but incurred utterly disastrous consequences as a result.

Symeon's account of the siege tells how it was abandoned after Duncan had lost the greater part of his cavalry to the defending forces. Taking flight in confusion, all his foot-soldiery were slain and their heads carried to the market place in Durham where they were impaled on stakes. 'And not long afterwards, when he had returned to Scotland, the king himself perished, slain by his own people.' That last sentence is, of course, confirmed by the Irish annal record, and most grandly by the entry in the *Annals of Tigernach* at the year 1040: 'Duncan, Crinán's son, high-king of Scotland (*airdrí Alban*) was slain by his own subjects.'

A more detailed and still more closely contemporary record of the death of Duncan was set down in Germany by an Irish monk who signed himself 'Máelbrigte the Recluse' but who is formally remembered as the meticulous chronicler Marianus Scotus. In the later years of his exile Marianus was in Mainz, and there he had the assistance of an Irish scribe who had recently arrived from Scotland in 1072 and would have been the likely source for the detail of the chronicle entry placed in the year 1040: 'Duncan, the king of Scotland, was killed in autumn, by his *dux Macbethad*, Findláech's son, who succeeded to the kingship for seventeen years.' Nowhere else in the sources is Macbeth assigned the Latin style of *dux* which, as Edward Cowan suggests, 'is probably best translated as "war-leader", an apt description of one of the functions of the mormaer'. It should be said, though, that despite any military implication of the title *dux* there is neither evidence nor likelihood of Macbeth having any part in Duncan's attack on Durham, which was more probably made, as Cowan suspects, 'in alliance with his Cumbrians'.[1]

That same scribe from Scotland would also have been a likely source of a marginal note in one manuscript of Marianus' chronicle which enters the precise date of Duncan's death as 'the nineteenth before the kalends of September [14th August in the modern calendar]'. One further detail of the slaying of Duncan by Macbeth – which is generally recognised as a death inflicted in battle – is found in the *Chronicle of the Kings*, which

---

1    Cowan, 'The Historical MacBeth', pp.122–3.

names the location as *Bothngouane* ('the smith's farm'), most convincingly identified as Pitgaveny near Elgin. That identification is further confirmed by Alexander II having endowed a chaplaincy in Elgin cathedral in 1235 to say mass for the soul of his great-great-grandfather King Duncan.

The location of Pitgaveny in the heartland of Moray lends credibility to Fordun's account of Duncan having been slain whilst engaged upon a regal progress through his kingdom for the purpose of dispensing justice – and, assuredly also, of collecting tribute. It was not at all unusual in Gaelic society, and especially in Ireland, for an overlord to be confronted with a refusal of such dues unless he could demonstrate his preparedness to collect by force. Had such a challenge been presented to Duncan by the men of Moray in 1040, it would have represented more than a mere formality when it followed so closely after the disastrous military performance at the siege of Durham. The inevitable damage which had been inflicted there upon his reputation and authority would have left Duncan dangerously vulnerable to a serious challenge – and so much so that the arrival of his royal progress in Moray in the August of 1040 effectively brought the high-kingship of Scots to within a sword-stroke of seizure by a formidable claimant from a rival kingly line.

Benjamin Hudson has pointed out that the identity of the successor to the kingship of Moray following the death of Malcolm mac Máelbrigte in 1029 'is not immediately obvious', and that the title of mormaer accorded Malcolm's brother Gillacomgain in the annal entry of his obituary in 1032 might signify nothing more than his having been a noble.[2] Yet Malcolm's predecessor Findláech had been recognised as king by his obituary in the *Annals of Ulster* at 1020, and what is now generally accepted as the first appearance of Findláech's son Macbeth in the historical record similarly recognises him as a Scottish king.

An entry under the year 1031 in the Worcester manuscript of the *Anglo-Saxon Chronicle*, set down in the later eleventh century, tells of the mighty Cnut (who had been king of England since 1016) having returned from pilgrimage to Rome and afterwards made an expedition to Scotland 'and the Scots king submitted to him and became his man,

2    Hudson, *Kings of Celtic Scotland*, p.136.

but kept to that only a short time'. There is an apparent allusion to that same meeting made by the immediately contemporary Icelandic *skald* Sigvat Thordsson, who had been court-poet to the Norwegian king Olaf the Saint. Lines of Sigvat's verse quoted in the version of Olaf's saga included in *Heimskringla* might even be taken to indicate its location in their reference to 'famous foreign lords [who] journey to Cnut – from Fife in the midst of the north'.

The Laud recension of the *Chronicle*, written at Peterborough in the first half of the twelfth century and considered to offer an especially detailed record of Cnut's reign, includes an account of the same visit to Scotland which is of particular value here by reason of its naming those 'famous foreign lords' as '*Maelcolm*, king of the Scots, . . . with two other kings, *Maelbeth* and *Iehmarc*'. While the 'Maelcolm, king of the Scots' in 1031 can only have been Malcolm II, the identities of the kings who accompanied him in that year are rendered less obvious by the chronicler's Old English name-forms, and more than a century of scholarly debate has pursued the true historical identities of these 'two other kings'. It was W. F. Skene who first recognised Macbeth mac Findláech as the chronicler's 'Maelbeth', although Skene was less successful in identifying 'Iehmarc' who has since been most convincingly identified as the Echmarcach Rognvaldsson who twice held the kingship of Dublin, although not until the year 1035.[3]

Echmarcach's father is recognised as 'king of the Isles' by his obituary in the *Annals of Ulster* at 1005, while Echmarcach himself is styled 'king of the Rhinns' by Marianus Scotus' entry of his obituary (presumably noticed by reason of Echmarcach having died whilst on pilgrimage to Rome in 1065). The Rhinns are almost certainly those of Galloway because Echmarcach is known to have held the kingship of Man (with territories scattered along the western seaboard as far north of the Irish Sea as the Isle of Lewis) in 1061 following his second expulsion from Dublin some nine years earlier. All of which led Benjamin Hudson to propose that when he 'was known as a ruler of lands in south-west Scotland to a contemporary familiar with Scottish affairs . . . Echmarcach's connection with south-west Scotland was neither recent nor insignificant'.

---

3   Skene, *Celtic Scotland*, vol. i, p.397; Hudson, 'Cnut and the Scottish Kings', pp.355–6.

Hudson's detailed study of the whole episode goes on to propose the likely political motive of Cnut's seeking some agreement with (if not actually the 'submission' of) the three Scottish kings having been related to the defeat of Olaf's bid to regain kingship of Norway at Stiklestad the year before. 'A king ruling in south-west Scotland, such as Echmarcach, and a king ruling in northern Scotland, such as Macbeth, were on the periphery of Norwegian-controlled lands [in the Western and Northern Isles]. Although Cnut was claiming lordship over the Norse before the death of St Olaf, he did not want Norse resistance to find support or shelter in Britain. So the meeting with the kings may have included a warning from Cnut against aiding his enemies.'[4]

If so, then the involvement of a king of Moray alongside a king of the Isles in such negotiations carries its own implications for the relationship between Norse and Gael along the frontiers of Scandinavian Scotland, but the immediate importance of the *Anglo-Saxon Chronicle* entry at this point bears specifically on Macbeth. His inclusion among the three Scottish kings meeting with Cnut must confirm his holding kingship in the north (although presumably acknowledging Malcolm II as his overlord) by the year 1031, so it would seem that it was he who had succeeded Malcolm mac Máelbrigte in, or fairly soon after, 1029. Macbeth would thus have reigned as king of the Cenél Loairn for some eleven years before he began his seventeen-year reign as high-king of Scots in succession to Duncan. While the *Duan Albanach* and most of the later king-lists confirm his seventeen years in the kingship of Scots, the *Prophecy of Berchán* – which knows Macbeth only as 'the red king' – would seem to have added in that earlier reign in Moray when his last stanza opens with the lines *fiche blíadhan is deich mblíadhna / for Albain airdrí ríaghla* . . . ('twenty years and ten years / the high-king ruling over Alba'). The apparent discrepancy between the reign-lengths indicated by the annal record and the round figure approximations supplied by the Berchán poet need present no great difficulty if due allowance is made for the demands of metre and a measure of poetic licence.

'The red king will take the kingdom,' according to the *Prophecy*, 'after slaughter of Gaels, after slaughter of *Gall* [Scandinavians]', and

---

4   Hudson, 'Cnut and the Scottish Kings', pp.356, 359.

presumably alludes to conflict preceding Macbeth's accession to the high-kingship. 'Slaughter of Gaels' might refer to the fatalities among Duncan's warriors on their flight from the siege of Durham (unless the majority of his force had been made up of Cumbrian Britons, of course), but might otherwise be read as a reference to contention surrounding the death of Duncan at Pitgaveny in 1040 which would assuredly have involved Gaels on both sides. There is, of course, no evidence of any *Gall* having been involved in either of those actions (unless the term might apply to Anglo-Danish defenders of Durham), and so the greater likelihood would be of both those Berchán references to slaughter alluding to another quite different campaign, and most probably to one fought against the Norse of Orkney, even though no such warfare is noticed elsewhere in the Scottish records or in the Irish annals. The only other sources likely to preserve a record of such warfare are the sagas, and most especially *Orkneyinga Saga*, even though it makes no reference, at least by name, to any Duncan or Macbeth as a king of Scots in these decades of the eleventh century.

There is, however, a lengthy chapter in *Orkneyinga Saga* telling of an extensive campaign conducted by Jarl Thorfinn, the son born to Jarl Sigurd by a supposed daughter of Malcolm II, but fought against a man whose name occurs nowhere else in the historical record. Malcolm, king of Scots, died some time after the reconciliation of Thorfinn and Brusi, his brother (*c.*1029–30), according to the saga-maker, 'and the next man to take power in Scotland was Karl Hundason, who claimed Caithness as earlier kings of Scots had done and demanded of it such tribute as was paid him elsewhere'. Not at all unexpectedly, Thorfinn insisted on his own claim on Caithness, believing it his rightful inheritance from his grandfather, and refused to pay the tribute demanded. This provoked a mutual hostility which began with each raiding the territory of the other until 'King Karl' appointed his nephew, 'a man called Mutatan or Moddan', as earl in Caithness. This Moddan mustered troops in Sutherland before arriving in his new earldom to find them greatly outnumbered by the forces Thorfinn had raised in Caithness and brought over from Orkney when forewarned of the Scots' approach. Confronted by such odds, Moddan made an immediate withdrawal which was pursued down through Sutherland and Ross by Thorfinn, who went on to plunder 'throughout Scotland' before returning to Caithness where he awaited further developments with 'five well-manned longships' held in readiness at *Dungalsbaer* (Duncansby Head).

Moddan reported back to Karl Hundason at *Beruvík*,[5] and it was from there that the angry Karl launched 'eleven longships' which eventually caught up with Thorfinn whilst he was on voyage back to Orkney. The fleets engaged off the coast of Deerness and after a 'long, hard battle' (vividly described in the saga and illustrated with verses by the Icelandic skald Arnor Thordsson) left the Scots facing defeat, Karl jumped from his own beleaguered ship to another, aboard which he made his escape back to Moray. In the meantime, Moddan had brought a land force up to Caithness and established himself in Thurso where he was surprised by Thorfinn's ally and former foster-father Thorkel Amundsson, who had secretly raised a local warband with which he seized the house in which Moddan was sleeping and set it afire. Moddan himself attempted to jump from an upstairs room in flight from the flames, but only to lose his head to Thorkel's axe-blade.

By this time Karl Hundason was already mustering forces for another contest in the north and ranging widely about Scotland, even as far as Kintyre, where he was joined by warriors earlier summoned from Ireland by Moddan, before advancing up to Ross where he was brought to battle at Tarbat Ness. 'Well the red weapons fed wolves at *Torfnes*,' according to the skald Arnor, 'slim blades sang there, south along *Ekkjalsbakki*' when Thorfinn led his warriors to a victory from which the saga-maker believed Karl Hundason to have once again taken flight. 'Although some say he was killed there.'

Thorfinn is said to have followed up his triumph by cutting a viking swathe 'deep into Scotland, conquering to the south as far as Fife'. In Fife, however, he appears to have met with some resistance which was, of course, swiftly suppressed with viking brutality and 'a great many captives herded like cattle' from burned-out villages where 'not a single cottage was left standing'. The historical authority of all this principally hinges on the immediately contemporary skaldic verses telling of the

---

5    Unconvincingly identified as Berwick-on-Tweed by Pálsson & Edwards, *Orkneyinga Saga*, p.247.

sea-fight off Deerness and the battle at Tarbat Ness, not least by reason of Arnor Thordsson – who is usually styled *jarlaskald* ('the jarls' skald') in the saga – having served Thorfinn (and others) as court-poet. He is even said to have accompanied Thorfinn on viking cruises and so there can be little, if any, doubt as to the historicity of the enigmatic 'King Karl' when he is mentioned by name in the quoted verses from Arnor. While the saga-maker's narrative is framed around Arnor's verses and presumably also draws on Orkney oral tradition, it is of a rather later construction and so can only be taken on the most cautious trust as an accurate account of the true sequence and character of the events it describes.

All of which raises the question long debated by historians as to which historical 'king of Scots' was known to the saga-maker as 'Karl, son of Hundi' and yet is unknown by that name anywhere else in the early sources. If the saga references can be taken to mean him having been the successor to Malcolm II, then 'Karl Hundason' must have been another name for Duncan, son of Crinán – as indeed the estimable W. F. Skene is joined by two recent biographers of Macbeth in believing it to be.[6] The currently prevailing opinion among academic historians, however, veers in a different direction when it proposes the alternative identification of 'Karl Hundason' as Macbeth, who followed Duncan into the high-kingship of Scots in 1040.[7]

In considering this not unimportant question it should first be pointed out that 'Karl, son of Hundi' must not necessarily be interpreted as a pejorative name (in the sense of 'churl, son of a hound'). Karl (or *Kali*) was not uncommon as a given name across the northern world, and certainly not in eleventh-century Norway where the sainted king Olaf named his principal warship 'Karl's Head' in honour of the Holy Roman Emperor Charlemagne. The same is also true of *Hundi*, a name presumably reflecting the nobility of a hunting-hound and, indeed, bestowed by Thorfinn on one of his own sons. It is curious nonetheless to find such a name attached to a Scots king whose Gaelic

---

6  Skene, *Celtic Scotland*, vol. i, pp.400–4; Ellis, *MacBeth*, pp.46–52; Aitchison, *Macbeth*, p.57.
7  Crawford, *Scandinavian Scotland*, pp.71–2; Cowan, 'The Historical MacBeth', pp.125–6.

name is found elsewhere rendered into Norse, in one case as *Dungadr* (Duncan) and in the other as *Magbjóðr* (Macbeth). To which might be added – especially in view of the recurrence of given names in Gaelic families – the occurrence among the notes in the *Book of Deer* of Gaelic names strikingly similar to the Norse *Moddan* and *Karl* in the entry of a *Matain*, son of *Cairell*, whose gift to the monastery of a 'mormaer's dues in Altrie' would seem to have been made in the last quarter of the eleventh century.

Edward Cowan's study of 'Caithness in the Sagas' suggests that the *Matain* in the *Book of Deer* may have been the same name as the *Moddan* of *Orkneyinga Saga*, just as the name of his father *Cairell* 'might recall the Karl of the saga', and goes on to propose that whoever the 'Moddan' of the saga might have been 'he was almost certainly the eponymous of the extremely important Celto-Norse family known as Moddan of the Dale'.[8] The name *Cairell* is also found in the *Chronicle of the Kings* as the patronymic of an otherwise unknown Domnall who died in the early 960s and so it evidently did have some currency in tenth- and eleventh-century Scotland, yet the absence of any record of a 'Cairell' having been 'king of Scots' north or south of the Mounth effectively leaves just two candidates for identification as the 'King Karl' known to the skald and saga-maker.

An attempt to choose between Duncan and Macbeth is perhaps best begun within the chronological framework, because *Orkneyinga Saga* places its Karl Hundason chapter after the reconciliation of Thorfinn with Brusi but before the return of Rognvald Brusason from Norway, which would date the events it describes to some time between *c*.1030 and *c*.1037, and thus into a period which inconveniently aligns with the deaths of two 'kings of Scots', both of them confusingly called Malcolm. It is quite possible, of course, that the original author of *Orkneyinga Saga* – who would have been an Icelander working from Orcadian traditions already a hundred and fifty years old – might have confused the two King Malcolms, and especially if Macbeth did succeed to kingship in Moray following the death of Malcolm mac Máelbrigte in 1029. Some five years after that date, Duncan mac Crináin succeeded his grandfather

8   Cowan, 'Caithness in the Sagas', p.33.

Malcolm II in the high-kingship of Scots, and yet all that is known of his sphere of activity before the very last year of his reign places it in the south of his kingdom and specifically in the direction of Northumbria. It is not at all impossible, then, that Duncan's short reign as a 'king of Scots' might have passed entirely unnoticed in the northerly orbit of the Orkney jarldom, just as it would seem to have done in Ireland where his name is similarly absent from the annal record.

There is a distinct likelihood, then, that Macbeth might have been the only 'king of Scots' of whom Orkney was aware through the later 1030s, and if so it was he who would have been remembered as 'the next man to take power in [certainly the north of] Scotland' following the death of whichever 'King Malcolm' the saga-maker believed to have been his predecessor. To these probabilities must be added the key item of evidence in support of the 'Karl Hundason = Macbeth' hypothesis found in *Njal's Saga*, which was set down in the penultimate decade of the thirteenth century and thus about a hundred years later than the original version of the Orkney saga.[9]

*Njal's Saga* tells of a battle fought by Jarl Sigurd, Thorfinn's father, against two 'Scots jarls' in Caithness and which is placed at a date very closely approximate to that of the battle which *Orkneyinga Saga* centres around its story of Sigurd's raven banner. While there are undeniable points of difference in detail in the two saga stories, sufficient similarity can still be found to suggest that both might be different recollections of the same battle, the one preserved as a family tradition of Njal's kindred (a prominent family in the south of Iceland) and the other retold over some two hundred winters around Orkney peat-fires.

Whereas the blood-fray described in *Orkneyinga Saga* was fought by prior arrangement with *Finnleik* at Skitten, *Njal's Saga* tells of Sigurd bringing a warband (including the Njalssons) across the Pentland Firth in pursuit of vengeance for one of his kinsmen slain by a Scots jarl called *Hundi*. Arriving in Caithness, Sigurd launched an attack on this 'Jarl Hundi' and 'another Scots jarl' called *Melsnati* at Duncansby Head. When Melsnati was slain by his own spear thrown back at him by an ally of the Njalssons, Hundi fled the field with the Orkneymen in

---

9   Apparently first discerned by A. O. Anderson, *ESSH*, vol. i, p.499.

pursuit until they heard that a 'King Malcolm' was gathering an army at Duncansby – at which point Sigurd and his men 'thought it better to turn back than to meet such a large force'.

The different locations identified by the two sagas are thought not to present any great difficulty, because Skitten (or Kilimster on modern maps) is just some ten miles south of Duncansby, which would probably have been a Caithness place-name more familiar than Skitten to an Icelandic family. The reference to 'King Malcolm' presents rather more of a problem if the saga's inferred dating of *c.*995 is to be accepted because there was no Scottish king of that name between the death of Malcolm I in 954 and the accession of his grandson and namesake in 1005, and neither is there any record of a Malcolm in power in Moray before 1020. Oddly enough, *Orkneyinga Saga* mentions no king of Scots by any name other than Malcolm until Duncan II, the son born to Malcolm Canmore by his Orcadian wife Ingibjorg, so the author of *Njal's Saga* might simply and not unreasonably have assumed a Scottish 'King Malcolm' reigning in the late tenth century.

Of most crucial bearing on the Karl Hundason question are the names given by *Njal's Saga* to the 'Scots jarls' in conflict with Sigurd at Duncansby, because *Melsnati* can be safely recognised as a Norse form of *Máelsnechtai*, the same name given to the son of Lulach and presumably one long current in the Moray dynastic kindred, while *Hundi* is a Norse name with no obvious Scottish Gaelic counterpart. Even so, if the battle fought in Caithness by Sigurd in *Njal's Saga* was indeed the same one described in *Orkneyinga Saga* then the man called *Hundi* in the one must be the *Finnleik* of the other, which would clearly infer Hundi's son Karl having been the same man as Findláech's son Macbeth. How and why such a curiously divergent naming of names occurred in the saga evidence has yet to be convincingly explained, even though it has been suggested that the name Macbeth – when translated from its original Middle Irish form of *Mac bethad* – means 'son of life' and 'may be thought to be an ecclesiastical name . . . presumably favoured by the monastic scribes and chroniclers who preserve much of what is known of him'.[10] There is no reason, of course, why Macbeth should not have

---

10    Cowan, 'The Historical MacBeth', p.129.

been known by more than one name, especially across a range of sources in different languages, although it does still seem strange that an apparently identically named (and presumably related) *Magbjóðr* had earlier appeared in the same saga.

Be all that as it may, the greater weight of contextual evidence would point to Macbeth as the more likely candidate for identification as the 'Karl Hundason' who is not only distinctly associated with the orbit of Moray by the saga-maker but also appears to have been possessed of naval forces and capability far superior to those which would have been available to Duncan. A supplementary perspective offered by Benjamin Hudson (who, as already explained, is convinced of Sigurd's wife having been a daughter of the Malcolm of Moray and not of Malcolm II) interprets the Karl Hundason chapter of *Orkneyinga Saga* to suggest 'the Cenél Loairn civil war being continued by Thorfinn Sigurdsson, the grandson of his [Macbeth's] predecessor Malcolm mac Máelbrigte'.[11] Clearly then, the identification of Karl Hundason with Macbeth has been accepted across a wide range of scholarly historical opinion, and might also serve here to cast its own light upon the significant event of the year 1040.

If Macbeth really had suffered those crushing defeats at the hands of Thorfinn which are described with such enthusiasm by both Arnor the Jarls' skald and *Orkneyinga Saga*, it would raise the question of how his kingly prestige in Moray might have fared in consequence – and especially when set beside the apparently comparable damage inflicted on Duncan's standing by his dismal performance at the siege of Durham. It is, of course, not at all unlikely that both skald and saga-maker would have greatly exaggerated Thorfinn's triumphs, and indeed just such might be read into the inclusion of such familiar features as hard-fought battles won against superior numbers and followed up with another grand viking tour of Scotland, all of which could simply have been plucked from the saga-maker's stock-in-trade. Even so, the passage describing Thorfinn's raiding, fighting and slave-taking in Fife is the sole reference in *Orkneyinga Saga* to that very distant (at least from an Orcadian perspective) southerly province of Scotland, and may indeed have its own specific bearing on Macbeth to be considered later.

---

11    Hudson, *Kings of Celtic Scotland*, p.140.

However suspect the aggrandising saga narrative might appear, it is quite unlikely that the skald would have been allowed to celebrate a defeat – or even a drawn game – as a famous victory when proclaiming his verses at Thorfinn's court, so there is genuine reason to believe Karl/Macbeth's forces having been the losing side at sea off Deerness and on land at Tarbat Ness. Following the chronology indicated by the sequence of events in *Orkneyinga Saga*, these battles would have been fought not so very long before Duncan suffered his great reverse at Durham and thus comparatively recent defeats inflicted on the two kings must have formed the political backdrop not only for Duncan's royal progress round his kingdom but also for the challenge which was to confront it in Moray. Whatever the meaning intended by Marianus' styling Macbeth as Duncan's *dux,* it does not amount to evidence for Macbeth having acknowledged Duncan as his overlord in 1040, if indeed he had ever acknowledged him as Malcolm's successor in the high-kingship. In which case, there would have been similar personal political imperatives on both sides at Pitgaveny, when Duncan had come tribute-collecting north of the Mounth as the most impressive way of reasserting his sovereignty after its undoubted setback at Durham and the challenge mounted so decisively by Macbeth would have been intended to restore his own standing in Moray by asserting his claim to the high-kingship of Scots.

It is interesting, nonetheless, to note that there is no reference in any of the sources to associate Macbeth with his ancestral heartland north of the Mounth between the killing of Duncan at Pitgaveny and the last year of his reign when he is said to have made his last stand at Lumphanan in Moray. All that is known of his activities between 1040 and 1057 – and, admittedly, there is little enough of it – finds Macbeth in locations south of the Dee. Indeed, the very earliest reflection of that association with the southern provinces of the Scots rather than his original kingdom in the north might be found in the first stanza bearing upon him in the *Prophecy of Berchán* where 'the red king' is swiftly transformed into 'the generous king of Fortriu'.

There may, however, be a greater significance contained in the fact of the Berchán poet having included Macbeth at all, because every other Scottish king of whom he writes was in some wise connected to the

Cenél nGabráin and so – as Benjamin Hudson points out in his study of the poem – the appearance of 'the red king' in the *Prophecy of Berchán* 'suggests that he had some ties of kinship with the Cenél nGabráin'.[12]

By reason of the secure identification of Macbeth's father in all the early sources, and the evidence of the Moray genealogies for his descent from Ainbcellach of the Cenél Loairn, any 'ties of kinship with the Cenél nGabráin' can only have been inherited from his mother. While more than one later medieval Scottish historian believed Macbeth's mother to have been related to Malcolm II, the oldest, and thus most reliable, evidence on the question is found in the chronicle compiled in 1291 by the canons of Huntingdon on the command of Edward I. The especial, if perhaps unexpected, authority of this source lies in the close links formed between Huntingdon and the Scottish court when David, son and eventual successor (as David I) of Malcolm Canmore, acquired the Honour of Huntingdon by his marriage to an English countess in 1113. On those grounds alone, the reference in the *Chronicle of Huntingdon* to Macbeth as *nepos* (literally 'nephew') of Malcolm II can be taken as impressive evidence for Findláech of Moray having married a sister of the king of Scots. Yet the same chronicle later also refers to Duncan as Malcolm's *nepos*, which raises the possibility that 'grandson' may have been the relationship intended in both cases, which would not only identify Findláech's wife as a daughter of Malcolm II, but also make Macbeth and Duncan first cousins.

John of Fordun, however, had been led to believe ('we read that . . .') Malcolm 'had no offspring but an only daughter named Beatrice [his form of the Gaelic *Bethoc*]', which, if true, would immediately dispute the claim made in *Orkneyinga Saga* for a daughter of that 'Malcolm, king of Scots' having been the wife of one Orkney jarl and the mother of another. The general opinion among modern historians is that Fordun intended 'Beatrice' having been Malcolm's only legitimate offspring, and that perfectly plausible interpretation would allow a daughter born out of wedlock to have been given in marriage to Jarl Sigurd. It would also, of course, conveniently provide for the likelihood of another such daughter having borne Macbeth to Findláech of Moray, although the

---

12   Hudson, *The Prophecy of Berchán*, p.224.

alternative possibility of that lady having been a sister of Malcolm II still cannot be dismissed out of hand.

Whether as nephew or grandson, the evidence for Macbeth's maternal kinship to the high-king of Scots would well correspond to his presence as one of Malcolm's kingly companions in the negotiations with Cnut in 1031. It might also strengthen the suspicion that Macbeth had at least some part – with or without the support of Malcolm II – in the death of Gillacomgain mac Máelbrigte in the following year. Gillacomgain, who is undeniably implicated by the annalists in the death of Macbeth's father, would have represented the most dangerous threat to Macbeth's kingship when he stood at the head of a rival branch of the house of Moray, yet he was also linked by marriage to the rival branch of the house of MacAlpin which Malcolm was evidently determined to eliminate from the succession. Into which can be introduced a further complication of kinship by marriage, and one still more securely confirmed by the historical record, because the Lulach who succeeded Macbeth in the kingship of Scots and was to become the forebear of all subsequent Cenél Loairn-descended claimants to that kingship, is entered in the twelfth-century Moray genealogies as the son of Gillacomgain, son of Máelbrigte.

Yet Lulach's entry in the *Chronicle of the Kings* makes no mention of his father, identifying him instead as the 'nephew of the son of Boite' (*nepos filii Boide*) which is more clearly rendered as 'the son of Boite's daughter'. The only daughter of Boite (or *Bodhe* in its Gaelic form) found in the early sources is the Gruoch whose name is known from the *Register of St Andrews*, which includes a Latin translation of an originally Gaelic record of donations made to the culdee community on St Serf's island in Loch Leven on the western edge of Fife before their monastery was assigned to the authority of the Augustinian canons of St Andrews by David I in 1145. Among those earlier land grants are two endowments of the 'hermits of Loch Leven' with income from *Kyrknes* (Kirkness, just to the south of Loch Leven) made by '*Machbet*, son of *Finlach*, and Gruoch, daughter of Bodhe, king and queen of Scots'. It was that same record, incidentally, which led Edward Cowan to his intriguing suggestion that 'it was perhaps in gratitude for Thorfinn's withdrawal from Fife that MacBeth and Gruoch granted Kirkness to Lochleven'

– to which he immediately adds a note admitting that 'the premise is as dubious as the notion that Thorfinn ever raided Fife'.[13]

These grants to the culdees of Loch Leven are approximately dated to 1037–54,[14] which would correspond to Macbeth having married his cousin's widow Gruoch – and presumably also adopted their son Lulach – within a few years of the death of Gillacomgain in 1032, and thus suggest the political purpose underlying their marriage having been the resolution of an internecine conflict which had been ravaging the house of Moray for a dozen years or more. Given that political dimension, suspicion of Macbeth's involvement in the death of Gillacomgain cannot necessarily be lifted by assuming that a widow would never knowingly wed the man who had killed her husband, because second marriages in just such circumstances were not at all uncommon either in Ireland or Scandinavia in the early medieval period. It should, perhaps, also be mentioned that neither was there anything unusual in the practice of arson as a weapon of warfare in this period, and certainly not in the Scandinavian world where the burning of Njal Thorgeirsson is the central episode of *Njal's Saga* and, rather closer to Moray, *Orkneyinga Saga* tells of numerous similar fire-raisings in Orkney and Caithness in the eleventh and twelfth centuries.

Of more immediate bearing on Macbeth himself are the wider political implications of Gruoch's marital history, because the grandson of Boite who had been killed by Malcolm II in the year before the king's own death would have been her nephew. If Boite was indeed the son of Kenneth III (as he is generally thought to have been) then Gruoch would have been of the branch of the house of MacAlpin which had long been at odds with Malcolm's family and even stands accused by Fordun of direct involvement in his supposed assassination. Whatever the truth of Fordun's allegation – which is nowhere corroborated in the earlier sources – marriage to a daughter of Boite would have implicated Macbeth, if only by association, in an intra-dynastic MacAlpin feud. That cannot have been the full measure of his dowry, of course, if only on the evidence of the endowments jointly granted to the culdees of

13   Cowan, 'The Historical MacBeth', p.127.
14   Reeves, *The Culdees of the British Islands*, pp.125–6.

Loch Leven which almost certainly drew upon Gruoch's own landhold-
ings when they were located in Fife rather than anywhere north of the
Mounth, and thus would have lain within the ancestral territory of her
line of descent from Malcolm I.

This then would have been a marital union of many-sided political significance, because – as Edward Cowan explains – 'by marrying
Gruoch Macbeth merged several claims to the kingship; his own as the
son of Findláech and those of his wife through previous kings'.[15] Indeed,
when seen from that viewpoint, there is good reason to allow Macbeth
a stronger claim on the kingship of Scots than Duncan because, while
Crinán had held a powerful office in Dunkeld, Macbeth's father had
been king of Moray in his own right and by direct descent from a long
line of kings of the Cenél Loairn.

Nonetheless, the evidence for Gruoch having been formerly the wife
of Gillacomgain confirms a precedent for intermarriage between the
Moray and MacAlpin dynasties (respectively, of course, representing the
ancient kingly lines of the Cenél Loairn and Cenél nGabráin) and so
there is little, if any, reason to doubt Findláech's wife having been a
kinswoman of Malcolm II. Indeed, as Benjamin Hudson has suggested,
the most persuasive evidence for Macbeth's maternal descent from the
house of MacAlpin might be found in 'the apparent peace among the
Scots during his reign'.[16]

'Apparent' is, of course, an essential cautionary qualifier when the reliable historical record of Macbeth's reign in the high-kingship is so very
sparse, comprising, as it does, scarcely half-a-dozen events (even when
the very approximately dated donations to Loch Leven are included)
through a period of seventeen years. Although there is one entry in
the annal record which could be read to suggest a residual element of
resistance centred on Dunkeld, there is no doubt whatsoever that when
opposition to Macbeth did eventually emerge, its driving force and
its cutting edge came from south of the Tweed. Interestingly – and in
striking contrast to the policy of the Canmore kings throughout their
ascendancy – there is no convincing evidence for Macbeth having

---

15    Cowan, 'The Historical MacBeth', p.122.
16    Hudson, *Kings of Celtic Scotland*, p.137.

pursued a campaign of attrition against Duncan's family (who are some-times, and not unreasonably, referred to as the 'house of Dunkeld'). Fordun, of course, tells a quite different tale when he claims that after Duncan's death, Macbeth 'went after his sons, Malcolm Canmore, who should have succeeded him, and Donald Bane, seeking, with all his might, to slay them. They, on the other hand, withstanding him as best they could and hoping for victory, remained two years in the kingdom. When they dare struggle no longer, Donald betook himself to the Isles and Malcolm to Cumbria, for it seemed to them that had they stayed, they would more likely have died than lived.'

The truth of the matter was more probably that the core of adherence to Duncan, presumably centred around his father Crinán at Dunkeld, had sheltered his young sons whilst hoping to contrive the overthrow of Macbeth. That hope having failed to materialise within a year or two, it was perhaps considered wiser – or more politic – to remove the boys to safety elsewhere. As the elder of the two, Malcolm would very probably have been sent first to Cumbria – of which, according to Fordun, he had been given tanist lordship in infancy – and yet shortly afterwards found his way into the orbit of Siward, earl of Northumbria. If Fordun was correct in claiming that Duncan's wife, and mother of his sons, was 'the cousin of Earl Siward' – and subsequent events would certainly corroborate his accuracy on that point – it would seem that Crinán had made something of a habit of marrying his sons into the Northumbrian aristocracy.

Symeon of Durham tells of Earl Uhtred (ealdorman of Northumbria, 1007–16) having given his daughter Aldgitha in marriage 'to Maldred, son of Crinán the thane', a style which itself attests Crinán's political status. The marriage of Duncan to a kinswoman of Siward, a Dane of Cnut's following who became earl of Northumbria in c.1033, would have been in line with the same policy – and would also mean that Malcolm, as the elder son of a marriage made sometime after that date, could not have been any older than seven or eight by the time he fled Macbeth's kingdom in 1042. His younger brother 'Donald Bane' (usually called by his Gaelic name-form of *Domnall Bán*) is said to have taken flight to the Isles, which would well correspond to the Gaelic orbit out of which he emerged to follow his brother Malcolm Canmore into the kingship in

1093. If Fordun's dating of events is accepted, Malcolm and Domnall apparently remained unharmed in Scotland through two full years after the death of their father, which must be taken as evidence for Macbeth having not tried so very hard – and certainly not 'with all his might', if indeed he had tried at all – to eliminate all potential rivals to his kingship. The despatch with extreme prejudice of rival claimants, especially ones so young, need have presented no problem to a ruthless high-king, as Malcolm II had demonstrated nine years earlier when he slew the grandson of Boite – and in so doing set an example followed by his successors of the house of Canmore even into the thirteenth century.

The solitary notice in the Irish annal record of the 1040s which could be taken as evidence of contention within Macbeth's kingdom is entered in the *Annals of Tigernach* at the year 1045 as 'a battle between Scots on one road [*ar aenrían*]; and Crinán, abbot of Dunkeld, was slain and a multitude with him, specifically nine score fighting-men'. The corresponding entry in the *Annals of Ulster* uses the phrase *etarru fein* ('among themselves') where the Tigernach annalist uses '*ar aenrían*', which is thought to be a corruption of an older term found elsewhere in the same source and others where it has been read to 'mean "upon a united expedition" or "in a mass-levy"; the implication here being that an army was composed of different elements, which divided into hostile parties'.[17] It would appear then that Crinán – who had evidently been allowed to remain in office for five years after his son was slain – had been at the head of his own warband as part of a hosting and been killed when fighting broke out between elements of the host, most probably a Moray faction affiliated to Macbeth in contention with an Atholl contingent still loyal to the house of Dunkeld.

While the Irish annals offer no detail as to the cause or the context of that incident in 1045, a connection has been suggested with an entry placed under the following year in the *Annals of Durham* which tells how 'Earl Siward came to Scotland with a great army and expelled king Macbeth, and appointed another; but after his departure Macbeth recovered the kingdom'. Compiled in the second half of the twelfth century, these annals would not, at least on first sight, be allowed the

---

17    Anderson, *ESSH*, vol. i, pp.583–4.

authority of a contemporary record. So when a comparison of their entry for the year 1046 with that found under 1054 in the Worcester text of the *Anglo-Saxon Chronicle* reveals close similarity of wording, it would appear that the Durham annalist might have simply misplaced a notice of Siward's invasion of that later year, which did, of course, inflict a serious defeat on Macbeth and install Malcolm Canmore in some measure of kingship in Scotland.[18] Yet the invasion of 1054 is also noticed under that year by the Durham annalist, even though in a very summary form quite different to that found in the Worcester *Chronicle*.

Despite there being no corroborating notice of that earlier incursion in any more contemporary source, the Durham record cannot be dismissed out of hand, because specialist research has shown that its compiler 'may have had access to early material now lost', and specifically so in the case of this entry under the year 1046.[19] Indeed, there may be a supporting reference to be found in the twelfth-century *Chronicle* of Henry of Huntingdon which includes an anecdote telling of one of Siward's sons having been killed in the course of a Northumbrian expedition 'to acquire Scotland' apparently made earlier than 1054. Thus an alternative interpretation of these fragments of evidence would suggest that Siward did indeed launch an earlier incursion into Scotland, presumably intending to reclaim Lothian for Northumbria by pushing the frontier of Macbeth's kingdom back to the Forth and installing a compliant recruit from the house of Dunkeld as his client ruler over the territory regained. The most likely candidate for that role in 1046 would have been Duncan's brother Maldred when Crinán had been slain in the previous year and Duncan's eldest son Malcolm had yet to enter his teens. If such an attempt had achieved any measure of success, it was to be only short-lived when the Durham annalist admits Macbeth's recovery of 'the kingdom' soon after the departure of the mighty Earl Siward from the picture – at least for the time being.

Whatever the true course of events in 1046, Macbeth must have been fully confident as to the security of his kingship and his kingdom by 1050 because in that year, and probably around the time of the Easter

---

18  Hudson, *Kings of Celtic Scotland*, p.140.
19  Offler, *Medieval Historians of Durham*, p.21.

festival, he completed a pilgrim's journey of almost twelve hundred and
fifty miles to Rome, and there – on the reliable authority of Marianus
Scotus – 'he scattered money like seed to the poor'. While there is no
good reason to doubt Macbeth's piety, if only on the evidence of 'the
utmost veneration and devotion' which accompanied a grant made
on his own behalf to the culdees of Loch Leven, it would seem that
pilgrimage to Rome had become something of a vogue among northern
magnates through the middle decades of the eleventh century. The
fashion may have owed something to the inspirational example of Cnut
who himself made at least one such visit from which he had returned
before his meeting with Malcolm II in 1031. Indeed, Echmarcach, the
aforementioned king of Dublin, Man and 'the Rhinns' who accompanied Macbeth in Malcolm's entourage on that occasion, was to make
his own pilgrimage to Rome at the very end of his life and died there in
1065. Another northern pilgrim to the Eternal City, and one of especial
importance here, was Jarl Thorfinn of Orkney who visited Rome in the
same year as Macbeth and may even have made the pilgrimage in his
company. Yet, as Edward Cowan has suggested, 'if the two did travel
together to Rome, then each held the other hostage for the safety of
their territories in their joint absence. They were, after all, civilised men
of the world.'[20]

The focal point of Macbeth's visit, however, is thought to have been
the newly-founded monastery of *Sanctae Trinitatis Scotorum* ('Holy
Trinity of the Scots/Irish') and it is likely that the source of information
for Marianus' entry would have been a first-hand account brought to
him by a monk from, or acquainted with, that community. Whether
or not the fulsome report of Macbeth's activity in Rome which reached
Marianus was, in at least some measure, coloured by his generosity to
that particular church, it will serve here to reflect other closely contemporary references associating Macbeth and his reign in Scotland with
munificence and abundance. The Berchán poet – who may have been
writing within a decade of Macbeth's own time – also recognises him
as 'the generous king' and describes his kingdom as 'brimful in the west
and the east during the reign of the furious red one'. The lines bearing

---

20    Cowan, 'The Historical MacBeth', p.128.

on Macbeth in the *Verse Chronicle* (inserted in the *Chronicle of Melrose* but somewhat older in origin) similarly acknowledge that 'in his reign were fruitful seasons'. Both of those references are thought to reflect the very much older belief in good harvests being evidence of the right of the reigning king to rule, an idea which would also recall the ancient pagan idea of an inauguration ritual symbolising the 'marriage' of the new king to the land he was to govern.

Thus what would now be considered nothing more than a fortuitous coincidence would in those times have been enthusiastically celebrated by a king's court-poets, and at least one fragment of evidence has been taken to suggest Macbeth's personal patronage of the bardic arts. Middle Irish verses believed to be of mid-eleventh-century origin and known from their opening line as *Cruithnigh cid dosfarclann* ('What assembled the Picts in Britain') comprise an account of the mythical origins and fate of the Picts, and the version of this poem preserved in the *Book of Ballymote* carries a dedication to a 'mac Bretach' (thought to have been Macbeth) reigning at the time of its composition. Of particular bearing here is Nick Aitchison's suggestion that 'this reference implies that the poem was intended for recital at Macbeth's court and was perhaps even composed under his patronage [when it] relates how Macbeth's ancestors conquered the Picts and founded the Scottish kingdom'.[21] All of which carries its own implications for the achievement of the Cenél Loairn ascendancy in Moray a century or two earlier as well as providing evidence of court-poets working in Macbeth's service, and even supporting the likelihood that the verses in celebration of 'the red king' in the *Prophecy of Berchán* might well preserve elements drawn from just such bardic praise-poetry.

There was also, of course, an important economic aspect to those 'fruitful seasons' in a society where a king's income came as tribute rendered in the form of predominantly agricultural commodities. Thus a king whose years of reign were blessed with abundant harvests would have enjoyed his own substantial share of the wider prosperity – and there is every reason to imagine such having been the case through the greater part of Macbeth's seventeen years in the high-kingship of Scots.

---

21    Aitchison, *Macbeth*, p.74.

Within some two years of his return from the pilgrimage to Rome, his court, and his reputation, were sufficiently impressive to attract the services of two soldiers-of-fortune from the English Midlands who can be recognised, for good or ill, as representatives of the most formidable military culture in mid-eleventh-century Europe. Ironic as it might now appear in retrospect, the entries in two reliable English chronicles of the earlier twelfth century leave no doubt of it having been Macbeth who welcomed the first Norman knights into Scotland. The entry under the year 1052 in the chronicle of Florent of Worcester (and likewise in that attributed to Symeon of Durham) is principally concerned with the terms of resolution of the dispute between Edward the Confessor and his powerful earl Godwine of Wessex which had grown out of the widespread English resentment of the Norman nobility whom Edward had brought back to England on his accession in 1042. Just a year after Godwine had been forced into a brief exile in Bruges in consequence of a quarrel with the king over the Norman question in 1051, he returned to England with more than enough support to compel Edward to rid the country of all but a handful of his Norman following, and most particularly of the hated knights called 'castle-men' whom the king had established as lords in the land along the troublesome Welsh Marches. Presumably most of those unwanted Normans made their way back across the Channel, but two who chose an alternative route out of England are named by the chronicler: 'Osbern surnamed Pentecost and his companion Hugh surrendered their castles and, by licence of the earl Leofric passing through his earldom, went into Scotland, and were kindly received by *Macbeoth*, king of the Scots.'

The fact of their requiring permission of Leofric, earl of Mercia, to pass through his domain probably reflects the declaration of Edward's Normans (even including the churchman Robert of Jumièges whom he had appointed archbishop of Canterbury) as 'outlaws'. It might, however, also be taken to indicate Osbern and Hugh having been accompanied on their journey north by a substantial military following, assuredly well-mounted, heavily armed and clad in the conical helmets and mail coats characteristic of the Norman fighting-man. Whether or not Macbeth had seen similar knights and men-at-arms in the lands through which he had recently travelled on pilgrimage to Rome and thus been already impressed by the latest continental military style, he would surely have been acquainted with the custom of maintenance of imported mercenary forces (called *gaill comlaind* in Irish) which appears to have long been a privilege allowed to kings in Celtic society.

Early historical examples of such mercenaries are the north British warriors who appeared in Ireland after the destruction of the king-doms of Rheged and the Gododdin by the Northumbrian Angles in the seventh and eighth centuries. The same custom can be recognised again and at least as early as the tenth century in the similar recruitment of Scandinavians who had become available to Irish princes as fighting-men for hire by the time their pirate nests around the coastline had grown into the trading townships which were to become the cities of a later Ireland. If the old legends can be believed, Irishmen themselves had earlier entered mercenary service with Pictish kings in centuries largely unknown to the formal historical record. So Macbeth's reception of those Norman castle-men into Scotland in 1052 can be recognised as his 'following in that tradition',[22] whether or not he himself realised that he was shortly to have urgent need of his new-found mail-clad mercenaries.

The entry in the Worcester manuscript of the *Anglo-Saxon Chronicle* under the year 1054 records 'at this time the earl Siward went with a great army into Scotland with both fleet and land-force; and fought against the Scots and put to flight the king Macbeth and slew the noblest in the land; and brought thence much war-spoil, such as no man had gained before; but his son Osbern and his sister's son Siward, and numbers of his housecarls as well as those of the king were slain there on the Day of the Seven Sleepers.' The same campaign, its causes and outcome are recorded with further detail and comparable authority by those twelfth-century English chroniclers best-informed on Scottish affairs, particularly by Florent of Worcester who asserts that the expe-dition was launched 'at King Edward's command' and adds that after putting Macbeth to flight Siward 'set up as king Malcolm, the son of the king of the Cumbrians, as the king [Edward] had commanded'.

Florent also records that the Northumbrian host 'slew many

22   Hudson, *Kings of Celtic Scotland*, p.143.

thousand Scots and all the Normans', a body-count recorded in greater detail by the otherwise peremptory notices from the Irish annals. The entry in the *Annals of Ulster* at 1054 simply records 'a battle between the men of Scotland and the English' but does add that 'in it fell three thousand of the men of Scotland, and one thousand five hundred of the English, including Dolfin, son of Finntur'. This Dolfin, although nowhere else recorded, was evidently fighting with Siward's forces and is thought likely to have been a kinsman of Malcolm because the same name occurs again in the later twelfth century when it is applied to a grandson of Maldred, Crinán's son and brother to Malcolm's father Duncan. The recurrence of the same given name so characteristic of Scottish pedigrees would infer the unusual name Dolfin being found in more than one generation of the house of Dunkeld, so the likelihood must be that Dolfin, son of Finntur, was related to Malcolm's family, although perhaps more probably resident in Cumbria than Atholl.

In which case, all the evidence would point to the hostile opposition to Macbeth in 1054 having come from south of the Tweed, and seemingly at the instigation of the English king. Florent of Worcester's assertion that Siward was acting on Edward's command is corroborated by a later Latin life of the Confessor and further supported by the reference in the *Anglo-Saxon Chronicle* to the king's housecarls having fought – and died – in Siward's ranks. The housecarl (from the Norse *huskarl*), a warrior-type introduced into England during Cnut's reign, was a fighting-man selected to serve in the personal bodyguard of a king or earl and soon became recognised as the elite component of the Anglo-Saxon military. While it is only to be expected that Siward would have brought his own housecarls to Scotland in 1054, the presence of some of Edward's personal bodyguard in his forces can be taken as good evidence for the king's active commitment to the campaign.

Of similar bearing is Fordun's plausible claim for the young Malcolm having been brought by Siward to the court of the Confessor who 'willingly extended his friendship unto him and promised him help', which he was indeed to supply some dozen years later. Indeed, one later medieval English king based his claim to overlordship of Scotland on the generosity of 'Saint Edward, who gave the kingdom of Scotland to Malcolm to be held by him', and was fully supported in that claim by almost all the English chroniclers.[23] It is nonetheless perhaps unlikely that any such grand ambition lay behind Siward's plan of campaign in 1054. His foremost responsibility as earl of Northumbria was 'the double task of defending the northern frontier of England and imposing the rudiments of public order on the most unquiet of English provinces',[24] so the extent of his territorial imperative need have been no greater than reclamation of the lands of Lothian and Cumbria won by the Scots in the reign of Malcolm II.

The installation of a grateful client with his own strong claim on Scottish kingship would have appeared to Siward as realistic a means to that end as the elder Malcolm's great-grandson and namesake (who by this time was a grown man of some twenty years of age) would have represented the ideal candidate for the role. Which raises the question of just what degree and extent of kingship of Scots actually was achieved for Malcolm Canmore by the great battle fought and won by Siward's host on the feast day of the Seven Sleepers of Ephesus (27th July), and not least because none of the king-lists reckon Malcolm's reign to have begun in the July of 1054. Indeed, while the various reign-lengths which they assign to Malcolm would correspond to the period between the dates of Macbeth's death in 1057 and Malcolm's obituary in 1093, the meticulous Marianus Scotus, who represents the most closely contemporary of all the sources, does not acknowledge Malcolm's accession to the kingship until after the death of Macbeth's successor Lulach in 1058.

All of which decisively refutes any suggestion of Malcolm having won the high-kingship of Scots in 1054, but it is nonetheless hardly likely that the territory of his kingship was confined to Lothian, Cumbria and Strathclyde. The location of the 'Battle of the Seven Sleepers' is nowhere recorded in the more contemporary records, although a somewhat later Latin account of the 'origins and exploits of Siward' claims he advanced as far north as Dundee, which would represent a fully credible port of entry for the naval contingent included in his forces by the scribe of the Worcester *Anglo-Saxon Chronicle*. It would also correspond to the detailed account of the campaign supplied by Andrew of Wyntoun

23    Edward I's letter to Pope Boniface, 1301; Anderson, *ESSH*, vol. i, p.593.
24    Stenton, *Anglo-Saxon England*, p.417.

in his vernacular verse *Orygynale Cronykil of Scotland* composed in the very early decades of the fifteenth century. Thought to have been born in a parish by Loch Leven and appointed prior on St Serf's island in 1395, Wyntoun assuredly had access to records and traditions bearing on Macbeth which have not survived for examination by more recent historians, and yet the authority of his *Cronykil* can never be considered any better than variable when its evidence ranges in quality from the arguably plausible to the wildly incredible. It is unfortunate then that Wyntoun represents the earliest source to locate the Battle of the Seven Sleepers at 'Dunsinane' and to associate it with Birnam woods, because if those locations do have any genuine historical basis they would have significant bearing on both the battle itself and on its political ramifications.

'Dunsinane' can be securely identified with Dunsinnan Hill, some seven and a half miles from Scone and thus close by the ceremonial centre of the early medieval kingdom of the Scots. When his lines are rendered into modern English, Wyntoun tells of Siward's forces having 'passed over Forth, down straight to Tay, up that water the high way, to the Birnam to gather whole'. Birnam lies just a couple of miles from Dunkeld, which might be quite reasonably taken to suggest Siward's host having joined up with forces loyal to Crinán's family before advancing upon Dunsinnan, which has been identified as the site of an ancient hill-fort. The remains of ramparts around its summit indicate its serving as a citadel or refuge in the Iron Age, and one which would have been well-suited to become an early medieval stronghold. So Dunsinnan would indeed have been a perfectly plausible location for Macbeth's capital fortress and as such the obvious target for Siward's advancing forces.

A full-scale assault on a heavily defended hill-fort would inevitably culminate in ferocious hand-to-hand combat, so a body-count estimated in the thousands by the Irish annalists need have been no wild exaggeration, but beyond that suggestion any attempt to reconstruct the course of the Battle of the Seven Sleepers would be pointless here. All that need be said is that Siward evidently did win an impressive victory, probably by sheer weight of numbers and possibly also, at least as regards his house-carl contingents, by the superior quality and weaponry of his military.

To which might be added the implication of Florent of Worcester's quite specific reference to all of Macbeth's Normans having been slain in the engagement, because it is not at all unlikely that the battle-fury of the housecarls would have been directed with enthusiasm against recognisable representatives of the hated Normans recently outlawed and expelled from Edward's kingdom. What is known with absolute certainty – despite some later medieval claims to the contrary – is that Macbeth himself survived the blood-fray and at some point thereafter made his way across the Grampians into his home country of Moray, where he will be found on his next and final appearance in the historical record.

As to the immediate political consequences of the Day of the Seven Sleepers, the *Anglo-Saxon Chronicle* and earlier twelfth-century English chroniclers, who make no further mention of Macbeth and none at all of his successor Lulach, apparently assumed Malcolm's kingship having been a *fait accompli* as of 1054. Yet Macbeth was to remain high-king of Scots for three more years, although he would appear (in Benjamin Hudson's reading of the situation) to have been forced to accept Malcolm into his ancestral lands, meaning those south of the Dee, but where he would still have been a subordinate client of the high-king.[25] Malcolm's ambition was rather greater than that, of course, and had not the ageing Siward died in the year after the battle of 1054, he may well have gone in pursuit of it sooner than he did. In the event, as the reliable dating of Marianus Scotus confirms, three more years were to pass before Malcolm came in arms north of the Mounth.

While Marianus' very summary entry for the year 1057 simply records 'Findláech's son killed in August', the Tigernach annalist is rather more generous both with style and detail in his notice of 'Macbeth, Findláech's son, high-king of Scotland, slain by Malcolm, Duncan's son'. Of the earlier sources of record, only the entry of Macbeth's seventeen-year reign in the *Chronicle of the Kings* is able to identify a quite precise location for his death: 'And he was killed in Lumphanan by Malcolm, son of Duncan; and was buried on the island of Iona.' Even though traditions from Perthshire and Aberdeenshire make their own dubious claims for local cairns and standing stones marking the site of Macbeth's

25    Hudson, *Kings of Celtic Scotland*, p.144.

resting-place, the statement by the *Chronicle* of his burial on Iona (even if it really represents nothing more than a standard formality) can still be recognised as 'yet another indication that he was regarded by his followers and perhaps even by his enemies as hailing from a traditional and ancient line of Scottish kings'.[26]

The record of his last stand having been made at Lumphanan is nowhere disputed, however, and can be recognised as of broader historical significance, especially if the thirteenth-century motte and bailey castle on the Peel of Lumphanan stands on the site of an earlier stronghold. Indeed, the location of Lumphanan, just some three miles north of a pass through the Mounth between Aboyne and Banchory on the river Dee, has been taken as evidence that 'Macbeth did not cower in the security of his royal centres on the Moray Firth' but may have 'prolonged the war in the north after 1054, perhaps by mounting raids south of the Mounth'.[27]

All of which would propose his having suffered his death-wound in combat (as distinct from an assassination) – and yet not necessarily having died on the field of a battle in which his forces may well have been undefeated. Such would most certainly be the implication of the last stanza bearing on 'the red king' in the *Prophecy of Berchán* which clearly indicates his having been wounded and yet brought alive from the field: 'In the middle of Scone he will spew blood on the evening of a night after a duel.' Neither is there any reason to doubt the feasibility of the Berchán poet's evidence, which might even derive from a bardic elegy composed at the time, because – as Benjamin Hudson has pointed out – 'even though hard riding would be necessary to cover the distance between Lumphanan and Scone in the time specified, it can be, and could have been, done'. Indeed, the whole point of such an arduous ride with a fatally injured man may well have been a deliberate political gesture, and one which would propose Macbeth's forces having won the battle against Malcolm, because as Hudson goes on to conclude, 'had Macbeth not defeated his foe, then Berchán would not claim that he had died at the ceremonial centre of his kingdom'.[28]

---

26   Williams, Smyth & Kirby (eds.), *Biographical Dictionary of Dark Age Britain*, p.175.
27   Aitchison, *Macbeth*, p.94.
28   Hudson, *The Prophecy of Berchán*, p.226.

It might be said that the strongest evidence for such a victory, and for the apparent failure of Malcolm to claim the high-kingship of Scots on the field of Lumphanan, is found in the closely contemporary evidence of the *Duan Albanach* with its entry of the lines 'after Macbeth of renown [or '*Mac bethad* with fame'], seven months in the reign of Lulach'.

Other than the violent circumstances which brought about its end, nothing is known of the events of Lulach's reign. Its length is variously estimated by the king-lists, but assuredly with most reliable accuracy by Marianus Scotus, who tells of his reigning 'from the Nativity [meaning the Assumption] of St Mary to the mass of St Patrick in the month of March'.[29] Rendered in the form of the modern calendar then, Lulach mac Gillacomgain held the high-kingship of Scots from 15th August 1057 (the day after that assigned by Marianus to Macbeth's death) to 17th March 1058, a period which would correspond quite precisely to the seven months claimed for him by the *Duan*.

Trusting once again in Marianus' chronological accuracy, 17th March would be the most precise date which can be assigned to the entry in the *Annals of Tigernach* at the year 1058: 'Lulach, king of Scotland, was treacherously slain by Malcolm, son of Duncan.' Although the nature of Malcolm's 'treachery' is unspecified by the annalist, there would seem to have been some story, still current in the thirteenth century but long since lost, which recalled Lulach having met his death by trickery or entrapment. The derogatory *fatuus* ('the simpleton' or 'the fool') attached to Lulach's name by some later versions of the *Chronicle of the Kings* assuredly refers back to the same source, as does the rather more sympathetic notice of 'the unfortunate Lulach' found in the corresponding entry in the *Verse Chronicle*, which goes on to identify a recognisable location when it adds that 'the man met his fate at Essie in Strathbogie'.

The location of Lulach's death at Essie, some eight miles to the south-west of Huntly, is corroborated by four versions of the *Chronicle of the Kings* and can be taken as evidence for his having been slain by Malcolm in the course – or probably as the objective – of an expedition

---

29    As amended by Anderson, *ESSH*, vol. i, p.602.

deep into Moray. There is, however, one aspect of that site which is rarely noticed, and yet might bear a significance of its own. The farm of Essie (still clearly identified by a signpost on the road out of Rhynie leading to the high moor of Cabrach) lies below and within sight of the massive prehistoric hill-fort called Tap o' Noth – and thus in a situation curiously similar to those of Dunsinnan and Lumphanan so firmly associated with the decline and fall of Macbeth. It might even seem as if the hill-forts which so regularly punctuated the annal record of the Cenél Loairn in Dalriada had risen out of the Highland mist to look grimly down on its decline and fall three hundred years later.

Even though the kingship of Scots was to pass forever from the Cenél Loairn after the death of Lulach, he can be said to hold a role of greater genealogical significance than that allowed to his very much more famous predecessor. The first importance of Macbeth here rests upon the recognition of his reign as the highest peak of Cenél Loairn ascendancy (and thus stands quite apart from what remains of the 'Shakespearean villain or Highland hero' debate) and so, having left no offspring known to any contemporary record, his place in this family history must effectively end in the August of 1057.

While the spectre of Macbeth assuredly haunted future generations of the Cenél nGabráin-descended house of Canmore, none of the subsequent rival claimants to kingship could have been a direct descendant of the son of Findláech and so any claim made for their Cenél Loairn ancestry must derive in some wise from the line of Lulach. Yet a dark shadow was to hang over that house for the most part of two hundred years because – as Edward Cowan has put it so well – the son of Gillacomgain slain at Essie in 1058 'stands at the head of a bloody procession extending all the way to the child at Forfar in 1230'.[30]

---

30   Cowan, 'The Historical MacBeth', p.134.

# REBELS IN THE NORTH

Other than an isolated entry in the Irish annals at the year 1065 – namely the obituary of 'Dubthach the Scot' who is thought to be the same Duthac of Tain convincingly identified as the author of almost all the stanzas telling of Scottish kings in the *Prophecy of Berchán* – the early sources preserve no record of events bearing on Moray for twenty years after the death of Lulach.

Even so, there is no doubt as to the identity and the ancestry of his successor in the kingship of the Cenél Loairn because it is the name of Máelsnechtai, son of Lulach, Gillacomgain's son, which stands at the head of the longer of the two Moray genealogies laid out under the title *Rig Albain* in the Rawlinson manuscript. Other than his prominent place in that pedigree and his obituary in the *Annals of Ulster* which recognises him as 'king of Moray' in the year 1085, Máelsnechtai makes only two other appearances in the early documentary record, and that modest assembly of notices must serve as the raw material of any account of his part in the history of the Cenél Loairn.

The name *Máel snechtai* – which has been translated as 'follower of the snows', but might perhaps commemorate some saint as yet unidentified – apparently did have an occasional currency among the ruling kindred of Moray, if only on the evidence of the 'Scots jarl Melsnati' who is placed in the last years of the tenth century by *Njal's Saga*. When the name is first found in the annal record almost a hundred years later, the recognition of Máelsnechtai as 'king of Moray' can be accepted as evidence for his having held the kingship (at least in the Irish sense) of the Cenél Loairn, although it has been further interpreted to imply Malcolm Canmore having 'let Lulach's son act as mormaer for him in Moray'.[1]

---

1   Grant, 'The Province of Ross and the Kingdom of Alba', p.102.

If such was indeed the case, it would infer some form of reconciliation, presumably involving at least nominal submission to overlordship, having been achieved between the men of Moray and the king of Scots after 1058.

The same explanation would also correspond to Malcolm having left Lulach's family apparently unharmed, when his widow and his daughter (neither of whom are named by the sources) as well as his son Máelsnechtai could otherwise have offered potential figureheads, even if no more than that, for renewed insurgency. An alternative possibility, of course, is that Malcolm's mercy might be attributed to the extreme youth of Lulach's offspring, because their father need have been no older than twenty-five when he became Macbeth's short-lived successor in 1057. Even if he was already into his thirties when he was slain in the following year, it is unlikely that either of his children would have been approaching adulthood by that time and so Máelsnechtai may not have been of an age to succeed his father until the later 1060s or even the early 1070s.

It is unfortunate then that the notes in the *Book of Deer* include no indication of the dates of the earlier land-grants they record, and particularly in the case of the gift of *Pett Malduib* ('the farm of Maldub') by *Málsnechta mac Lulóig* entered immediately after the note of similar endowments of the monastery by Malcolm II and Malcolm mac Máelbrigte. Máelsnechtai's gift was presumably made whilst he was mormaer and so an indication of its date would allow at least some approximation of his reign. As it is, all that can be said of his gift to the monks of Deer is that it was quite certainly made before 1078 on the evidence of an entry under that year in the Worcester manuscript of the *Anglo-Saxon Chronicle* which, although slightly damaged, represents the only record of his fall from power in Moray: 'In this year king Malcolm captured the mother of *Maelslaehta* . . . and all his best men, and all his treasures, and his cattle, and he himself escaped with difficulty . . .'[2]

Whatever might have been the disposition of provincial government arranged between Malcolm Canmore and the men of Moray in the wake of the death of Lulach, it had evidently crumbled into contention

---

2  Ellipses indicate some seven lines left blank in the Worcester manuscript.

by 1078. Further to which an anecdote included in his *Scotichronicon* by Walter Bower, abbot of Inchcolm in the first half of the fifteenth century, has some likely bearing when it tells of Malcolm, having learned that 'one of his chief nobles had arranged with his enemies to kill him', confronting the man face to face, with no hint of his forewarning, and shaming him into begging his king's forgiveness. The modern editor of the *Scotichronicon* has suggested a link between these 'enemies' and the house of Moray, and the position given to the story in the chronology of Bower's narrative would place the events it describes within the first decade of Malcolm's reign. 'If this dating is correct,' suggests R. Andrew McDonald in his study of the enemies of the Canmore kings, 'it then becomes tempting to associate the unnamed enemies with the Moray dynasty, perhaps even Máelsnechtai himself.'[3]

To indulge such a temptation is surely allowable when the evidence of the sources is so sparse, and especially at this point where it enables the construction of a credible time-frame around the events of 1078. Had there already been rumblings of hostile intent towards Malcolm in Moray by the later 1060s (as Bower's chronology can be taken to imply), it would quite probably have been centred around Máelsnechtai, who might well have been into his teens and crossing the threshold of manhood within some ten years of his father's death. By the early 1070s, however, Malcolm Canmore was confronted by the new ascendancy in England which had delivered its first impact on the Sussex coast in October 1066. Almost six years later, in the August of 1072, the Norman duke William, remembered as 'the Conqueror' who had already made himself king of England, brought a fleet to Scotland and an army across the Forth (seemingly following much the same course of advance as had Siward in 1054). Florent of Worcester tells how 'Malcolm, king of Scots, met him at the place called *Abernethiei* (Abernethy on the Tay, south-east of Perth) and became his vassal', a claim supported by Symeon of Durham, and by the Peterborough manuscript of the *Anglo-Saxon Chronicle* which also mentions Malcolm having given William hostages. Fluctuating relations with William the Conqueror, as with his son and successor William II (called Rufus), continued through the last

---

3    McDonald, *Outlaws of Medieval Scotland*, p.21.

two decades of Malcolm's reign and quite possibly distracted his attention away from the northern outlands of his own kingdom. If so, then there must have been some genuinely compelling reason for his forceful intervention in Moray in 1078.

The specific reference made by the Anglo-Saxon chronicler to the seizure of livestock might perhaps be read as Malcolm's response to an earlier refusal to render tribute, which had subsequently escalated into an open rebellion and one presumably led by Máelsnechtai. If so, and if he himself had made his escape while his principal supporters were taken captive, then his mother would probably have been held as a hostage against any renewal of insurgency. The further likelihood is of Máelsnechtai having escaped a similar fate or worse by taking refuge in a monastic sanctuary (quite possibly at Old Deer) and having been forced to accept the religious retirement in which he was to die seven years later – at least on the evidence of the annalist's form of his obituary indicating a death in religion and its inclusion alongside those of a number of ecclesiastics entered in the *Annals of Ulster* at 1085.

Another obituary entered separately by the same annalist at that year is shrouded in obscurity, and yet has still been read to imply some possible bearing on Moray in its record of a 'Donald, son of Malcolm king of Alba, [who] ended his life unhappily'. This Donald, who is nowhere else recorded, must have been a son of Malcolm Canmore, either the illegitimate offspring of a youthful liaison or a second son by his first wife Ingibjorg of Orkney (the elder being the Duncan rendered to William the Conqueror in 1072 as a hostage for his father's good faith), and would have represented 'an obvious candidate for authority in Ross'.[4] Or even in Moray, because the form of words chosen by the annalist for the obituary of this Donald suggests a death by violence and prompts a speculative Moray connection between the two obituaries entered at 1085 if 'the killing of Donald (whoever he was) represented vengeance for Malcolm's raid against Máelsnechtai in 1078'.[5]

Some thirty years were to pass before the next reference to Moray is found in the early sources, but that vacuum in the formal historical

---

4    Grant, 'The Province of Ross and the Kingdom of Alba', pp.104–5.
5    McDonald, *Outlaws of Medieval Scotland*, p.21.

record cannot be taken as evidence for quietude in the Gaelic outlands of the north. Whether or not the men of Moray had any part in the contentions which punctuated the reigns of the first two successors to Malcolm Canmore – and there is every reason to believe that they would have done – the descendant line of the second of those kings commands a position of key significance in the later history of the Cenél Loairn and so an account of the house of Canmore on its passage into the twelfth century will serve to supply some useful context here.

When Malcolm Canmore was slain by a Norman knight near Alnwick on 13th November 1093 (in the course of his fifth invasion of Northumbria), his chosen successor – Edward, the eldest of the six sons born to him by his second wife, Margaret – sustained his own death-wound beside his father, which still left no fewer than three immediate claimants to the succession. While Edgar, the next in line of the sons of Margaret (who herself died of grief just three days after her husband was slain), would eventually follow his half-brother Duncan into the king-ship, Malcolm's immediate successor was his own brother, the Domnall Bán said (by Fordun) to have taken flight to the Isles some two years after Macbeth's accession. The influence of those long years in the Gaelic–Norse milieu of the western seaboard is reflected in Domnall's name-form (the cognomen *bán* meaning 'the white' or 'the fair') as perhaps also in the account of his succession found in the Peterborough *Anglo-Saxon Chronicle* which tells how 'the Scots elected Donald, the brother of Malcolm, as king and drove out all the English who were with the king Malcolm before'.

Thus the immediate choice of Domnall Bán as his brother's successor, presumably made by native Scots magnates, can be recognised as a reaction against the Anglo-European (as yet distinct from any specifically Norman) influence introduced into Malcolm Canmore's court by the English entourage accompanying his second queen Margaret, herself a granddaughter of the West Saxon king Edmund Ironside although born and raised in exile in the fiercely evangelistic climate of a recently converted Hungary. The likelihood that the 'English' promptly driven out on Domnall's accession included the surviving sons of Margaret is confirmed by a folio inserted in the *Chronicle of Melrose* which makes specific reference to the 'sending into exile of Edgar, Alexander and

David', who would assuredly have found a welcome in the Anglo-Norman kingdom which had passed to William Rufus on the death of his father in 1087. While all three were eventually to enter history as fully-fledged Canmore kings of Scotland, their elder half-brother Duncan was first in the field to challenge the kingship of Domnall Bán.

Duncan's mother is identified in *Orkneyinga Saga* as 'Ingibjorg the Jarls' mother', the widow of Jarl Thorfinn the Mighty who had borne his two sons and successor jarls Paul and Erlend. Sometime after Thorfinn's death in *c.*1065, or possibly before that date if the jarl had divorced her,[6] 'Ingibjorg the Jarl's mother married *Melkolm Skota-konung* called *langháls* [or 'long-neck', and presumably the Norse equivalent of *cenn mór*]. Their son was *Dungadr.*' An alternative proposal, and one not unreasonably based upon factors of age and fertility, suggests it is more likely that the Ingibjorg who married Malcolm would have been a daughter of Thorfinn who had been named for her mother. On the other hand, Ingibjorg is thought to have been born around the year 1020 which have would put her in her mid-forties and thus not necessarily beyond child-bearing age at the time of her second marriage, so the very specific saga evidence cannot be dismissed out of hand, and especially so when it would better correspond to Ingibjorg having died sometime around 1069 and just a year or so before Malcolm's marriage to Margaret.

Whatever might have been the real relationship of his mother to Jarl Thorfinn, there is no discernible evidence of any Orkney–Norse character in what is known of Duncan's adult persona which would appear to have been shaped by the Norman courtly culture in which he had grown to manhood. Having earlier released him from whatever nominal constraints would have been imposed upon a princely hostage, William Rufus made Duncan a knight and admitted him into his own service. Indeed, it is fully possible that Duncan was in Normandy with the king at the time of his own father's death in November 1093, but both were back in England before the end of the year when news from the north would seem to have reminded Duncan of his own claim on the kingship of Scots.

The entry of Domnall Bán's succession in the *Anglo-Saxon Chronicle* goes on to tell how Duncan, having 'heard that all this had happened,

---

6    Sellar, 'Marriage, divorce and concubinage in Gaelic Scotland', p.476.

came to the king [William] and did such fealty as the king would have of him; and, with his consent, went to Scotland with such English and French assistance as he could obtain, and he deprived his kinsman Donald of the kingdom and was received as king. But afterwards some of the Scots gathered together and slew almost all of his followers; and he himself escaped with but a few. Thereafter they became reconciled, but on condition that he should never again introduce English or French into the land.'

In fact, the date under which the Peterborough chronicler entered his account of Duncan's accession and its immediate aftermath is misleading because the *Chronicle of the Kings* allows six months to the first reign of Domnall Bán, which does read rather like an approximation but would still seem more realistic than the date of entry in the *Anglo-Saxon Chronicle* by effectively placing Duncan's invasion of Scotland in the later spring of 1094. Presumably then the rebellion against Duncan, the slaughter of his followers and his 'reconciliation' with the opposition would all have taken place through the summer, perhaps even into the autumn, of the same year. Further to which an eminent modern Scottish historian has commented that 'the rising is interesting for, unlike earlier revolts, it was not made in the interests of a rival; it seems to have arisen only from the strongest antipathy to the mail-clad knight and the foreign culture which he represented'.[7]

If so, then the surge of hostility to Duncan and his following in the mid-1090s represented the first emergence of what has since been recognised as the twelfth-century 'anti-feudal faction which included the great Somerled of Argyll and Harald Maddadsson, earl of Orkney',[8] as well as the rebel kindreds associated with Moray, which reared up in response to the much more extensive 'Normanisation' of Scotland in the reign of David I. In the immediate context of 1094, however, the slaughter of Duncan's Anglo-Norman warband and the conditions under which he was allowed to cling on to his kingship assuredly served the interest of Domnall Bán when Duncan had been left so dangerously exposed to challenge that his reign was not to outlast the year. As

7    Duncan, *Scotland: The Making of the Kingdom*, p.125.
8    Cowan, 'The Historical MacBeth', p.131.

indeed the Peterborough chronicler confirms in the concluding passage of his entry for 1094: 'In this year also the Scots entrapped and slew Duncan, their king, and thereafter took to themselves as king, a second time, his paternal uncle Donald on whose counsel and instigation he was betrayed to his death.'

Duncan's downfall is noticed across a wide range of early sources, none of which doubt the involvement of Domnall Bán in his nephew's fate. The entry at 1094 in the *Annals of Innisfallen*, for example, represents an immediately contemporary Irish record: 'Duncan, Malcolm's son, king of Scotland, was killed by Domnall, son of Duncan; and that Domnall took the kingship of Scotland afterwards.' Although somewhat confused as to the family relationships of the parties involved, the *Annals of Ulster* still supplies an item of further detail when it blames the killing of Duncan on 'his own brothers, Domnall and Edmund'. Domnall was actually Duncan's uncle, of course, while Edmund – by that date the second in line of the sons born to Malcolm and Margaret – would have been more accurately identified as Duncan's half-brother.

Presumably attracted by the prospect of greater advancement under his uncle (because he may even have been rewarded with half the kingdom during Domnall's second reign), Edmund had evidently chosen to stay in Scotland while his brothers sought a more congenial courtly refuge in Norman England. Although both he and his uncle probably were, at least in some wise, complicit in Duncan's demise, neither stands accused of the act itself by the (more detailed and assuredly more reliable) evidence of a thirteenth-century Latin version of the *Chronicle of the Kings*: 'Duncan, Malcolm's son, reigned for six months [and] was killed by *Malpeder, comite de Moerns* [Máelpetair, mormaer of the Mearns], in Mondynes [south-west of Stonehaven]; and Donald, Duncan's son, reigned again for three years.'

The corresponding entry in the *Chronicle of Huntingdon* appears to have been copied from the folio inserted in the *Chronicle of Melrose*, and yet the process of transcription somehow rendered the original phrase 'a certain earl, the earl of Mearns' into 'a certain Scottish earl, the earl of Moray'. Possibly mere scribal error, of course – especially when the original Latin form of Mearns could have been so easily mistaken by a Huntingdon canon for the more familiar Moray – and yet one which can still be taken as evidence for his immediate association of the men of Moray with rebellion against the sons of Malcolm Canmore. Whether or not they did have any part in the passage of arms at Mondynes (and it is not at all impossible that they could have done), Geoffrey Barrow certainly considers it 'likely that the men of Moray backed Domnall Bán in his unsuccessful four-year struggle to wrest the throne from his Normanising nephews'.[9]

Domnall's struggle was brought to its grim conclusion in 1097 when William Rufus sent an army into Scotland to install Edgar, by now the eldest surviving son of Malcolm Canmore, as his client king of Scots. While Edmund is said by one twelfth-century English chronicler to have been carried off in chains and apparently forced into religion, Domnall was more cruelly served, first of all being condemned – in the words of the *Chronicle of Melrose* – to 'perpetual imprisonment' and then, a year or two later according to the Irish annals, suffering the blinding of both of his eyes. There are differing accounts of Domnall's ultimate fate, but he may have survived as a mutilated captive for a full decade on the closely contemporary evidence of Orderic Vitalis, an English-born chronicler resident in Normandy who claims Domnall had been put to death by Alexander when he succeeded to the kingship on the death of his brother Edgar in 1107.

It was in the first decade of Alexander's reign that the men of Moray were to make their next appearance in the historical record, and specifically in an entry in the *Annals of Ulster* at the year 1116: 'Ladhmunn, Donald's son, grandson of the king of Scotland, was slain by the men of Moray.' This *Ladhmunn* (apparently a Middle Irish form of the Norse name *Lodmund*) might be quite reasonably identified as a son of the Donald whose obituary had been entered by the same annalist at 1085 and who is thought to have been a son of Malcolm Canmore appointed by his father to some position of government north of the Grampians. An alternative proposal which suggests this Lodmund as a son of Domnall Bán would conveniently link his Norse name with Domnall's supposed exile within the Gaelic–Norse culture of the Hebrides, but it does seem hardly likely that Alexander would have assigned any role in

9    Barrow, 'Macbeth and other mormaers of Moray', p.118.

the administration of the north to a son of the uncle his own brother had so viciously deposed twenty years earlier and he himself is said to have only recently put to death. When the given name of an individual so often points to the background of his or her mother, it is fully possible that the 'Donald, son of Malcolm king of Scots' might have followed his father's example and taken an Orkney–Norse wife, which would equally well explain the Norse name given to his son.

The death of Lodmund at the hands of the men of Moray might be better placed into context if it can be linked to an anecdote told in slightly different forms by Wyntoun and by Bower but seemingly describing the same incident in which Alexander was attacked at Invergowrie, near Dundee, by an enemy said by Bower to have been 'ruffians of the Mearns and Moray'. Whereas Bower tells of Alexander having withdrawn to the south where he mustered a greater force for a campaign of retribution in the Highlands, Wyntoun's version has Alexander going in pursuit of his attackers 'over the Stokfurd [probably the cattle-ford on the Beauly river] into Ros'. Both those later medieval accounts seek to associate this expedition in the Highlands with Alexander's reputation as 'the Fers' (or 'fierce') and claim his foundation of Scone priory to have been a gesture of thanksgiving for victory. When the date of that foundation is approximately placed between 1114 and 1120, Andrew McDonald finds it 'very tempting to connect the events related by the Irish annals for 1116 with those described by Bower and Wyntoun, linked as they are not only by a coincidence of chronology but also by the apparent involvement of the men of Moray'.[10] If Lodmund had held a similar position in the government of the north under Alexander to that assigned to his probable father, the Donald slain in 1085, under Malcolm Canmore, then it is not unlikely that Lodmund might have been killed at Invergowrie, and so Alexander's campaign in the north would represent an act of vengeance for the death of his nephew.

Nothing more is heard of those men of Moray until the reign of the youngest of the sons of Malcolm and Margaret who succeeded to the kingship as David I on the death of his brother Alexander I in 1124. Orderic Vitalis tells of a rebellion against David in the very first year of

---

10    McDonald, *Outlaws of Medieval Scotland,* p.24.

his reign which may have had a link to Moray, but if so Orderic makes no specific reference to such a connection, at least in this instance, and the rebellion is noticed in no other source. The first widely recorded, and undeniably momentous, Moray rising of David's reign does not appear in the historical record until 1130, while the king himself was in England at the court of his brother-in-law Henry I, the youngest son of William the Conqueror, who had succeeded on the death of his brother William Rufus in 1100 and, in the same year, married Matilda, one of the daughters born to Malcolm Canmore by Margaret.

It may very well have been David's absence from his own kingdom which offered the house of Lulach its first opportunity in a generation to assert its claim to the kingship of Scots. When Máelsnechtai died, seemingly without male issue, in 1085, the line of descent passed to his sister who is unnamed in the early sources but whose son Angus had almost certainly been brought up to believe himself the successor to the ancient kingship of the Cenél Loairn and thus also to the high-kingship of Scots.

His assertion of that claim is recorded in the *Annals of Ulster* at 1130: 'A battle between the men of Scotland and the men of Moray; and in it fell four thousand of the men of Moray, including their king Angus, the son of the daughter of Lulach; and a thousand – or, more correctly, a hundred – of the men of Scotland fell in that encounter.' While the Ulster annalist's distinction between 'the men of Moray' and 'the men of Scotland' implies recognition of Moray as a kingdom in its own right even in the second quarter of the twelfth century, the stark entry of the same blood-fray as 'the slaughter of the men of Moray in Scotland' in the immediately contemporary *Annals of Innisfallen* offers a chilling evocation of what was undoubtedly a massacre. In striking contrast to the brevity of the Innisfallen annalist, the similarly contemporary account set down in Normandy by Orderic Vitalis offers more detail than any other record.

Orderic confirms David having been away in England at the court of Henry I when 'Angus, earl of Moray, entered Scotland with Malcolm and five thousand armed men, and strove to subdue the whole region to himself. But Siward's son Edward, who was tribune of the Mercians under king Edward [the Confessor], leader of the knighthood and cousin of king David, collected an army and suddenly opposed the army of the enemy. At last a conflict took place and Edward slew the earl Angus and overwhelmed, captured and routed his forces. Thereafter with his cohorts, now elated with triumph, he eagerly pursued the fugitives and entered Moray which lacked a defender and lord, and with God's help obtained the entire lordship of that expansive province.'

That reference to pursuit of the remnants of Angus' host into Moray indicates the battle having been fought south of the Mounth and thus corroborates Fordun's location of the field of conflict at Stracathro near Forfar, but other elements of Orderic's account are not so easily identified. A. O. Anderson's thorough survey of likely candidates for identification as 'Siward's son Edward' disentangles apparent confusions in Orderic's text to conclude that the Edward who evidently served as constable to David I, 'more probably may have been [a grandson, rather than a son, of the] Siward, earl Siward's nephew, who was associated with his uncle in the campaign against Macbeth in 1054' and fell in battle at Dunsinnan on the day of the Seven Sleepers.[11]

Even more – in fact, very much more – scholarly ink and effort has been expended on the identification of the Malcolm (usually, but not yet, called 'Malcolm MacHeth') who is said by Orderic to have been Angus' ally at Stracathro. He had already been mentioned by the same chronicler under the year 1124, where he is described as 'the base-born son of Alexander' who attempted 'to snatch the kingdom from his uncle and fought against him in two fierce battles. But David . . . conquered him and his followers.' When placed beside Orderic's reference to Malcolm's part in Angus' rising of 1130, it would appear that an illegitimate son of Alexander had failed in his challenge to his uncle's succession in 1124 and subsequently thrown in his lot with the house of Moray in order to make a second attempt. The king's absence in England might have been thought by one or both parties to offer them every prospect of success – at least until they crossed the Esk and came up against the evidently superior forces available to David's constable. Yet when Angus was slain at Stracathro, Malcolm not only escaped with his life but somehow evaded capture for four more years on the evidence

---

11    Anderson, *ESSH*, vol. i, pp.596–7.

of an entry in the *Chronicle of Melrose* under the year 1134 which records that 'Malcolm was taken captive and placed in custody at the town of Roxburgh'.

It would not seem, however, that a lone fugitive had been caught on the run, on the evidence of the speech reportedly made to David I by Robert de Brus before the 'Battle of the Standard' fought on Cowton Moor near Northallerton in 1138 (and so called by reason of a ship's mast hung with the banners of great northern saints mounted on a wagon to accompany the English army). David's incursion across the Tweed in that year (made, at least officially, in support of his niece Matilda, daughter of Henry I) had advanced into North Yorkshire and already come to Thirsk when the king was met by two Anglo-Norman barons, Robert de Brus and Bernard de Balliol, seeking to dissuade him from further 'ravaging the land of Saint Cuthbert' (in the words of a contemporary prior of Hexham). To which end, Robert de Brus (who held the lordship of Annandale from David) is said to have reminded the Scottish king of all that he and his house owed to the Norman nobility of England. 'Remember when you called upon the aid of the English against Malcolm, the heir of his father's hatred and persecution . . . how willing to help, how ready for danger came nobles of the English to meet you at Carlisle, how many ships they prepared, how they made war and with what forces they made defence; how they terrified all your enemies, until they took Malcolm himself, surrendered to them; taken, they bound him; and delivered him over bound. So did the fear of us while binding his limbs bind still more the courage of the Scots, and by quenching all hope of success remove the presumption to rebel.'

Although there is very reasonable doubt as to whether these words – which are known only from the account of the battle set down by Ailred of Rievaulx – actually were those spoken on that occasion, or whether they were of Ailred's own devising and only attributed by him to Robert de Brus, there is nonetheless good reason to trust the substance of their evidence. Just four years before the events he describes, Ailred had himself held office under David before becoming a monk of the Cistercian community at Rievaulx where he was to be eventually appointed abbot in 1147. So he may well have been still at David's court when Malcolm was delivered there as a captive in 1134, and neither is it unthinkable that he could have been chosen, in his new capacity as an English churchman, to accompany the embassy to David at Thirsk. If so, then the detail included in the speech he attributes to de Brus would have the authority of first-hand recollection – and so too would his account of those negotiations being brought to an abrupt end by the intervention of 'William, the king's nephew, a man of high spirit and the chief provoker of war, [who] with greatest fury accused Robert of treason'.

That contemporary reference to 'William, the king's nephew' (a son of David's half-brother, the Duncan slain in 1094) is worthy of especial notice here by reason of the unexpected role of his descendants in the later history of the Cenél Loairn-descended house of Moray, but the more immediate importance of Ailred's account of the de Brus oration at this point lies in its evidence for the capture of Malcolm. If David really did need to call upon such exertions by Anglo-Norman barons to find and seize Malcolm, the man must have represented not only a serious threat in his own right to the house of Canmore but one with access to formidable forces in his support. As Andrew McDonald observes, 'this suggests a combined land-based and naval campaign . . . possibly even that a series of engagements was fought'.[12]

All of which raises further questions as to the associations of this man who is thus far known from Orderic Vitalis as an allegedly illegitimate son of Alexander I who twice rebelled against David I. Some new light is thrown upon those questions by the chronicles of Holyrood and Melrose, but not until after the death of David and the succession of his grandson as Malcolm IV in 1153 – by which date the prisoner at Roxburgh would have already been incarcerated for almost twenty years. An entry in the *Chronicle of Holyrood* under that year, and specifically assigned to 6th November, tells how 'on that day in Scotland, Somerled and his nephews, the sons of Malcolm, having allied themselves with very many men, rebelled against the king Malcolm and disturbed and disquieted Scotland in great part'.

Somerled mac Gillabrigte – of Gaelic–Norse parentage yet most often remembered in more recent times as the founding dynast of the

---

12   McDonald, *Outlaws of Medieval Scotland*, p.152.

Clan Donald Lordship of the Isles – was styled 'king of the *Innsegall* and Kintyre' by his obituary entered in the *Annals of Tigernach* at 1164 and acknowledging his seizure of the Hebrides from the Norse king of Man and the Isles. Although Somerled does not make his first appearance in the contemporary sources until the 1150s, he is already recognised by the *Chronicle of Man* as '*regulus* [a title comparable to mormaer] of Argyll' and so would probably have been rising to power on the western seaboard through the 1130s. The marriage of his sister to Malcolm must have been made either before or very soon after 1130 to allow for the birth of at least three children (the sons mentioned by the chronicler and a daughter later identified by *Orkneyinga Saga*) before his capture and imprisonment in 1134, so Malcolm had either fled to Argyll after the battle at Stracathro and there taken a daughter of Gillabrigte as his wife, or possibly been based somewhere in the west before he had joined Angus' rebellion.

Either of those possibilities would lend a significance to the reference made in the de Brus speech to the barons having met with David at Carlisle which was his principal court of residence (and where he died in 1153), but which would also have been ideally situated for the assembly of a seaborne expedition around the coastlands of south-west Scotland where Malcolm had presumably found refuge and support in the years between Stracathro and his capture in 1134. There evidently was no shortage of support for 'the anti-feudal faction' around the shores of the Irish Sea – in Galloway and Man as well as Argyll – as is illustrated by the extraordinary career of Wimund, the rebel bishop of Man. This Wimund is said by the chronicler William of Newburgh (informed at first-hand on personal acquaintance) to have 'feigned to be the son of the earl of Moray . . . deprived of the inheritance of his father by the king of Scotland' and to have twice 'ravaged the isles and provinces of Scotland' between 1134 and 1151 in support of his claim (which will bear further consideration here).

The same region must also have incorporated the power-base from which 'Somerled and his nephews, the sons of Malcolm, disturbed and disquieted Scotland' in 1153, even though the Holyrood chronicler is less than specific as to the geographical detail of that rising. There is, however, a quite precise reference to a location at the edge of the Irish

Sea in the next notice of a son of Malcolm, entered in the *Chronicle of Holyrood* for 1156 and under the same year but with additional detail in the *Chronicle of Melrose*, which records 'Donald, son of Malcolm, taken captive at Whithorn; and imprisoned with his father in the tower of Roxburgh'.

The location of Whithorn in the southern coastland of Galloway would put Malcolm's son within Somerled's orbit of activity, especially in 1156 when he had recently engaged Godred, king of Man, in the sea-battle off Islay by which he won possession of the Inner Hebrides. Indeed, it is not impossible that Donald might himself have taken part in that battle, because he and his unnamed brother would have been raised by their mother, presumably somewhere in their uncle's heartland of Morvern and Lorn, while their father was imprisoned. Donald's capture at Whithorn raises another question, however, because the lordship of Galloway was at that time held by the famous Fergus, whose shifting political alignments – as regards Somerled and Godred (both of whom were Fergus' kinsmen by marriage) – are difficult to ascertain. So too are his relations with David I because, unless the Galloway contingent included in the Scottish host at the Battle of the Standard had been simply hired as mercenaries, its presence would indicate Fergus' acknowledgement of David as his overlord, just as the inclusion of 'the men of Lorne' in the same force has been taken to indicate Somerled of Argyll having been loyal, and even tributary, to the king at least until 1153.[13] 'On the other hand,' as Andrew McDonald has pointed out, 'it might be argued that Donald MacHeth was actually apprehended by Fergus, who then turned him over to the king, [because] it is difficult to imagine Donald being taken in Galloway without at least the tacit approval of the ruler of the region.'[14]

Nothing more is known of Donald after 1156 because, once consigned to captivity in the tower of Roxburgh, he makes no further appearance in the historical record. It is fully possible, however, that he might have been free within the twelvemonth unless he had remained a prisoner held hostage for his father's future loyal conduct – in view of the next

13    Duncan, *Scotland: The Making of the Kingdom*, p.166.
14    McDonald, *Outlaws of Medieval Scotland*, p.88.

entry in the *Chronicle of Holyrood* stating that 'in the year 1157 Malcolm *Machet* [MacHeth] was reconciled with the king of Scots'.

So well reconciled, indeed, as to be granted an earldom by the king by 1160, and certainly before 1162, on the evidence of a charter authorising 'Malcolm, earl of Ross, to protect and maintain the monks of Dunfermline' (presumably in respect of their property at Auldearn, not far from Ross), which is corroborated by the obituary entered in the *Chronicle of Holyrood* under the year 1168 and recognising him as 'Malcolm *Machbeth* [MacHeth], earl of Ross'.

Such then is the historical record of the man who demands attention here, by reason of his alliance with Angus of Moray and also because one, and possibly two, of his descendants were to follow him in what had apparently become a family tradition of alliance with the Moray cause which was to continue even into the first decades of the thirteenth century. The question of the true origin and descent of this Malcolm who is said to have been an illegitimate son of Alexander I on his first appearance in the sources, only to reappear under the surname or patronymic of 'MacHeth' and recognised as the earl of Ross, has been variously answered across a wide range of opinion which can be categorised into three distinct schools of thought.

One of these proposes that the record preserved in the early sources actually refers to two different Malcolms, the first being the 'base-born son of Alexander' said to have risen against David I in 1124 and again with Angus in 1130, before being captured and imprisoned at Roxburgh in 1134. The second Malcolm thus becomes the 'Malcolm MacHeth' who was reconciled with Malcolm IV in 1157 and afterwards received the earldom of Ross which he held at the time of his death in 1168. This proposal would resolve the disparity of an illegitimate son of Alexander I being known as 'MacHeth' (which would represent or be derived from a Gaelic patronymic meaning 'son of Aed'). It would also correspond to Ailred's description of the Malcolm of 1134 as 'the heir of his father's hatred and persecution', which has been read as a reference back to the contentious relationship between the reigning Alexander and his ambitious younger brother David.

While there is an alternative interpretation of that de Brus reference (which will also bear consideration here later), the first objection to the 'two Malcolms' hypothesis is its ultimate dependence upon the claim made by Orderic Vitalis and endorsed by Robert de Torigni for the Malcolm of 1124 and 1130 having been the illegitimate son of Alexander I. Both of those chroniclers, although close contemporaries and possibly drawing on another source since lost,[15] were writing far away from Scotland and making a claim nowhere corroborated by any of the similarly contemporary but more local sources such as the Scottish and English chronicles and the Irish annals. To which can be added the very reasonable observation that the sequence of events between 1124 and 1168 – especially including the imprisonment of Donald, son of Malcolm 'with his father in the tower of Roxburgh' in 1156 – presents no chronological impediment to the same man having been the Malcolm intended throughout. The introduction of the surname or patronymic 'MacHeth' in 1157 might be otherwise explained as having been intended to distinguish the newly appointed Malcolm, earl of Ross, from another Malcolm, earl of Atholl, who is found as witness to charters from 1154 onwards and of whom the Holyrood chronicler entering the later notices of Malcolm MacHeth would assuredly have been aware.

A second proposal hinges upon the distinctly Gaelic patronymic MacHeth and the possibility of kinship with the Cenél Loairn implied by the long-standing association of the MacHeths with Moray, which extends over three quarters of a century from the alliance of Malcolm with Lulach's grandson Angus in 1130 to the involvement of Malcolm's great-grandson Kenneth in the MacWilliam rising of 1215. Máelsnechtai, son of Lulach, having seemingly left no son on his death in 1085, the male line of Cenél Loairn descent passed in the next generation to the son of Lulach's daughter, and so it is crucially unhelpful that neither she nor her husband are identified by name in the historical record.

The absence of those two key pieces from the genealogical jigsaw of the Cenél Loairn and its descendent house of Moray presented an invitingly open door to a proposal that the Aed identified in the patronymic 'MacHeth' might have been the otherwise unnamed husband of Lulach's daughter and thus the father of Angus, earl of Moray, as well as

---

15   Anderson, *SAEC*, p.167.

of Malcolm, earl of Ross. Reliable evidence for the existence of an Earl Aed who witnessed two early charters of David I adds a handful of grist to the same mill – and yet there are at least as many problems with its proposal as there were with the 'two Malcolms' hypothesis. There is, for example, nowhere any hint by the early sources of Angus and Malcolm having been brothers, or even half-brothers, which might perhaps be explained by Malcolm having been the son of Aed by an earlier marriage – and yet that would not have allowed Malcolm so much as a fingertip hold on the Moray claim to kingship.

Another possibility is that 'MacHeth' may have already been a family surname (as distinct from a personal patronymic) by Malcolm's time, as it evidently had become by the early thirteenth century when Malcolm's apparent great-grandson Kenneth is also surnamed MacHeth. A similar objection has been found in the name Aed itself, and particularly in view of the Gaelic custom of the same given name recurring time and again in the same family, because Aed (from the Gaelic *Aodh*) is nowhere to be found either in the genealogies of the Moray dynasty or among the records of its Cenél Loairn ancestors. Yet the name does occur in the Cenél nGabráin-descended house of MacAlpin, as do those of Donald and Kenneth which also occur in later generations of MacHeths – and it is this factor which forms an important component of another proposal of the origin and ancestry of the elusive Malcolm MacHeth.

This last of the three schools of thought on the MacHeth question, as developed by Alexander Grant,[16] is centred around the appointment of the recently released and reconciled Malcolm MacHeth to the earldom of Ross. Proposing 'MacHeth' as a straightforward patronymic rather than a family surname when applied to Malcolm, he suggests the Aed found among the witnesses to the two charters of David I (and perhaps also to Alexander I's foundation charter for Scone priory) as the only reliably identified father of Malcolm. While none of those documents assigns a province to this earl Aed, the only Scottish earldoms not otherwise accounted for at that time are those of Moray and of Ross. Since Angus, grandson of Lulach, is recognised as 'earl of Moray' in 1130 by the Melrose chronicler, Grant comes to the reasonable conclusion that

---

16   Grant, 'The Province of Ross and the Kingdom of Alba', pp.107–9.

'Ross is the better bet – which would indicate that in the 1160s Malcolm MacHeth was restored to his father's earldom'.

Proposing that the province of Ross had probably come under the control of the king of Scots in the reign of Malcolm III, he goes on to suggest that 'it is likely to have been entrusted to a member of the royal kindred'. Referring also to the presence of an Aed in the MacAlpin king-list and the absence of the name from the pedigrees of the house of Moray, 'a royal descent for Earl Aed is entirely reasonable', which leads him on to the suggestion that the Aed, father of Malcolm MacHeth, had been a son of the Donald, Malcolm Canmore's son, who had died in 1085, 'and hence perhaps a brother of the Lodmund who was killed in 1116'. An extension of the same proposal could also supply an alternative explanation of Ailred's description of the Malcolm of 1134 as 'the heir of his father's hatred and persecution' in terms of Aed having supported Alexander I and worked for him 'in the troublesome north' after the death of Lodmund. In view of the fractious sibling rivalry between Alexander and David, a supporter of Alexander with a power-base in the north might well have resented his successor's Anglo-Norman followers, and so bequeathed the paternal hatred ascribed to Malcolm MacHeth which would thus have been quite specifically directed against David I himself.

To which can be added the comparison, made by Alexander Grant and other historians, of the very different fates of the two rebels of 1130. While Angus had suffered a violent death similar to those inflicted on his grandfather Lulach and on Lulach's step-father Macbeth, Malcolm MacHeth was punished only by imprisonment when taken captive, and not only eventually released but soon afterwards granted an earldom. That alone can be taken as evidence for his relationship with the current ruling kindred of Cenél nGabráin descent having been quite unlike that of the house of Moray – and so must also effectively exclude him and his descendants from the Cenél Loairn pedigree of central importance here. Nonetheless, that long line of descent from Ferchar Fota can be picked up again within a dozen years of the death of Malcolm MacHeth when the rebel house of MacWilliam makes its first entry into the historical record.

When Malcolm IV died without issue (hence his posthumous epithet of 'the Maiden') in 1165, the succession passed to his younger brother William, recognised for some reason by a contemporary source as 'the lion of justice' – from which later writers derived his more familiar by-name of 'the Lion'. The peace and stability of the first decade of William's long reign was not to endure beyond the year 1174 when he was captured at Alnwick on one of the invasions of Northumberland which seem to have become established as a family tradition in the house of Canmore. Having been brought as a shackled prisoner to Henry II at Northampton, he was afterwards taken with the English king to France, and in company with other political prisoners kept under guard. News of an uprising in Galloway demanded William's urgent return to Scotland, and so he could do no other than accept whatever terms Henry demanded to allow his release. The resultant Treaty of Falaise not only cost him castles and hostages but effectively consigned himself and his kingdom to English overlordship for the next fifteen years.

The complex politics of Galloway were of most immediate concern to William on his eventual return to Scotland in the summer of 1175 and attracted greater attention from the chroniclers than did the situation in the north, which is scarcely noticed in the sources until the end of the decade. There is every reason, nonetheless, to suspect resentment of David I's feudalisation of Moray and Ross in the wake of Stracathro steadily swelling into the flood tide of rebellion which was to engulf the north in, even if not before, the 1180s. The entry for the year 1163 in the *Chronicle of Holyrood* concludes with the words 'and King Malcolm *transtulit* ['transferred' or 'transported'] the men of Moray'. Interpretations of that curious statement range from a transferral of the bishopric of Moray to something akin to the (very much) later Highland Clearances having been imposed in reprisal for insurrection – as is claimed by the corresponding entry in the *Gesta Annalia* appended to Fordun's chronicle.

At this time the rebel nation of the *Moravienses*, whose former lord, Earl Angus, had been killed by the Scots would, for neither prayers nor bribes, neither treaties nor oaths, leave off their disloyal ways, or their ravages among their fellow-countrymen. So having gathered together a great army, the king removed them all from the land of their birth . . . and scattered them throughout other parts of Scotland, both beyond the hills and this side thereof, so that not even one native of that land abode there; and he installed therein his own peaceful people.

Allowing for biblically inspired exaggeration (the Old Testament references having been omitted here), there is every likelihood that this represents a record of the eviction of freeholders to make way for the feudal tenants of imported Normans and Flemings. Even so, it is still unclear whether the reference to 'their ravages' harked back to 1130 or referred to more recent risings unnoticed elsewhere in the sources, because – as Andrew McDonald has recognised – 'taken altogether the indications are that Moray continued to be troubled into the second half of the twelfth century'.[17]

An entry in the *Chronicle of Melrose* for the year 1179 offers the first real evidence for such troubles in its record of William's expedition into Ross 'with a great and strong army; and there they strengthened two castles, the one called Dunscath [Dunskeath at the mouth of the Cromarty Firth], the other named Ederdower [now Redcastle in the south of the Black Isle on the shore of the Beauly Firth]'. While those fortifications may have been intended as defences against Harald Maddadsson of Orkney (of whom more anon), the expedition itself is linked to another of the king's enemies by the corresponding entry in the *Gesta Annalia* which tells of William having 'advanced into Ross against MacWilliam'. That reference to the name MacWilliam in 1179 (in fact, its first appearance in the historical record) supplies its own evidence for an earlier active presence in the north of the same Donald identified by Roger of Howden, a northern English chronicler well-informed on Scottish affairs, in his entry for the year 1181.

While the king of Scotland tarried with his lord the king of England in Normandy, the son of William fitz Duncan, the Donald who had very often claimed the kingdom of Scotland and had many a time made insidious incursions into that kingdom, by a mandate

---

17   McDonald, *Outlaws of Medieval Scotland*, p.31.

of certain powerful men of the kingdom landed in Scotland with a numerous armed host, wasting and burning as much of the land as he reached; and he put the people to flight, and slew all whom he could take . . . William, king of Scotland, hearing that the above-named Donald and his accomplices were wasting his land, received from the lord king leave to go home and returned to his native land.

Even though the threat posed by this invasion was considered sufficiently serious to bring William the Lion back from Normandy yet again, another six years were to pass before he was to take any action against it, thus allowing Donald MacWilliam – on the evidence of the *Gesta Annalia* – to 'wrest from his king the whole of Ross . . . and for no little time hold the whole of Moray'.

All of which raises the question of how a son of the William last heard of here in the entourage of David I in 1138 (when he wrecked negotiations with Robert de Brus before the Battle of the Standard) came to make his first entry into the historical record some forty years later under an unmistakably Gaelic name and at the head of a rebellion in the north. His father – who is invariably called by the Anglo-Norman patronymic name-form of William fitz Duncan – is first noticed as an 'infant' in an early charter of Duncan II, the son born to Malcolm Canmore by his first wife Ingibjorg of Orkney, who had seized the kingship from his uncle Domnall Bán in 1094 but only to reign for a matter of months before he was slain later in the same year. His son William, who would have grown to manhood through the reigns of Edgar and Alexander I, was a Norman knight in his every aspect and held a prominent position at the court of David I, as is attested by his frequent appearance as a witness to David's charters.

Some time around 1140, he married a Cumbrian heiress, Alice de Rumilly (*de Romille*), who bore him a son (also named William, but usually remembered as 'the boy of Egremont' by reason of his premature death) and three daughters, which effectively identifies Donald as William's son by another liaison, presumably an earlier marriage. Further light has been thrown on that former relationship by a reference to William fitz Duncan as 'earl of Moray' in a Cumbrian genealogy (the 'Chronicon Cumbrie') compiled in the thirteenth century, and it is this which underlies Geoffrey Barrow's proposal of William's first wife having been either a cousin or a sister of Angus whose earldom had passed back to the king after his death in battle at Stracathro. It would probably have been around that time (if not in 1130, then shortly afterwards) that David would have granted the earldom to his nephew in an attempt to assign the Moray claim on the kingship to a trusted kinsman and close companion of his own, who would thus have been earl of Moray as much by right of his wife as by formal royal grant.

While it is doubtful how long William remained as earl of Moray (perhaps only until his first wife's death, because he is nowhere styled with the title of earl whilst lord of Craven and Coupland by right of his second marriage), he evidently left a son by that earlier marriage and one whose given name and form of patronymic 'testifies to his upbringing in a Gaelic-speaking milieu' where he might have expected to succeed to the earldom of Moray when he came of age. No such succession was to be allowed him, of course, because the earldom appears to have been effectively suppressed by the end of the 1130s (as was the earldom of Ross after the death of Malcolm MacHeth in 1168), and yet all that is known of Donald MacWilliam's claims, and of the support they received, corresponds to the Barrow hypothesis.[18]

To which might perhaps be linked the claim of Wimund, the rebel bishop of Man, to have been 'the son of the earl of Moray'. While William of Newburgh does not name the earl, it is usually assumed to have been the Angus who was slain in 1130, and yet the fragment of Cumbrian evidence for another 'earl of Moray' has suggested an alternative candidate when 'the Cumbrian associations of both Wimund and William fitz Duncan raise the possibility that Wimund was in fact an otherwise unknown son of William . . . Moreover, Wimund's treatment at the hands of David strongly suggests that he stood in some relationship to the royal house'.[19] Wimund is said by the Newburgh chronicler to have been born in 'a most obscure part of England' but is linked to Cumbria by his having been a monk of Furness before going

---

18    Barrow, *The Acts of William I*, pp.12–13.
19    McDonald, *Outlaws of Medieval Scotland*, p.102.

to Man in 1134, and by the inclusion of Furness in the land grant by which David I negotiated an end to his last rising in 1151. While it is possible that Wimund could have been a son of William fitz Duncan by a youthful liaison somewhere in the north of England, he must have been an adult by the time he became bishop of Man soon after 1134 and so could hardly have been born to William by the kinswoman of Angus whom it is suggested he married sometime after 1130. Whether David's merciful generosity to a rebel cleric implied his kinship to the ruling house (which, indeed, it may well have done) or otherwise simply represented the king's deference to a man of the cloth, there is nonetheless no evidence to support any realistic possibility of Wimund's descent from the Cenél Loairn.

By contrast, the proposal of Donald MacWilliam as a son of William fitz Duncan by a first marriage to a woman of the house of Moray is fully credible in the light of the subsequent history of the MacWilliam rebellions. His father's direct descent from the eldest of the sons of Malcolm Canmore bequeathed him a claim on the kingship 'which had laid dormant for over sixty years',[20] while his mother's descent from the line of Lulach would have put him at the head of the Cenél Loairn – and those two lines of kingly ancestry endowed Donald MacWilliam with a right to the kingship of Scots bearing comparison to that held by Macbeth more than a century earlier. The 'anti-feudal faction' (meaning those adherents to the old tradition of alternating kingship opposed to the 'feudal' system of a single line of succession based on primogeniture), which the later course of events shows to have had a broad base of support in the Scotland of the later twelfth and very early thirteenth centuries, would have needed to look no further for a perfectly qualified candidate.

If Donald MacWilliam had been born in the mid-1130s and raised by his mother's people in the north, he would have come of age in the last years of the reign of David I and already seen something of the 'gradual but far-reaching changes [which] meant the extinction of the old mormaerdom and almost all that it stood for'.[21] The rising of the sons of MacHeth following

---

20   Barrow, *The Acts of William I*, p.12.
21   Barrow, 'Macbeth and other mormaers of Moray', p.119.

the succession of Malcolm IV and the death of their uncle Somerled when his invasion of the Clyde was defeated at Renfrew a decade later can only have aggravated his resentment of the increasingly entrenched feudal order and, at the same time, confronted him with the dwindling possibility of receiving whatever he believed to be his own due inheritance. Although the name MacWilliam is not noticed in any source before 1179, that first reference in the *Gesta Annalia* implies that he had already been in revolt against William the Lion, as is corroborated by Roger of Howden's statement that Donald had 'many a time made insidious incursions' before his dramatic enterprise of 1181. It would follow then that Roger's reference to Donald having 'landed in Scotland with a numerous armed host' in that year indicates his having earlier fled, or been forced to flee, the kingdom and found an offshore power-base, possibly in the Hebrides but perhaps more probably in Ireland because it was from there that two later generations of MacWilliam rebels appear to have arrived in Scotland. As it happens, either of those two locations would correspond to the record (found in another manuscript of the Howden chronicle) of Donald having 'despoiled along the sea-coast [probably meaning that of Wester Ross]'.

For all the importance of Roger of Howden as a source for the invasion in 1181, his evidence reflects the attitude of the Scottish king and court to their rivals, as is illustrated by his insistence on Donald's 'wasting and burning as much of the land as he reached', putting the people to flight and slaying 'all whom he could take'. Yet, as Andrew McDonald observes, 'stock images of fire and slaughter aside, there appears to be little real detail that can be recovered relating to the impact of these insurrections on the Scottish land, people and kingdom'.[22] Remarkably, in view of the statement by the *Gesta Annalia* that he seized 'the whole of Ross . . . and for no little time held the whole of Moray', the only item of detailed evidence for his six years of control of that region is found in a charter of William the Lion referring to the forfeiture of lands by one Gillecolm, the king's marshal who had 'feloniously surrendered my castle of *Heryn* [Auldearn, just south of Nairn] and then went over to my mortal enemies in the manner of a wicked traitor and stood with them against me to do as much harm as he could'.

---

22    McDonald, *Outlaws of Medieval Scotland*, p.129.

Neither was Gillecolm alone in his support for the MacWilliam, as indeed Roger of Howden confirms when he states quite plainly that Donald's invasion of 1181 was made with 'the mandate of certain powerful men of the kingdom'. The identities of a number of these 'powerful men' were unfortunately lost to history with a record which disappeared after being carried off to England by Edward I in 1296, but it is said by an official inventory of Scottish documents to have contained 'old charters of the time of King William and King Alexander [II] his son [listing] those to whom the said kings formerly gave their peace and those who stood with MacWilliam'. There is general agreement among historians, however, that one of the most powerful men 'who stood with MacWilliam' was Harald Maddadsson – the son of Maddad, mormaer of Atholl, by a daughter of the Orkney jarl Hakon Pálsson – who had become sole earl of Orkney and Caithness by 1059 and whose compliant relations with the king of Scots would have been cemented by his own marriage to a daughter of the earl of Fife.

Yet Harald was scarcely less ambitious than Orkney jarls of centuries past, and especially so in the direction of Ross and Moray. The first signal of such ambition was his decision to put aside his wife and marry a daughter of Malcolm MacHeth (who was earl of Ross when he died in 1168 which is thought to have been around the time of Harald's remarriage). So when Ross and Moray were the undoubted targets of Donald MacWilliam's invasion in 1181, 'all the circumstances point to Earl Harald Maddadsson as one of its instigators'.[23]

Another discernible, if not immediately obvious, MacHeth association with the MacWilliam rising has been found in an entry in the *Chronicle of Holyrood* for the year 1186.

On the fifteenth day before the kalends of December [17th November], the peace of the holy church was outraged at Coupar [Angus] by the violence of Malcolm, earl of Atholl; because Adam surnamed Donald's son, who was the king's outlaw, was seized, and one of his associates was beheaded before the altar; and the rest, fifty-eight in number were burned and killed in the abbot's dwelling.

---

23    Duncan, *Scotland: The Making of the Kingdom*, p.193.

When the chronicler's 'Adam' is read as his Latinised equivalent of the Gaelic name *Aed*, a MacHeth connection becomes immediately apparent and allows the convincing identification of this 'Adam' as Aed, a son of the Donald MacHeth last noticed by the same chronicler some thirty years earlier when he had been captured in Galloway and imprisoned with his father Malcolm.

It would appear then that the MacHeth alliance with the house of Moray had reappeared in the third generation and found common ground with the MacWilliam heir to the Moray cause. Nothing further is recorded of this 'Adam', who appears to have escaped the fate of his followers and so was presumably lost to history in some unidentified place of imprisonment. What might be inferred from this incident in Coupar Angus (less than twenty miles west of Forfar) is that a warband allied to Donald MacWilliam had made an incursion into Gowrie, and thus so far south of the Grampians as to compel the Lion king of Scots to the action he took in the following year. Roger of Howden's entry for 1187 includes some unexpected references to the MacWilliam cause.

> William, king of Scotland, assembled a great army and set out for Moray to subdue a certain enemy of his, who was named MacWilliam; who also said he was born of royal stock, and by right of his parents, so he affirmed, claimed the kingdom of Scotland, through consent and counsel of the earls and barons of the kingdom . . . The king William, therefore, considering that he must either lose the kingdom of Scotland or slay MacWilliam, or else drive him from the confines of his kingdom, set out to go into Moray . . .

Presumably quite unintentionally, Roger of Howden's opening paragraph reflects key components of the MacWilliam claim in its statements of Donald's believing himself 'born of royal stock' and – still more significantly here – claiming the kingdom by right of both his parents.

The Howden chronicle goes on to tell of William deflected from his intention to go in person with his forces when he was persuaded by 'the people' to stay and support them in the city. 'And the king remained in the castle which is called Inverness. And he sent his earls and barons with the Scots and the men of Galloway to subdue his enemy.' Interestingly then, Inverness had remained loyal to the king and thus presumably lay outwith control of the MacWilliam. The king's professed intention to lead his own army against MacWilliam must have called to mind his ancestor's venture into Moray in 1040 and, still more ominously, its momentous outcome. Neither, it would seem, could he have had full confidence in the loyalty of his commanders in the field, because 'when they set out, treason arose among the chiefs; for certain of them loved the king not at all, and certain of them loved him. And the latter wished to proceed, but the others did not permit it. And after dissension they agreed that the chiefs of the army should remain, and send forth scouts to seize food.'

If Roger of Howden can be trusted – and there is no reason to doubt him on this occasion – sympathy, if not active support, for the MacWilliam cause was seemingly not restricted to the outlands north of the Grampians. There is, nonetheless, a measure of irony in the outcome of events, because included among the 'three thousand warlike youths . . . sent to seek out the king's enemy' were men of Galloway, 'the household of Roland, Uhtred's son'. Roland, a grandson of Fergus of Galloway, had been an intransigent rebel in his own right until the previous year when, threatened with an army sent against him by Henry II, he rendered hostages and swore fealty to Henry and to William of Scotland. It was this same Roland, then, 'upon whose nod hung the decision of all' when his warband came upon 'the army of the MacWilliam, made an attack upon them and slew MacWilliam himself and many of his forces. And they cut off the head of MacWilliam and carried it away and presented it to the king of Scotland.'

To which the Scottish chroniclers can add a precise location and date. The *Chronicle of Holyrood* records 'Donald, William's son, slain in Ross', but the *Chronicle of Melrose* tells how 'they found MacWilliam with his followers upon the moor called Mam Garvia, near Moray, and presently they fought with him, and with God's help slew him, with many others; on the day before the kalends of August, the sixth day of the week [Friday, 31st July, 1187]'. The chronicler's Latin form of the Gaelic *màm garbh* (literally 'the rough, rounded hill') which would seem to be on the border of Ross and Moray has been convincingly identified on the moorland around Garve beside the main road linking Inverness with the coastland of Wester Ross, a stretch of country in a location which would correspond equally well to the direction of William's forces as to what is known of Donald's range of operations. It would seem though that Donald was defeated by an impromptu attack rather than in a 'set-piece' battle, which might suggest the likelihood of his smaller warband having been outnumbered by enemy forces. Whatever had been the actual course of the conflict, its outcome is left beyond doubt when Donald is said to have been slain in the blood-fray and his head severed as a trophy to be brought before the king.

The name MacWilliam does not appear again in the historical record until almost a quarter of a century after that day in July 1187, but even so the north was not to be left undisturbed through those years because Harald Maddadsson enters into contention with William the Lion by the later 1190s. On at least one occasion dated to *c.*1196/7, William brought a large army north to expel Harald from Moray and pursued him into Caithness where the earl refused battle and fled to his ships, leaving the king free to destroy one of his castles thereabouts. Harald was forced into submission, if only to save his lands from devastation, and yet when he failed to deliver the promised hostages he found himself taken captive and held in chains in Edinburgh. Released after surrendering his son as hostage in his place, Harald returned to Caithness and offered to buy it back from the king, a proposal to which William was prepared to agree but only on the condition that the earl put aside his MacHeth spouse and restore his first wife in her place. When Harald refused that condition, Caithness was held back from him and so he launched another campaign to reclaim it in 1201, inflicting penalties and punishments on those he accused of treason against him. When William brought yet another army north, the bishop of St Andrews somehow negotiated a settlement under which Caithness was at last restored to Harald Maddadsson, although his son held hostage had already suffered blinding and emasculation in retribution for his father's behaviour. Harald himself lived on until 1206, when his obituary at the very end of *Orkneyinga Saga* ranked him beside the first Sigurd and the second Thorfinn as 'the most powerful jarls of Orkney'.

Five years later a new generation of MacWilliams enters the historical record when Guthred, a son of the Donald who was slain in 1187, is said by Bower to 'have come to those parts [meaning Ross] from Ireland'. In fact, Walter Bower – who was writing more than two hundred years after the event but is thought to have had access to a contemporary source – supplies the most detailed account of this second MacWilliam rising. He tells how 'in 1211, William, king of Scotland, sent a huge army with all the nobles of the kingdom into Ross against Guthred MacWilliam. The king himself followed when he was able [and] on the way he built two castles, laid waste nearly all of Ross, and took or killed as many of Guthred's supporters as he could find.' Yet Guthred was evidently well-accomplished in guerrilla warfare and 'always avoided the king's army, all the while laying ambushes whenever he could by night or day, and driving off plunder from the lord king's land'.

Eventually a royal force four thousand strong managed to engage the rebels in a skirmish and force their retreat, but it was now towards the end of September when the campaigning season customarily came to its end, so William withdrew his army and assigned responsibility for Moray to the earl of Fife. Guthred meanwhile was still in action and took the opportunity to besiege and destroy one of the castles the king had earlier built in Ross. This incident offers a remarkable illustration of the military capability of the rebel forces, because Bower tells of Guthred having 'made ready his siege engines and was on the point of capturing the castle when the garrison within . . . surrendered it, of their own accord to save their lives. This Guthred granted to them, and setting fire to the castle burned it down.' It is difficult to know exactly what Bower (or his source) meant by 'siege engines', which could be something as basic as a battering ram or as elaborate and costly as the great siege towers used by the best-equipped medieval armies. More modest devices such as the mangonel (basically a heavy-duty mobile crossbow) or stone-throwing ballista were perhaps the most likely 'siege engines' available to Guthred, unless his guerrilla tactics had included the acquisition of more sophisticated machinery from a weapon train which might have accompanied William's forces.

However impressive his accomplishment in siege warfare, it was not to bring Guthred victory because another royal army was sent against him in the next campaigning season, and (nominally) commanded by the king's son who was to succeed his father as Alexander II in a couple of years' time. This second expedition is said by the immediately contemporary English *Annals of St Edmunds* to have been reinforced by the generosity of Henry II's son and successor when it records that 'King John sent many Brabantines to the aid of the king of Scotland, their leader being a certain English noble'. In the end, though, it was treachery in his own ranks which put an end to Guthred's rising, on the evidence of Bower's account which tells of him betrayed by his own followers, put in chains and brought to the Comyn earl of Buchan who had been appointed justiciar in Moray by the earl of Fife. 'The justiciar, who wanted Guthred brought before the king alive, got as far as Kincardine. There, when he learned the king's will, which was that he did not want to see him alive, they beheaded Guthred, dragged him along by his feet, and hung him up. He was already very close to death for he had refused food ever since his capture.'

A footnote to Bower's account of Guthred's fate might be found in the corresponding entry in the *Gesta Annalia*, which also records his 'being seized and fettered through his own men's treachery' but goes on to tell of him 'brought before the king's son, the lord Alexander, at the king's castle and manor of Kincardine'. There are at least three places called Kincardine in Scotland, but the one referred to by the *Gesta* and Bower would have been that now known as Kincardine O'Neil in Aberdeenshire, situated on a pass through the Grampians and nearby to a castle of the thirteenth century on the Peel of Lumphanan where Macbeth is said to have fought his last battle.

A closely contemporary English account in the *Chronicle of Barnwell* says nothing of Guthred betrayed by his own people, but does add a reference of especial interest here in its acknowledgement of Guthred's being 'of an ancient line of Scottish kings; and supported by the aid of Scots and Irish, had practised long hostility against the modern kings, now in secret, now openly, as had also his father Donald'. The Barnwell chronicler goes on to identify what he believed to have been the underlying cause of rebellion – and in so doing assuredly reflects the manifesto of the 'anti-feudal faction' – 'for the more recent kings of Scots profess themselves to be rather Frenchmen, both in race and in manners, in language and culture; and after reducing the Scots to utter servitude, they admit only Frenchmen to their friendship and service'.

The death of King William in the early days of December 1214 and the succession of his son 'the lord Alexander', even now only sixteen years old, offered the traditional opportunity for another rising from the outlands of the north or the west against another new king of the house of Canmore, and it was taken up by another son of Donald MacWilliam, evidently undaunted by the fate which had befallen his own brother just three years before. Neither was he acting alone on this occasion, because the entry for the year 1215 in the *Chronicle of Melrose* identifies his ally as a representative of the latest generation of another disaffected kindred.

> The lord king of Scotland's enemies entered Moray – namely Donald Bán, the son of MacWilliam; and Kenneth MacHeth; and the son of a certain king of Ireland – with a numerous band of malignants. Maccintsaccairt attacked them, and mightily overthrew the king's enemies; and he cut off their heads, and presented them as new gifts to the new king; on the seventeenth day before the kalends of July [15th June]. And because of this, the lord king appointed him a new knight . . .

The Melrose chronicler's concise, and yet most informative, account of this third MacWilliam rising serves to illustrate how much had changed in those three years, when the forces which had been deployed in 1211–12 are compared with those seemingly required to suppress the insurgency of 1215. Guthred's guerrilla campaign evidently posed so great a threat that two full-scale expeditions, one of them reinforced with Brabantine mercenaries, were sent north in 1211 and 1212, and yet no royal army was required to finish off the MacWilliam and MacHeth alliance, even though it had the support of an Irish prince who would have been accompanied by his own warband. Presumably this brother of Guthred (seemingly named for his father and distinguished from him with the by-name *Bán*, 'the fair') had stayed in Ireland in 1211, and thus survived to challenge the new king of Scots in 1215. Yet the fate of his rising reveals how drastically support for the MacWilliam cause had diminished in those few years.

While Guthred had been capable of outfighting a royal army by astute deployment of guerrilla tactics in wild Highland country and success-fully besieging a royal fortress, the alliance led by his brother Donald Bán was apparently defeated by forces no greater than the levy available to a regional nobleman. In fact, it is the identity of that nobleman which has been widely recognised by historians as the factor of paramount signifi-cance, because the man known as 'Maccintsaccairt' in the chronicle entry is elsewhere identified as Farquhar Machentagar (or Ferchar MacTaggart in its modern form), who was knighted by Alexander for his efforts in 1215 and later (certainly by 1226, possibly a few years earlier) granted the earldom of Ross. His patronymic (from the Gaelic *macc an t-sacairt*) identifies him as 'son of the priest' and the Ross connection first led to the proposal that he was descended from the lay abbots of Applecross, yet it now seems more likely that he belonged to the line of hereditary priests of St Duthac at Tain. Whichever was the case, Geoffrey Barrow has 'no doubt that he was a leader of the old native aristocracy. If such men would no longer support the MacWilliams, their cause was clearly lost.'[24] So indeed it was, and yet it would be another fifteen years before darkness fell on the last of their line of Cenél Loairn descent.

The fourth and final MacWilliam rebellion must be placed in the 1220s, even though its very few events recorded in any detail are dated to the last three or four years of that decade. What would seem to be a reference to their last rising is appended to the year 1223 in Bower's *Scotichronicon*, where he first mentions the appearance of Gillescop (probably *Gilleasbuig* in the original Gaelic) 'of the race of MacWilliam', with his sons and his accomplice Roderic, 'in the farthest limits of Scotland' and their later being 'brought summarily to justice'.

Although nowhere else supported in the sources, Bower might have been recording an early intrusion by Gillescop, almost certainly a grandson of the Donald MacWilliam slain in 1187, of whom he writes again when, in 1228, 'a certain Scot named Gillescop set fire to some wooden defen-sive works in Moray and killed a thief called Thomas of Thirlestane after attacking his castle by surprise in the night. Afterwards he burned a great part of Inverness, and about [the time of the feast of] the Nativity of the Blessed Mary he plundered some neighbouring lands of the lord king.'

---

24    Barrow, 'Macbeth and other mormaers of Moray', p.121.

It may, of course, have been that Bower simply introduced Gillescop into Scotland five years too soon, and that 1228 represents the true date of his rebellion, but it is equally possible that 1223 was the date of an initial raid in league with this 'Roderic', who has been convincingly identified as the piratical Ruairi mac Ranald, the grandson of Somerled who was to became the eponym of the MacRuairis of Garmoran and the Uist island group.[25] It was in the early 1220s that Alexander II made his first attempt at action against Somerled's descendants and he may have forced a redistribution of lands between Ruairi and his brother Donald, which would have provided Ruairi and Gillescop MacWilliam with a common ground of hostility towards the king of Scots. Their alliance could also have been rooted in kinship by marriage, because David Sellar has discerned a fragment of Clan Donald tradition which can be read to suggest Ranald mac Somerled having married a sister of Donald MacWilliam. All of which would support the likelihood of Ruairi's involvement in the supposed MacWilliam incursion of 1223, and yet he need not necessarily have had any part in the events of 1228–9, and so may well have lived on until 1247, if he was indeed the same *Mac Somurli* whose death in battle at Ballyshannon in the west of Ireland is entered at that year in the Irish annals.[26]

The reference to Thomas of Thirlestane, however, supplies a firm foothold in the historical record, because Thomas is known to have been of English descent and a tenant of the honour of Lauder in the Borders who had probably found his way north with a Galloway contingent on one of King William's expeditions. He later become lord of Abertarff, a motte-and-bailey castle near Fort Augustus at the southern end of Loch Ness, where Bower's description of him as 'a thief' might be recognised as an admonitory allusion to his appropriation of lands belonging to the church, thus 'leaving the priest with only toft and croft'.[27]

As for Gillescop, he would seem to have created sufficient disruption in 1228 to bring the king himself to the north where Bower reports the royal appointment of William Comyn, earl of Buchan, to the control

25  McDonald, *The Kingdom of the Isles*, p.82; *Outlaws of Medieval Scotland*, pp.162–6.
26  Sellar, 'Hebridean Sea Kings', pp.200–1.
27  Duncan, *Scotland: The Making of the Kingdom*, pp.197–8.

of the region, and the assignment to him of 'a large number of troops' for that purpose. The subsequent course of events is obscure, at least until 1229 when Bower records Gillescop and two of his sons slain and decapitated to supply the king with what by now seems to have become the customary trophy of a suppressed MacWilliam rising.

The last record of the MacWilliams is preserved in the *Chronicle of Lanercost*, where it is entered under the year 1230 after an apparent reference to earlier events.

> And after the enemy had been successfully overcome, a somewhat too cruel vengeance was taken for the blood of the slain: – the same [Gillescop] MacWilliam's daughter who had not long left her mother's womb, innocent as she was, was put to death in the burgh of Forfar, in view of the market place, after a proclamation by the public crier: her head was struck against the column of the [market] cross, and her brains dashed out.

Such then was the fate of the last in the long line of descent from the Cenél Loairn kings of Dalriada, inflicted exactly a hundred years after the death of Angus of Moray and just nineteen years before the inauguration at Scone of the last king of Scots of the Cenél nGabráin-descended house of Canmore.

# APPENDIX

## OF GIRIC, KING OF SCOTS

It could once have been said of Macbeth, and with every confidence, that he was the first king of the Cenél Loairn to achieve over-kingship of the Cenél nGabráin after those two dynastic kindreds had moved out of Argyll and established themselves in the lands of the Picts east of Druim Alban. In recent years, however, Benjamin Hudson has put together an imaginative case for another candidate having a prior claim on that achievement.[1]

This man was the Giric who is said by various sources to have slain Aed – the second and last of the sons of Kenneth mac Alpin to follow their father into the kingship – in 878. The earliest, and often most informative, version of the *Chronicle of the Kings* enters Aed's successor as 'Eochaid, son of Rhun, king of the Britons [of Strathclyde, and] grandson of Kenneth by his daughter, [who] reigned for eleven years; although others say that *Ciricius* [or Giric], the son of another, reigned at this time, because he became Eochaid's *alumpnus* ['foster-father'] and *ordinator* ['steward']'.

Other sources are able to put a name to Giric's father but, for some reason, that name would appear to have changed by the twelfth century. While the earlier king-lists from the *Synchronisms* onwards identify Giric as 'Dúngal's son', a later sub-group follows the *Verse Chronicle* in the *Chronicle of Melrose* to call his father *Dofnaldus* (or 'Donald'), which has led to the identification of Giric as a son of Donald mac Alpin, the brother of Kenneth who followed him into the kingship in 858 and reigned until 862. This school of thought would thus – and

---

1   Hudson, *Kings of Celtic Scotland*, pp.55–7, 129–32; *The Prophecy of Berchán*, pp. 44–5, 85–6, 205–8.

not at all unreasonably – propose Giric killing his cousin Aed and afterwards claiming the kingship with another cousin's young son as 'a family affair' within the ruling house of MacAlpin, 'whereby the son of Kenneth's brother (Donald I) intervened violently to stake a claim to the kingship in opposition to Kenneth's sons'.[2] The same intra-dynastic feud would thus appear to have been continued when – according to the version of the *Chronicle* quoted earlier – 'Eochaid, with his foster-father, was expelled from the kingdom', presumably by Aed's nephew who succeeded as Donald II.

W. F. Skene, on the other hand, preferred to follow the earlier sources' identification of Giric as 'Dúngal's son', proposing his father as a Briton from Strathclyde, the *Dumnagual* entered in the old Welsh genealogies (appended to Nennius' *Historia Brittonum*) as the father of Artgal, king of Strathclyde, and thus the grandfather of Eochaid's father Rhun.[3] Benjamin Hudson also prefers the identification of Giric as 'Dúngal's son', but goes on to identify his father as a different Dúngal, the one entered in the later Latin king-lists as the great-grandson of Muiredach, son of Ainbcellach. If so, then the Giric who slew Aed in 878 and held the kingship of Scots with Eochaid would have been of the Cenél Loairn.

Hudson finds support for this proposal from Fordun whose *Chronicle* claims that, 'according to the rule of the kingship', Giric (or *Gregorius* in Fordun's Latin form), son of Dúngal, should have become king before Aed, who died of wounds suffered 'in a battle fought at Strathallan'. Fordun evidently had access to the later king-list interpolating three generations of descent from Muiredach mac Ainbcellach into kingship through the later eighth century and into the ninth, because he had recorded the accession of its 'Dúngal, Selbach's son' (as *Dungallus*, son of *Selwalchius*) in 824. Having already accepted their contrived descent from 'Loarn, son of Erc', Fordun's assertion that Dúngal's son Giric 'should have become king before Aed' corresponds to the tradition of kingship alternating between branches of a ruling kindred under which the Cenél Loairn would have had a pressing claim on the over-kingship

---

2   Smyth, *Warlords & Holy Men*, pp.215–17.
3   Skene, *Celtic Scotland*, vol. i, pp.329–31.

of Scots already monopolised by two generations of the Cenél nGabráin-descended Mac Alpin dynasty.

Placing all of this into its ninth-century context, Benjamin Hudson refers back to the reign of Constantine, the son of Kenneth mac Alpin who followed his uncle Donald into the kingship in 862 and later assumed overlordship of Strathclyde after allegedly instigating the murder of its king Artgal in 872. Hudson then suggests that 'in the aftermath of their discomfiture, the men of Strathclyde looked for allies and found them among Cenél Loairn'. As part of that alliance, the young Eochaid (who was, of course, a grandson of both Artgal and Kenneth) might have been sent to be fostered by Giric mac Dúngail, 'a descendant of Ferchar *fota*'. On the death of Constantine in 877, his brother Aed followed him into the kingship, and the Strathclyde Britons allied with the Cenél Loairn to mount the challenge to his succession which led to the death of Aed in (or after) the battle at Strathallan. At which point, Eochaid would have been recognised as king by the Cenél nGabráin while his foster-father Giric would have risen to power as his *ordinator*, 'the most important of the overlord's subordinates'. Hudson goes on to suggest that, after a brief and supposedly unhappy reign, Eochaid 'may have been forced to acknowledge the lordship of Giric, who would then have been king of the Cenél Loairn and overlord of the Cenél nGabráin . . . This would have reintroduced the status quo found in Dalriada a century earlier and would explain why Giric, not Eochaid, is remembered in the later histories.'[4]

He is certainly generously remembered by Fordun, who elaborates the claim made by later versions of the *Chronicle of the Kings* that Giric 'subdued to himself Ireland and nearly all England' into his having also 'subdued the upper and western districts' seemingly at the expense of the northmen who were already settling the western seaboard. Whatever might be meant by Giric's supposed subjugation of Ireland (which is nowhere noticed by any of the Irish annalists), the claim for his subjugation of 'nearly all England' (presumably intended in the sense of 'territory of the Angles') is generally thought to apply to Lothian (at that time the northern extent of Northumbria), as indeed is indicated

---

4  Hudson, *Kings of Celtic Scotland*, p.57.

by the later versions of the *Chronicle* which make specific reference to Northumbria, and in one instance to its northern province of Bernicia.

The *Prophecy of Berchán*, although set down three centuries earlier than Fordun's *Chronicle*, is similarly generous to Giric, who is welcomed as 'the son of fortune . . . who will knead Alba into one kingdom' (in striking contrast to Eochaid who had been earlier greeted with 'alas! . . . that a Briton should take lordship over the Gael'). The Berchán poet's 'prophecy' that Giric was to 'knead Alba into one kingdom' is interpreted by Hudson as 'possibly a reference to the union of Cenél Loairn and Cenél nGabráin under Giric's lordship', while another stanza by the Berchán poet tells of his having had 'slaves with him in his house, *Saxain* (English), *Gaill* (Scandinavians), and *Brethnaigh* (Britons)', which Hudson recognises as 'an obvious listing of the peoples against whom he warred'. It might also be read to suggest that Giric himself was not a Briton, but a Gaelic Scot, and thus further support the proposal of his having been of the Cenél Loairn. Indeed, Hudson reads the stanzas in which the Berchán poet describes the reigns of Eochaid and Giric to imply the relationship between the two (who are usually supposed to have succeeded to the kingship together and ruled jointly) as 'adversarial', even to the extent 'that Eochaid ruled alone [until] he was forced to flee by the efforts of Giric'.[5]

There is one point, however, on which the *Prophecy of Berchán* fully accords with the *Chronicle of the Kings*, as also with Fordun, and it is the location of Giric's principal stronghold, a subject which would have wider implications for what is known of the Cenél Loairn in the ninth century if he was indeed of that kindred. The Berchán poet tells of 'the son of fortune' having built 'the strong house on the bank of the Earn' where he would 'fall by the hands of the men of Fortriu', a 'prophecy' which closely aligns with the statement 'Giric, Dúngal's son, died in Dundurn' made in a version of the *Chronicle* dated to the late eleventh century and followed by Fordun three hundred years later. A hill-fort at the eastern end of Loch Earn, Dundurn is first mentioned as the site of a siege entered in the *Annals of Ulster* at the year 683, but would appear, from evidence found in the course of modern archaeological

---

5    Hudson, *Kings of Celtic Scotland*, pp.56–7; *The Prophecy of Berchán*, p.206.

excavations, to have been extensively rebuilt in the ninth century when it would have been in use as Giric's capital fortress.

The location of Dundurn in what is now Perthshire does not fit easily into all the other evidence for the migration of the Cenél Loairn out of northern Argyll and into Moray having been already well advanced, if not fully established, at the time of Giric's reign in the kingship of Scots. It is not impossible, of course, that a branch of the Cenél Loairn might have remained in or around their traditional heartland when others were moving, or had moved, up the Great Glen. Such would seem to be implied by Benjamin Hudson when he makes the point that Dundurn would have been 'equally accessible from three western areas: the Cenél Loairn stronghold of Dunollie; the Dál Riata ceremonial centre at Dunadd and the British fortress at Dumbarton Rock [while] control of Dundurn would have been most useful to someone who needed to control Strathearn and did not want to be too far from the area around Oban'.[6] Even so, the former Cenél Loairn territories in Argyll do seem to have been distinctly peripheral to a power centre at Dundurn in the light of what little is known from the earliest sources of Giric's orbit of activity as king of Scots. Neither does the Berchán poet's claim for 'Alba kneaded into one kingdom' necessarily bear on the Cenél Loairn, and especially when their descendent 'men of Moray' were still recognised as distinctly separate from the 'men of Alba' even into the second quarter of the twelfth century. In fact, the poet may simply have been alluding to Strathclyde, which had already been brought under the kingship of Alba after the death of Artgal and might be thought to have become further welded to that kingdom during Giric's reign.

Such points of alternative interpretation have come to mind whilst giving Benjamin Hudson's proposal of Giric as a ninth-century king of the Cenél Loairn the lengthy and sympathetic consideration which it justly demands. It has been a process which has involved changes of mind almost beyond counting before reaching a conclusion which was finally determined by the genealogical hinge upon which his hypothesis ultimately depends. To accept Giric, king of Scots, as a son of the 'Dúngal' who is entered in the late Latin king-lists as a great-great-grandson of

---

6    Hudson, *Kings of Celtic Scotland*, p.132.

the genuinely historical Ainbcellach would of necessity require accept-ance of the extended Cenél Loairn pedigree which is found only in those lists and which has already been rejected here.[7]

So if Giric was not the son of a descendant of Ferchar Fota, then who was this man variously identified as the son of another Dúngal (or 'Donald')? The name (which is also found as a patronymic in the notes to the *Book of Deer*) must be the Gaelic form of *Ciricius*, which is used for Giric in the earliest version of the *Chronicle of the Kings* and represents the Welsh version of the name of Cyricus (or Cyriacus), the fourth-century saint of Tarsus who is commemorated in the place-name Capel Curig in Gwynedd. That origin for the name would point in a Britonic/Welsh direction and my own feeling is that Skene was on the right track in his proposal of Giric as a son of the *Dumnagual* entered in the Welsh genealogies. A much more recent discussion of the subject by Alan Bruford also recognises Giric as the great-uncle of Eochaid – and then goes on to offer a most convincing explanation of how his patro-nymic came to appear in the two different forms found in the Scottish king-lists.

Bruford suggests that the 'early Welsh Dumnagual, later Dyfnwal, resembles the Irish Dúngal on paper but is actually cognate with Domnall and might be translated as such by a bilingual scholar: this could explain the confusion'. Dumnagual was the name of the father of Artgal, the king of Strathclyde killed in 872 on the advice of Constantine, son of Kenneth mac Alpin, and so the Giric who killed Constantine's brother Aed in 878 'could well have been Artgal's avenging brother, who added old-style legitimacy to his reign in Pictland by nominally sharing it with his great-nephew, the small son of Aed's sister'.[8]

It is for that reason that Giric has been consigned to this appendix and was omitted from the main body of the foregoing history of the Cenél Loairn.

---

7 See pp.72–4 above.
8 Bruford, 'What happened to the Caledonians?', p.65.

# GENEALOGIES

NB: The spelling of names in Genealogies 2 and 4 has been adapted from the variant forms foun in the manuscript copies of the original texts so as to correspond with those used in the relevar chapters above.

– I –

## Cenél Loairn Kings of Dalriada
(from the Irish annal records)

(Dates of reign shown in parentheses)

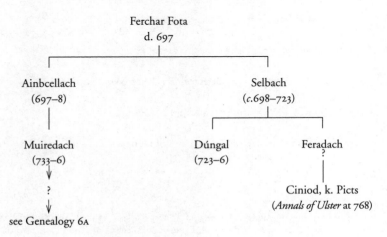

Ferchar Fota
d. 697

Ainbcellach
(697–8)

Selbach
(*c.*698–723)

Muiredach
(733–6)

↓

?

↓

see Genealogy 6A

Dúngal
(723–6)

Feradach
?

Ciniod, k. Picts
(*Annals of Ulster* at 768)

## – 2 –

Genealogies from the *Genelaig Albanensium*
appended to the *Senchus fer nAlban*

*Genelach Cenél Loairn mar*

—— Ainbcellach
son of Ferchar *fota*
son of Feradach
son of Fergus
son of Colman
son of Báetán
son of Echdach
son of Muiredach
son of Loarn Mór *
son of Erc
son of Eochaid Munremar

—— Morgán
son of Domnall
son of Cathamail
son of Ruadri
— — — — — — —**
son of Erca
son of Muiredach
son of Báetán

* John Bannerman assigned 'the five Dalriadic pedigrees [in the *Genelaig Albanensium*] . . . to the eighth century' (*Dalriada*, p.110). If so, the original must have been amended by a later scribe to make 'Loarn Mór' one of the 'three sons of Erc' contrived by the tenth-century editor of the *Senchus*.

** If this is the same Morgán, son of Domnall, known from the annal record and from the Moray genealogies, he flourished in the mid-tenth century, so a number of generations must have been omitted when this genealogy was interpolated beneath that of Ainbcellach in the *Genelaig Albanensium* – presumably in the later tenth or early eleventh century.

— — — — — — — — — — — — — — — — — — — — — — — — — — — — — — —

*Genelach Cenél Gabráin*

—— Congus
son of Consamla
son of Cano *garb*
son of Gartnait
son of Aedán

— — — — — — — — — — — — — — — — — — — — — — — — — — — — — — —

## - 3 -

## Kings and Mormaers of Moray
### (from the Irish annal records)

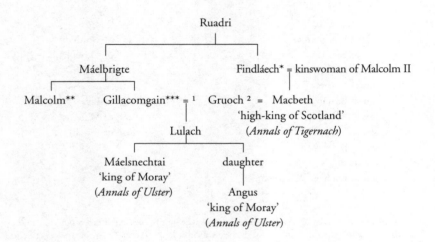

* Styled 'king of [or 'in'] Scotland' by the *Annals of Ulster* and 'mormaer of Moray' by the *Annals of Tigernach* at 1020.

** Styled 'king of [or 'in'] Scotland' by the *Annals of Tigernach* at 1029.

*** Styled 'mormaer of Moray' by the *Annals of Ulster* at 1032.

# – 4 –

## Moray Genealogies from the Rawlinson B 502 Manuscript

*Item Ríg Albain**

– *Máel-snechtae* (Máelsnechtai)
son of Lulach
son of Gillacomgain
son of Máelbrigte
son of Ruadri
son of Domnall (?)**
son of Morgán
son of Domnall***
son of Cathamail
son of Ruadri
son of Ainbcellach
son of Ferchar Fota
son of Feradach
son of Fergus
son of Nechtan
son of Colmán
son of Báetán
son of Echdach
son of Muiredach
son of Loarn
son of Erc
son of Echdach Munremar

*Item Ríg Albain*

– *Mac-bethad* (Macbeth)
son of Findláech
son of Ruadri
son of Domnall
son of Morgán

---

* headed *Genelach Clainde Lulaig* in the *Book of Leinster*.

** in Rawlinson B 502 – but entered as *Dondgusa* in the *Book of Leinster*.

*** from the *Book of Leinster* – omitted from Rawlinson B 502.

– 5 –

Proposed descent of the MacWilliams from the Cenél Loairn

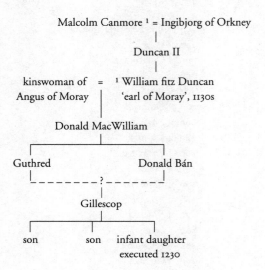

# – 6 –

## Alternative Genealogies for Giric, son of Dúngal

A
*Cenél Loairn descent*

Ainbcellach
son of Ferchar Fota
|
Muiredach
|
Eogan*
|
Selbach*
|
Dúngal*
|
Giric

\* only in later Latin king-lists – see Anderson, *ESSH*, vol.i, pp.cxxxiii, cxxxvi.

– – – – – – – – – – – – – – – – – – –

B
*Strathclyde descent*

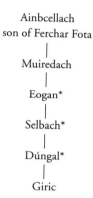

Dumnagual

Artgal          Giric
k. Strathclyde
|
Rhun = daughter of Kenneth mac Alpin
|
Eochaid
k. Scots

# BIBLIOGRAPHY

Adomnán/Adamnan   see under Anderson, Sharpe, Skene

Aitchison, N., *Macbeth: Man and Myth*, Stroud, 1999

—— *The Picts and the Scots at War*, Stroud, 2003

Anderson, A. O. (ed./trans.), *Scottish Annals from English Chroniclers, AD 500 to 1286*, 1908; rep. Stamford, 1991

—— *Early Sources of Scottish History, AD 500 to 1286* (2 vols), 1922; rep. Stamford, 1990

—— & M. O. (eds./trans.), *Adomnán's Life of Columba*, rev. London & Edinburgh, 1961

Anderson, M. O., *Kings & Kingship in Early Scotland*, rev. Edinburgh, 1980

—— 'Dalriada and the creation of the kingdom of the Scots' in Whitelock *et al.* (eds.), *Ireland in Early Mediaeval Europe*, Cambridge, 1982

*Anglo-Saxon Chronicle*   see under Garmonsway

Baldwin, J. R. (ed.), *Caithness: A Cultural Crossroads*, Edinburgh, 1982

—— *Firthlands of Ross & Sutherland*. Edinburgh, 1986

Bannerman, J. W. M., *Studies in the History of Dalriada*, Edinburgh, 1974

—— 'The Scots of Dalriada' in McNeill & Nicholson (eds.), *Historical Atlas of Scotland*. St Andrews, 1975

Barrow, G. W. S. (ed.), *The Acts of Malcolm IV, King of Scots, 1153–1165*, Edinburgh, 1960

—— (ed.), *The Acts of William I, King of Scots, 1165–1214*, Edinburgh, 1971

—— 'Macbeth and other mormaers of Moray' in Maclean (ed.), *The Hub of the Highlands*, Inverness, 1975

—— *Kingship and Unity: Scotland 1000–1306*, rev. Edinburgh, 1989

Batey, C. E., Jesch, J. & Morris, C. C. (eds.), *The Viking Age in Caithness, Orkney and the North Atlantic*, Edinburgh, 1995

Bede   see under Sherley-Price & Farmer

Brown, D., 'The Seven Kingdoms in *De Situ Albanie*' in Cowan & McDonald (eds.), *Alba*, Edinburgh, 2005

Bruford, A., 'What happened to the Caledonians?' in Cowan & McDonald (eds.), *Alba*, Edinburgh, 2005

Chadwick, N. K., 'The Story of Macbeth: A Study in Gaelic and Norse Tradition', *Scottish Gaelic Studies* VOL.6, 1949 & VOL.7, 1951

Clancy, T. O. (ed.), *The Triumph Tree: Scotland's Earliest Poetry* AD *550–1350*, Edinburgh, 1998

Cowan, E. J., 'Caithness in the Sagas' in Baldwin (ed.), *Caithness: A Cultural Crossroads*, Edinburgh, 1982

—— 'The Historical MacBeth' in Sellar (ed.), *Moray: Province & People*, Edinburgh, 1993

—— & McDonald, R. A. (eds.), *Alba: Celtic Scotland in the Medieval Era*, rev. Edinburgh, 2005

Crawford, B. E., 'The Making of a Frontier: The Firthlands from 9th to 12th Centuries' in Baldwin (ed.), *Firthlands of Ross & Sutherland*, Edinburgh, 1986

—— *Scandinavian Scotland*, Leicester, 1987

—— *Earl & Mormaer: Norse-Pictish Relationships in Northern Scotland*, Rosemarkie, 1995

Duncan, A. A. M., *Scotland: The Making of the Kingdom*, rev. Edinburgh, 1978

Ellis, P. B., *MacBeth, High King of Scotland, 1040–57*, Belfast, 1990

—— & Ellsworth, R., *The Book of Deer*, London, 1994

Farmer, D. H., *The Oxford Dictionary of Saints*, Oxford, 1987

Fordun, John of see under Skene

Fraser, I. A., 'Norse & Celtic Place-Names around the Dornoch Firth' in Baldwin (ed.), *Firthlands of Ross & Sutherland*, Edinburgh, 1986

Garmonsway, G. N. (ed./trans.), *The Anglo-Saxon Chronicle*, London, 1972

Grant, A., 'The Province of Ross and the Kingdom of Alba' in Cowan & McDonald (eds.), *Alba*, Edinburgh, 2005

Henderson, I., 'Pictish Territorial Divisions' in McNeill & Nicholson (eds.), *Historical Atlas of Scotland*, St Andrews, 1975

Hudson, B. T., 'Cnut and the Scottish Kings', *English Historical Review* 107, 1992

—— *Kings of Celtic Scotland*, Westport, Connecticut & London, 1994

—— *The Prophecy of Berchán: Irish and Scottish High-Kings of the Early Middle Ages*, Westport, Connecticut & London, 1996

Jackson, K. H., *The Gaelic Notes in the Book of Deer*, Cambridge, 1972

Kenney, J. F., *The Sources for the Early History of Ireland: Ecclesiastical*, Dublin, 1968

Kirby, D. P., 'Moray – prior to *c.*1100' and 'Moray in the 12th Century' in McNeill & Nicholson (eds.), *Historical Atlas of Scotland*, St Andrews, 1975

McDonald, R. A., 'Monk, Bishop, Imposter, Pretender: The Place of Wimund in Twelfth-Century Scotland', *Transactions of the Gaelic Society of Inverness* VOL. 58, 1994

—— *The Kingdom of the Isles, Scotland's Western Seaboard* c.1100– c.1336, East Linton, 1997

—— *Outlaws of Medieval Scotland: Challenges to the Canmore Kings, 1058–1266*, East Linton, 2003

—— see also under Cowan, E. J.

Maclean, L. (ed.), *The Hub of the Highlands: The Book of Inverness and District*, Inverness, 1974

——— *The Middle Ages in the Highlands*, Inverness, 1981

McNeill, P. & Nicholson, R. (eds.), *An Historical Atlas of Scotland, c.400–c.1600*, St Andrews, 1975

Mac Niocaill, G., *Ireland before the Vikings*, Dublin, 1972

Magnusson, M. & Pálsson, H. (eds./trans.), *Njal's Saga*, London, 1960

Nicolaisen, W. F. H., 'Gaelic Place-names' in McNeill & Nicholson (eds.), *Historical Atlas of Scotland*, St Andrews, 1975

——— 'Scandinavians and Celts in Caithness: the place-name evidence' in Baldwin (ed.), *Caithness; A Cultural Crossroads*, Edinburgh, 1982

——— 'Names in the Landscape of the Moray Firth' in Sellar (ed.), *Moray: Province & People*, Edinburgh, 1993

——— *Scottish Place-names*, Edinburgh, 2001

Offler, H. S., *Medieval Historians of Durham*, Durham, 1958

O hOgain, D., *Myth, Legend & Romance: An Encyclopaedia of the Irish Folk Tradition*, New York, 1991

Pálsson, H. & Edwards, P. (eds./trans.), *Orkneyinga Saga: The History of the Earls of Orkney*, London, 1978

Reeves, W., *The Culdees of the British Islands*, Dublin, 1864; rep. Felinfach, 1994

Reid, N. H. (ed.), *Scotland in the Reign of Alexander III – 1249–1286*, Edinburgh, 1990

Ritchie, A., *Picts*, Edinburgh, 1989

——— & Breeze, D. J., *Invaders of Scotland*, Edinburgh, 1991

Sellar, W. D. H., 'The Origins and Ancestry of Somerled', *Scottish Historical Review* 45, 1966

——— 'Marriage, divorce and concubinage in Gaelic Scotland', *Transactions of the Gaelic Society of Inverness* 51, 1978–80

——— 'Highland Family Origins – Pedigree Making and Pedigree Faking', in Maclean (ed.), *The Middle Ages in the Highlands*, Inverness, 1981

——— (ed.), *Moray: Province & People*, Edinburgh, 1993

——— 'Sueno's Stone and its Interpreters' in *Moray: Province & People* (above)

——— 'Hebridean Sea Kings: The Successors of Somerled, 1164–1316' in Cowan & McDonald (eds.), *Alba*, East Linton, 2000

Sharpe, R. (trans.), *Adomnán of Iona: Life of St Columba*, London, 1995

Shepherd, I. G., 'The Picts in Moray' in Sellar (ed.), *Moray: Province & People*, Edinburgh, 1993

Sherley-Price, L. & Farmer, D. H. (eds./trans.), *Bede: Ecclesiastical History of the English People*, rev. London, 1990

Skene, W. F., (ed.), *John of Fordun's Chronicle of the Scottish Nation*, 1871–2; rep. Felinfach, 1993

—— *Celtic Scotland: A History of Ancient Alban* (2 vols), Edinburgh, 1886–90

—— (ed.) & Forbes, A. P. (trans.), *Life of Saint Columba, Founder of Hy, written by Adamnan*, Edinburgh, 1874

Smyth, A. P., *Warlords and Holy Men: Scotland AD 80–1000*, Edinburgh, 1989

Stenton, F, M., *Anglo-Saxon England*, rev. Oxford, 1989

Stokes, W. (ed.), *The Annals of Tigernach*, Paris, 1895–6; rep. Felinfach, 1993

Taylor, A. B., 'Karl Hundason, "King of Scots"', *Proceedings of the Society of Antiquaries of Scotland* VOL. 71, 1937

Watson, W. J., *The History of the Celtic Place-names of Scotland*, 1926; rep. Dublin, 1986

Whitelock, D., McKitterick, R. & Dumville, D. (eds.), *Ireland in Early Mediaeval Europe*, Cambridge, 1982

Williams, A., Smyth, A. P. & Kirby, D. P. (eds.), *A Biographical Dictionary of Dark Age Britain*, London, 1991

# INDEX

ABBREVIATIONS

| | |
|---|---|
| ab. | abbot of |
| bp. | bishop of |
| dtr. | daughter of |
| e. | earl of |
| j. | jarl of |
| k. | king of |
| mor. | mormaer of |
| s. | son of |
| s-k. | sub-king of |
| w. | wife of |